The Origins and Early Develop
of Witham, Essex

*A Study in Settlement and Fortification,
Prehistoric to Medieval*

by Warwick Rodwell

with sections by

B. K. Davison, Roland Flook and Owen Bedwin

and contributions by

Marion M. Archibald, Nigel Brown, C. A. I. French,
D. B. Harden, Robin Holgate, Hilary Major,
Peter Murphy, David Rudling and Val Williams

Oxbow Monograph 26
1993

Published by
Oxbow Books, Park End Place, Oxford OX1 1HN

ISBN 0 946897 50 6

This book is available direct from
Oxbow Books, Park End Place, Oxford, OX1 1HN
(Phone: 0-865-241249; Fax: 0-865-794449)

and

The David Brown Book Company
PO Box 5605, Bloomington, IN 47407, USA
(Phone: 812-331-0266; fax: 812-331-0277)

**Publication of this report has been aided by grants from
Essex County Council and English Heritage**

Printed in Great Britain by
The Short Run Press, Exeter

Contents

List of Illustrations

Preface and Acknowledgements

This volume brings together the results of excavations, chance discoveries, fieldwork and research carried out intermittently at Witham over a period of nearly sixty years. The story began with a research project instigated by Sir (then Dr) Mortimer Wheeler in the early 1930s, on the site of the supposed *burh* of Edward the Elder. The results of that excavation were never published, and it was not until 1969 that there was a serious revival of academic interest in Witham. Over the next few years investigations and research took place, quite independently, on several fronts.

The present writer's own research into the archaeology and topography of Witham and its environs began in 1971, as a by-product of the extensive investigations that he and Mrs Kirsty Rodwell were then conducting in the adjacent parishes of Rivenhall and Kelvedon. The study of Witham was embraced when it became apparent that the ecclesiastical, and to some extent the tenurial, history of Rivenhall was closely intertwined with that of Witham. Further impetus was provided by the discovery in 1970 of a major and wholly unsuspected Iron Age earthwork at Witham Lodge. The discovery and initial recording, by Mr Paul Drury, led to further investigations in 1971 and 1972. At the same time as this work was in progress, Mr Brian Davison was undertaking rescue excavations on the Iron Age plateau fort and putative Anglo-Saxon *burh* at Chipping Hill Camp, also in Witham parish.

Subsequent discussion with the late Professor C. F. C. Hawkes concerning problems of the Middle Iron Age in central Essex, and in particular the inter-relationship of the prehistoric earthworks at Witham, led to the decision to attempt the compilation of a report on the unpublished excavations at Chipping Hill Camp of 1933–35. Professor Hawkes kindly made available the finds that had been in his custody since 1945, and he further contributed from his own personal knowledge of the site. Mr Davison readily agreed to become a collaborator, contributing a report on his excavations of 1969 and 1971. A fresh opportunity for excavations on the defences of the camp arose in 1988, and a report on these has been prepared by Dr Owen Bedwin and Mr Roland Flook, who also readily agreed to its incorporation in the present volume.

I am indebted to all of the above mentioned colleagues, not only for making available material evidence, but also for many years of stimulating and fruitful discussion. Much assistance has also been given by the following: Mr David Buckley and Dr David Andrews of the Archaeology Section, Essex County Council; the staff of the Colchester and Essex Museum, especially Mr David Clarke (lately Curator) and Dr Paul Seeley; the staff of the Essex Record Office, especially Mrs June Beardsley; Miss Gillian Sheldrick, who carried out historical research on Rivenhall and its environs; Mr Paul Drury and Mrs Kirsty Rodwell. I am indebted to Mrs Janet Gyford, who provided several critical references and to Dr John Blair for the opportunity of consulting his paper 'Anglo-Saxon Minsters: A Topographical Review', in advance of publication. Grateful thanks are also due to Jeremy Haslam for the benefit of much fruitful discussion concerning the history and topography of Anglo-Saxon *burhs* in eastern England, and the interpretation of the Witham evidence in particular.

The illustrations have mostly been prepared by the author, assisted by Mrs Kirsty Rodwell and Miss Helen Fuller. Illustrations relating to the 1988 excavations have been prepared by Essex County Council's Archaeology Section.

Warwick Rodwell

Downside,
April 1991

Summary

For almost three centuries the earthworks at Chipping Hill, just outside the town of Witham in eastern Essex, have attracted the attentions of antiquaries who initially interpreted them as a Roman camp, and later as Edward the Elder's *burh* of 913 (now corrected to 912). Excavations by F. Cottrill in 1933–35 sectioned the defences of the two concentric enclosures, revealing predominantly Iron Age material. Both circuits were again sectioned in 1969–71, by B. K. Davison. The inner earthwork, containing 3.5 ha, was confirmed as prehistoric, while the outer circuit (10.3 ha) unexpectedly proved to have had at least two phases, the first of which was undated and the last was certainly medieval.

Further work elsewhere on the defences in 1988, by Roland Flook, yielded only Iron Age and earlier material, and indicated a Late Bronze Age date for the inner earthwork, and possibly for the outer one too. The excavations also revealed evidence for late Neolithic settlement, as well as yielding a scatter of Mesolithic flints. No tangible evidence for an Anglo-Saxon re-fortification of Chipping Hill has been found, and the site is now totally submerged beneath housing.

Three further earthwork sites, all defining major enclosures, have been discovered at Witham in recent years. First, excavations in 1970–72 at Witham Lodge, to the south-west of the town, located a large Iron Age enclosure containing some 56 ha, within which lay a Roman temple and early Christian site (Ivy Chimneys); secondly, at Rivenhall End, on the north-eastern border of the parish, topographical studies revealed a sub-rectangular enclosure of 18 ha, known as Burgate Field; and, thirdly, beneath the medieval 'new' town of Witham another earthwork has been identified, enclosing a 27 ha arc of land in a bend of the river Brain. Several smaller earthworks and the principal field systems in the parish are also discussed.

The object of this volume is to present the evidence for, and to discuss the significance of, each of the earthwork enclosures, their associated settlements, and the landscapes in which they lie. Using all available topographical, archaeological and documentary evidence, the development of Witham is traced from the prehistoric era to the Middle Ages. Chipping Hill Camp is assigned primarily to the Late Bronze Age with refortification in the Middle Iron Age, and the earthworks at Witham Lodge are dated to the Late Iron Age. Both sites were associated with Roman-period activity, which in one case included an important religious complex. The enclosure at Rivenhall End is considered to be the most plausible candidate for Edward the Elder's *burh*, and it is argued that the earthwork beneath Witham town marks the site of the lost *Wulvesford*. It may have been either a Danish fortification, or belonged to an earlier phase of Edwardian activity. Neither site spawned a late Saxon town with churches, a mint, market and other recognisable urban paraphernalia: it is therefore claimed that Witham represents a failed *burh*.

Study of the ecclesiastical geography of the district suggests that a major Anglo-Saxon minster and royal estate lay at Witham, which was also the hundredal centre. The parish church of St Nicholas lay outside the earthworks at Chipping Hill, and became the focus of a small late Saxon settlement. In the early twelfth century a modest planned town was established here (Chipping Witham), but its inconvenient siting in relation to the main London-to-Colchester road stunted growth. This 'proto-town' was effectively superseded in 1213 by a new urban foundation of the Knights Templar, sited on the main road and known as Newland Witham. The planning and complex development of Witham in the twelfth and thirteenth centuries has been elucidated.

Other key sites in the Witham area are described and their significance assessed, including a posited prehistoric circular enclosure around St Nicholas's Church, two short-lived earthen castles (one at Chipping Hill, the other at Blunt's Hall), and a moated manor at Howbridge Hall.

1

Introduction

Until recently, Witham was a small market town in eastern-central Essex, lying on the former main road from London to Colchester (A12), 14 km north-east of Chelmsford (Fig. 1); it is now a sprawling commuter settlement and designated 'overspill' area for Greater London. Topographically and historically, the settlement consisted of two distinct units: a medieval 'new' town laid out in the early thirteenth century by the Knights Templar astride the main (Roman) road, and an older core at Chipping Hill, 1 km to the north (Fig. 2; Beresford 1967, 436–7, fig. 36; Britnell 1968). Witham is largely contained in the angle formed by the confluence of two rivers, the Blackwater and the Brain, where it controls an important crossing point. The Blackwater is one of the major rivers of Essex, which debouches into the North Sea at Bradwell-on-Sea.

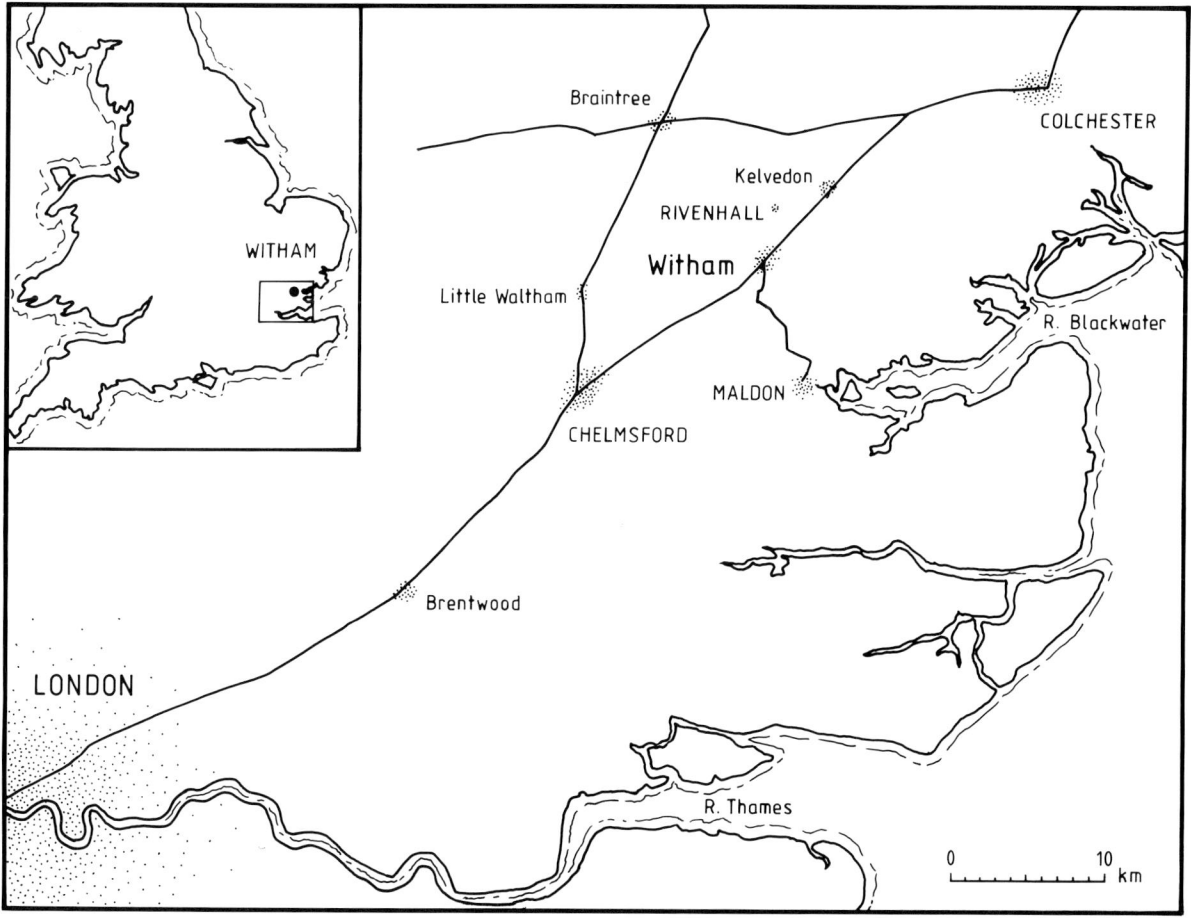

Fig. 1. *Location map, showing the line of the Roman road (later A12) from London to Colchester, and the principal sites in the Witham area that are mentioned in the text.*

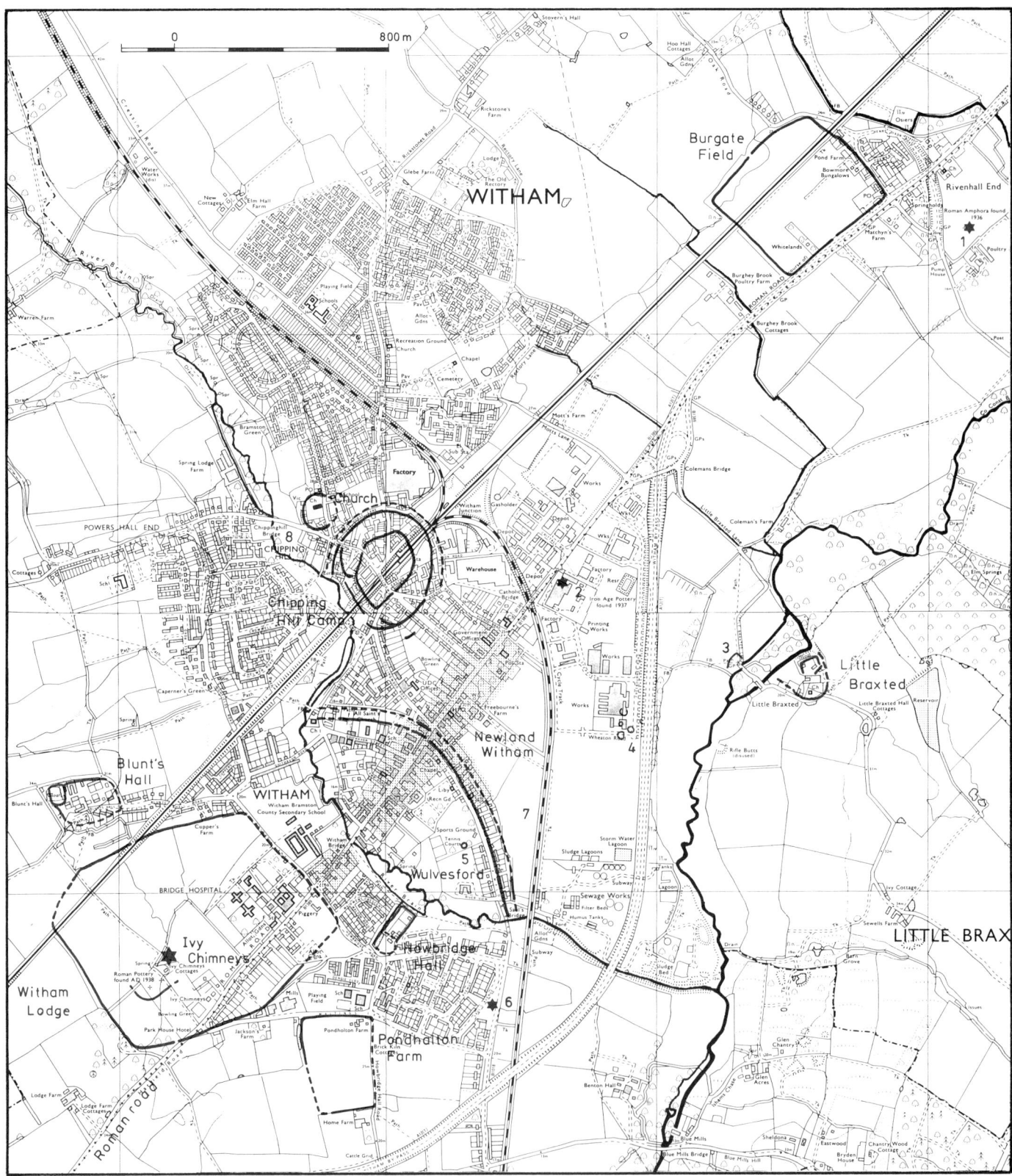

Fig. 2. *Reduced extract from the Ordnance Survey 1:10,000 map of Witham, with the rivers Brain and Blackwater emphasised. The major earthworks are outlined, and areas of medieval planned town are indicated by stipple. Lesser archaeological sites are numbered:* **1.** *Rivenhall End (burial?);* **2.** *Step Field (settlement);* **3.** *Cropmark enclosure, Little Braxted;* **4.** *Ring ditches, Barn Field;* **5.** *Mount Field;* **6.** *Maldon Road (cemetery);* **7.** *'Potlids';* **8.** *Mount Meadow. Since the date of this survey (1968), the majority of the open areas to the west of the A12 by-pass have been infilled by development. Scale 1:20,000. (Crown Copyright).*

Chipping Hill

At Chipping Hill, lie the last vestiges of two almost concentric earthworks of sub-circular plan, commonly known as Chipping Hill Camp (Fig. 2). This occupies a small spur on the 30 m (100 ft) contour on the east bank of the river Brain, a tributary of the Blackwater. Owing to modern development, the Witham spur is now ill-defined, but in antiquity the land fell away gently to the east and south, and there was a much steeper slope to the floodplain of the Brain on the west (Fig. 3).

The interior of the camp stood some 10 m above river level, on a terrace of mixed gravels and clays. Geologically, the Chipping Hill spur is glacial sand and gravel (Chelmsford Gravels), capped by a thin layer of Boulder Clay (Springfield Till), and underlain by further Boulder Clay (Maldon Till). Beneath these Pleistocene deposits is the older London Clay, which forms the floor of the Brain valley.

The camp is transected by several roads, and early maps demonstrate that four breaches in the outer defences are not modern; the inner circuit is broken in only two places. Immediately outside the north-west entrance is the parish church of St Nicholas, Witham, and a roughly triangular green which was formerly a market place (Figs. 4B and 5). The settlement at Chipping Hill remained distinctly separate from the 'new town' (with its own market place) on the main road until late in the last century, but the two elements have now fully coalesced.

Most of the county and local historians of the eighteenth and early nineteenth centuries alluded to the Chipping Hill earthworks. They were also noticed by some of the greater antiquaries, including Edmund Gibson. Opinions concerning the origin of these works were divided: some writers attributed the camp to the Roman period, equating it with the settlement of *Ad Ansam* or that of *Canonium*, recorded in the Antonine Itinerary. Both associations are demonstrably erroneous, *Ad Ansam* being at Stratford St Mary, and *Canonium* at Kelvedon (Rodwell 1975).

The identification with *Ad Ansam* was first promulgated by Gibson (1695, 358), accepted by William Holman, *c.* 1720[1] and by John Horsley (1733, 445), sceptically repeated by Philip Morant (1768, 106), firmly restated by Thomas Wright (1836, 216), and followed by some subsequent authors, even down to recent years. The alternative identification, *Canonium*, was proposed by Richard Gough (1789, 56), accepted by James Dugdale (1819, 411–12), and championed by John Adey Repton (1848, 320). A radically different view, especially for its time, was advanced by Joseph Strutt (1774, 25), who proclaimed Chipping Hill as a 'Saxon castle'.

Fig. 3. *View of Chipping Hill, Witham, from the south in 1832. The inner defences on the west side of the prehistoric earthwork appear on the right; the outer defences, on the terrace below, had been levelled by this time. For the location of the view-point, see plan Fig. 10. (After Wright 1836, opp. 216).*

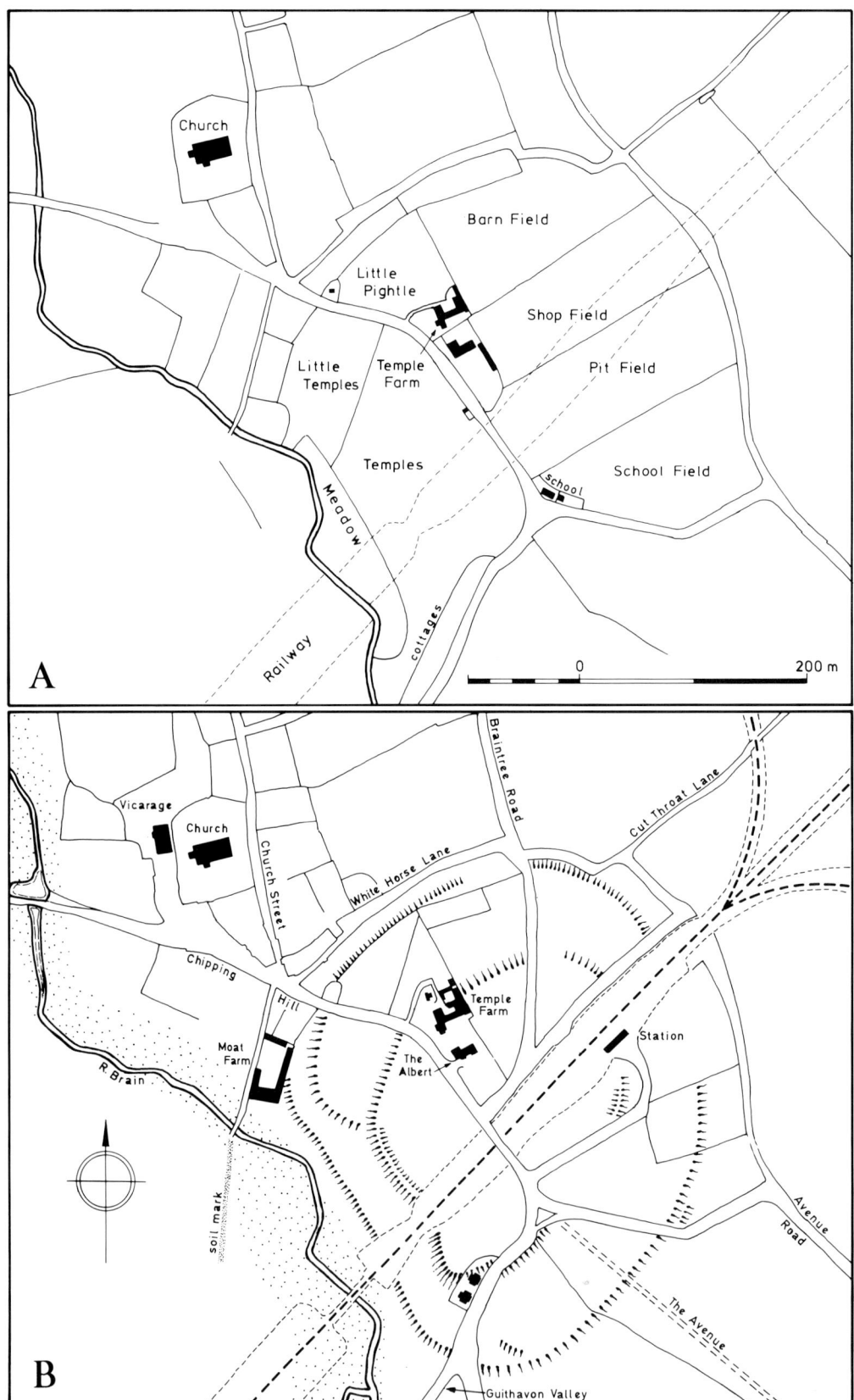

Fig. 4. A. Plan of Temple Farm, Chipping Hill, in 1839, as shown on the Witham Tithe map, replotted to an Ordnance Survey base. The line of the proposed Eastern Counties Railway had just been determined when the survey was made.
B. The local topography of Chipping Hill in the early twentieth century, showing earthworks surveyed by D. H. Montgomerie in c. 1911, together with minor additions made by F. Cottrill in 1934. The river flood-plain is lightly stippled.

A shift of opinion away from Roman associations gradually occurred during the nineteenth century — as antiquarian interest began seriously to embrace post-classical monuments — and the earthworks were more generally asserted to be those of the *burh* of Witham which, according to the *Anglo-Saxon Chronicle*, was constructed by Edward the Elder in 913 (now recalibrated to 912: see Whitelock 1961). The site was briefly mentioned in this context by several of the county historians (eg. Anon., 1818, 28; Coller 1861, 368). Notwithstanding, local opinion adhered firmly to the Roman affiliation, and in the 1882 sale particulars the site was described as 'An Ancient Roman Camp'.[2]

Fuller descriptions of the site were given by local antiquaries, W.J. Lucas (1884), F.C.J. Spurrell (1887) and I.C. Gould (1903). Witham was also accorded prominent treatment in several general accounts of fortifications (eg. Armitage 1912), and its burghal status received the imprimatur of the Victoria County History (Gould 1903) and the Royal Commission on Historical Monuments (RCHM 1921).

Excavations at Chipping Hill, 1933–1988

In the early 1930s, when Dr (later Sir) R.E.M. Wheeler was assembling material for his handbook *London and the Saxons* (Wheeler 1935), he was acutely aware of the paucity of later Anglo-Saxon artifacts from excavated sites in the London region, and accordingly instigated a research excavation designed to shed light on a period that was then largely untouched by field archaeology. Wheeler's attention turned to Witham, a moderately preserved earthwork site, accessible for excavation, and seemingly securely dated. The site was known to him from his days as a pre-war (1914–18) investigator with the Royal Commission on Historical Monuments. The resultant Chipping Hill project, begun in 1933 under the supervision of the late Frank Cottrill (then a member of Wheeler's staff at the London Museum), was sponsored principally by the Society of Antiquaries, the Royal Archaeological Institute and the Essex Archaeological Society.[3]

Cottrill's first excavation sectioned the defences on the west side of the camp in Temples Field (Figs. 4 and 10), yielding small quantities of Iron Age and Roman material, as well as 'grass-tempered' pottery which was initially accepted as being of later Saxon date, despite some reservations concerning its early Saxon affinities (Cottrill 1934). Further work, on a larger scale, was undertaken in 1934–35, on the west and south defences, and in the interior of the camp. Some of the artifacts recovered were overtly of Iron Age type, and doubts began to arise concerning the attribution of much of the pottery to the Saxon period. The preconception that

Fig. 5. *View of Chipping Hill, looking north-west from the inner rampart in Temples Field (1933). Moat Farm is centre left, and the river Brain is concealed by the trees alongside. (Photo: T. C. Gall).*

Chipping Hill had to be the Edwardian *burh* was so strong that it even coloured the initial identification of non-ceramic finds from the site. A fragment of iron was unhesitatingly claimed as a Saxon sword (*scramasax*), a late Roman glass bowl was also held to be Saxon, and British potin coins were assigned to the ninth century.

In due course, the plain truth could no longer be ignored: excavations ceased, and in August 1935 Cottrill summarised the dating of Chipping Hill in a letter to Wheeler. He noted four coins, 'chief among the dating evidence', describing them as 'British base metal ones, uninscribed, with irregular clipped flan (Evans [1864] ch. VII, and pl. H). They are supported by a fragment of triangular loomweight, two clay sling bullets and part of a bone comb of the prehistoric form with ring-and-dot ornament ... two bronze rings and some ironwork give the impression of being the same period. So I think the problem of period is at last settled ... It will be amusing to find out what queer local sort of Iron Age the place represents. It is certainly non-Belgic — there was not one fragment of Belgic pottery in the place — perhaps it is Trinobantian!'[4]

Although it was to remain unappreciated for another three or four decades, Cottrill had stumbled upon the elusive Middle Iron Age in Essex, but that was no consolation at the time. Cottrill was despondent: Wheeler was furious. For various reasons, no detailed report on Chipping Hill was ever written, although some of the finds were illustrated in preparation for one. Over the course of time, and particularly in consequence of the Second World War, the finds and records became dispersed and many were lost.[5]

Considerable academic confusion then ensued. It is necessary to outline this in order to explain how Chipping Hill has acquired a dual identity in archaeological and historical writing. Cottrill's only published account of Witham (1934) maintained unequivocally that Chipping Hill was the site of Edward's *burh*. He was merely following the lead already given by the Victoria County History and the Royal Commission on Historical Monuments. Many recent scholars too have accepted this viewpoint without demur, including Stenton (1947, 321), Beresford (1967, 159, 436) and Petchey (Eddy and Petchey 1983, 91). In local historical writing, Chipping Hill Camp is still resolutely identified as the Edwardian *burh* (eg. Gyford 1985; Henderson 1986).

Other scholars, particularly prehistorians, were however privy in the 1950s and '60s to Cottrill's unpublished dating evidence, and once it was accepted by them that most of the artifacts initially labelled as Anglo-Saxon were in fact Iron Age, a reaction set in, and it was widely denied that the Chipping Hill earthworks were the *burh* at all. Witham was firmly included in Cotton's survey of Iron Age hillforts in southern England (Cotton 1960), and it appeared as a

multi-vallate enclosure on the Ordnance Survey's *Map of Southern Britain in the Iron Age* (1962). The most recent discussions of the camp have been by Rodwell (1976a; 1976b), and Morris and Buckley (1978).

Meanwhile, the search for Edward the Elder's *burh* continued, and the possibility that it might be located at an alternative site in the Witham area was countenanced by Dr David Trump who, in 1958, sectioned the sub-rectangular earthwork at Blunt's Hall, 1.2 km south-west of Chipping Hill (Figs. 2 and 32). This site was shown to be a moated manor of eleventh and twelfth-century date (Trump 1961). Attention switched back to the Chipping Hill earthworks, and in 1969 and 1971 Brian Davison sectioned the northern defences in advance of the construction of a new link-road. Although in 1930 nearly half of the site was free from development, by 1969 very little open space remained, and the ramparts had almost entirely disappeared without any excavation or recording during the intervening period.[6] Far from resolving the question of dating, the 1969–71 sections raised fresh problems. At least two periods of earthwork construction were revealed, but without close dating evidence: prehistoric and medieval. There was, however, still no direct evidence for an Anglo-Saxon phase, although an undated phase of the outer ditch could conceivably be assignable to the Edwardian era.

The erosion of Chipping Hill by housing and factory development continues, and the camp is no longer visible as a field monument. The redevelopment in 1988 of the site of the glove (later button) factory in Temples Field facilitated a fresh examination of a small area at the south-west corner of the site, including the inner rampart and what may have been the outer ditch, as well as ground between the two lines of defence. This work, which was carried out by Essex County Council, affirmed the prehistoric date of both earthwork circuits, at this point. Pottery evidence pointed to the probability that the inner earthwork was constructed in the Late Bronze Age. The presence of Late Neolithic flints and pottery indicated an even earlier settlement site here. The collection of flints from the 1988 excavation extended knowledge of human activity back to the Mesolithic period.

Other Enclosed Sites at Witham

Up to the late 1960s, there were only vague records of nineteenth and early twentieth-century discoveries of prehistoric and Roman artifacts at a few other locations in Witham parish. Most interesting amongst these appeared to be the site at Ivy Chimneys Cottages, 1.8 km south-west of Chipping Hill (Fig. 2). Bronze Age pottery had been reported in the mid-nineteenth century, and Romano-British finds were made in 1938 (Hull 1963, 201–2). Excavations in the late 1960s by the

Witham Archaeological Research Group yielded a high proportion of small-finds, some of which indicated votive activity (Frere 1970; Henig *et al*. 1972).

In 1970 the redevelopment of an adjacent property, Witham Lodge, was begun and the contractors' trenches were observed by P.J. Drury, who discovered substantial ditches belonging to a levelled earthwork alongside the Chelmsford to Witham road. Thus a new dimension was added to the problem of the Witham earthworks. Further excavations in 1971 by W.J. and K.A. Rodwell revealed a major Iron Age enclosure and further Romano-British material (Figs. 2 and 29). There was a hint of Anglo-Saxon occupation too (Rodwell forthcoming). Although the considerable extent and importance of the site were fully established, it was nevertheless mostly built upon without archaeological investigation. Only the posited site of a Roman temple was excavated, in 1979–82, by the Archaeology Section of Essex County Council. A Roman religious complex, which included an early Christian baptistery, was revealed (Turner, forthcoming).

The number of possible candidates for the site of Edward's *burh* was increased yet again in 1977, when a 18 ha, rectangular enclosure with the evocative name of 'Burgate Field' was discovered, as an incidental by-product of topographical and historical research, alongside the Colchester road at Rivenhall End, 1.6 km north-east of Chipping Hill (Figs. 2 and 31; Rodwell and Rodwell 1985 and 1992, forthcoming). At the same time, a topographical study of the Witham area resulted in the recognition of another earthwork enclosure beneath the 'new town'. This enclosure cut off a bend in the river Brain, as well as straddling the Roman road (Figs. 2 and 28).

Finally, in addition to the four major defensive earthworks at Witham, there are several enclosures of lesser magnitude that deserve notice, even though they are not serious contenders for the status of *burh*. Perhaps the most interesting of these is the former circular enclosure at Chipping Hill, containing the parish church, vicarage and graveyard (Figs. 2 and 23). The Blunt's Hall earthwork, previously mentioned (p. 6), is readily identifiable as a fortified manor house (a diminutive motte-and-bailey castle); and it is possible that a similar site existed at Howbridge Hall (Figs. 32 and 33).

In sum, it is now clear that the river crossing at Witham has not only been favoured as a location for continuous settlement since the late Neolithic — and probably since the Mesolithic — but has also been of recurrent importance as a defensive position. Despite the bewildering number of earthwork enclosures at Witham, and the paucity of archaeological evidence derived from excavation, unreserved claims for the Anglo-Saxon primacy of Chipping Hill continue to be made: 'it can be stated confidently that the outer rampart of the Chipping Hill earthwork is the defensive circuit of the Saxon *burh* (Eddy and Petchey 1983, 91; see also Petchey 1980, 113). The time is therefore ripe for a presentation of the evidence relating to all the known earthworks and major archaeological sites in and around Witham, and for an overall assessment of their significance in the history and topography of the locality.

2

Chipping Hill Camp

The Site and Early Discoveries

The earliest reference to the earthworks (TL 820151) is contained in Gibson's edition of Camden's *Britannia*, where it is reported that 'between the church and the street are still visible the remains of a large old camp; though much of the fortifications are digg'd down to make way for the plow, and a road lyes through the midst of it'[7] (Gibson 1695, 358). A specific act of destruction, apparently datable to the closing years of the seventeenth century, was reported by Holman: 'Mr Barwell, in levelling some hills belonging to the Roman worke', found two coins, the legends on which he accurately noted. The incident was not published until the mid-eighteenth century by the county historian, Morant (1768, 106).[8] Robert Barwell, who died in 1697, was probably clearing the central-southern segment of the outer earthworks in preparation for the construction of 'The Avenue' through the park associated with his new house, The Grove (Figs. 26 and 49).[9] It was later reported that the road leading out of the camp to the south-west (Mill Lane) ran on top of the inner bank for part of its course (Gough 1789, 56).

The subdivision of the interior of the camp into several fields, as depicted on the Tithe map (Fig. 4A), did not occur until sometime in the eighteenth century. In *c.* 1720 Holman noted, 'The whole by ye name of Temples'; but by 1839 the name applied only to the western half of the camp, and that was subdivided into 'Temples' and 'Little Temples'.[10] Holman was also responsible for the earliest known plan of Chipping Hill, although it has neither been published nor its existence mentioned by any previous writer (Fig. 6).

The first detailed description of the camp was by the Essex antiquary, Joseph Strutt. His account should be read in conjunction with his perspective view and plan of the earthworks (Fig. 7, A, B, respectively). 'The middle circle A contains the keep or castle and is about 160 yards in diameter, and 486 yards round; the ditch B is now much filled up with the digging down of the keep, and is in its

present state 260 feet in breadth; beyond the ditch is the external vallum, which is yet in a very perfect condition full 4 feet high and 18 or 20 feet in breadth; the circumference of the whole is about 1,000 yards. Where the external vallum is broken off at D there is a steep precipice down to the river so that here the ditch seems only to be a common surface of earth below the keep, but this has been effected in labouriously digging down the external vallum, for the more easy ploughing up the ground about it.' (Strutt 1774, 25).

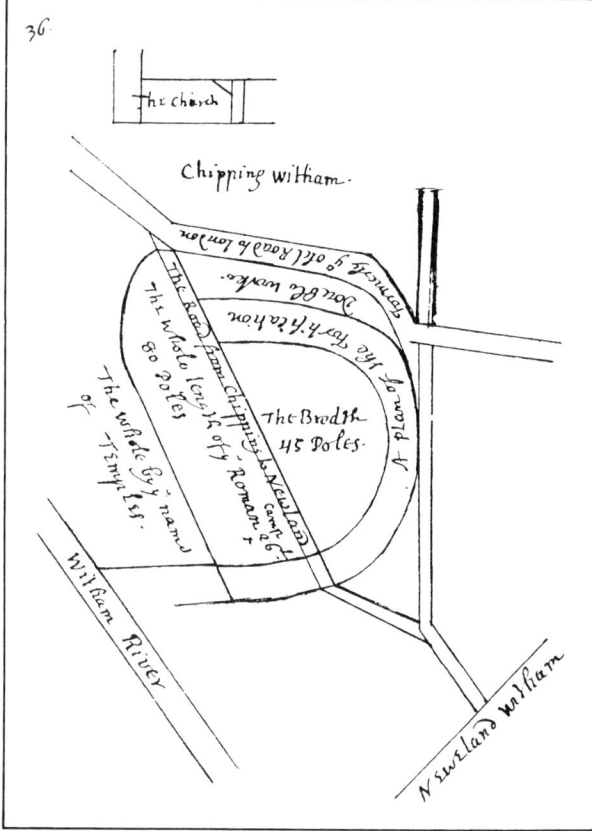

Fig. 6. The earliest known plan of Chipping Hill Camp, made by William Holman, c. 1720. North is at the top. (Reproduced by courtesy of the Essex Record Office).

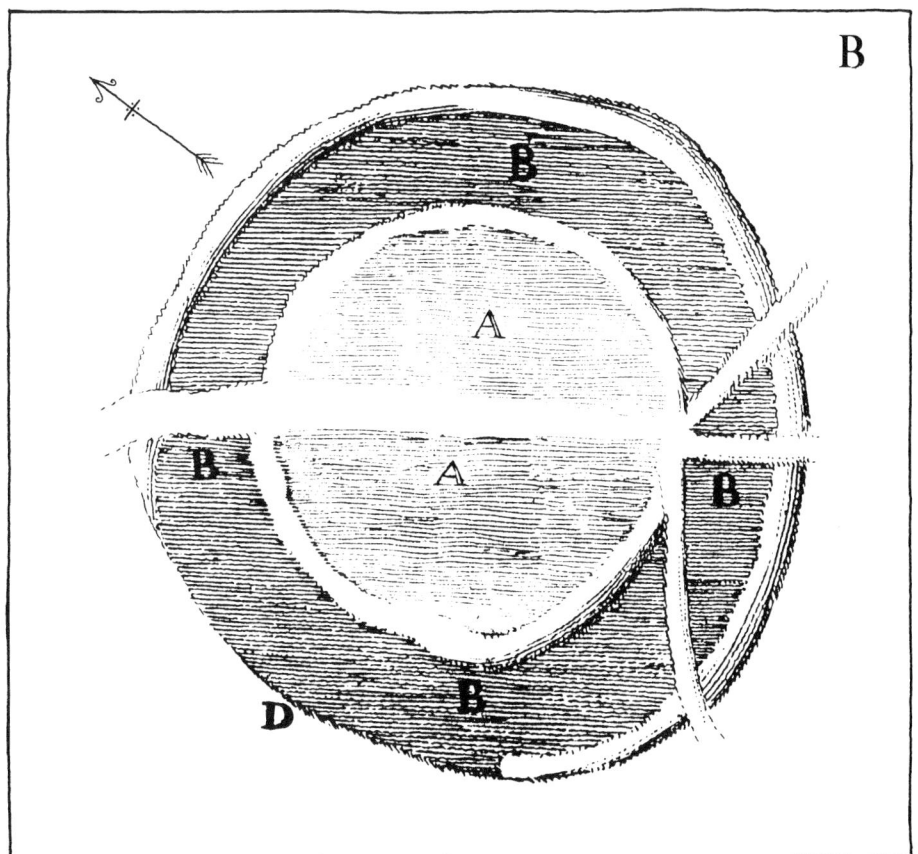

Fig. 7. A. *Perspective view of Chipping Hill Camp, Witham, from the west in 1774. Roads, hedges and Temple Farm have been omitted. The drawing was made from the river bank, the flanking vegetation of which appears at the bottom of the picture. The indentation in the inner earthwork was possibly an old quarry, through which the railway cutting passed in 1844.*
B. *Plan of Chipping Hill Camp in 1774; roads passing through the site are shown, but Temple Farm is omitted. Compass orientation added. (After Strutt 1774, pl. II.5, 6).*

While it may be accepted that Strutt's illustration contains a certain amount of artistic licence, it does however ante-date some of the recorded destruction.[11] Moreover, it was published before Gough's 1789 edition of *Britannia*, wherein the camp is described as 'defended by a double vallum, almost levelled within on the south side, but very plain on the west' (Gough 1789, 56). Some idea of the relationship between the western defences and the flood plain can be seen from an engraving of 1832 (Fig. 3, after Wright 1836, opp. 216).

The greatest act of depredation suffered by the camp came in 1844, when the Eastern Counties (Great Eastern) Railway drove its main line from London to Colchester through the middle of the site, in a deep cutting. At the centre of the camp the cutting was enlarged for the construction of Witham station. There are no records of archaeological observation during the sectioning of the defences, although local antiquaries were almost certainly present: Coller (1861, 369), in support of his refutation of the supposed Roman date of the camp, added, 'the railway navvie, when he came to assault the hill for the formation of the line, settled the question by the report that his pick had not brought to light a single weapon or other fragmentary record to sustain the theory' (of Roman origin).

Curiously, Coller had overlooked a report of the finding of skeletons and three 'weapons or instruments in iron, much corroded, on the site of an ancient camp in Witham, called Temple Field' (Anon. 1844, 393). It has already been noted that Temple(s) Field lay in the western part of the camp, where it spanned the outer and inner defences (Fig. 4A). Although the three iron objects, which attracted little attention at the time, were correctly described as fire pokers by Lucas (1884, 208), Baldwin Brown included them amongst his discussion of spears and angons, on the presumption of their being Saxon in date (Brown 1915, 603). Consequently, Witham entered the literature as an early Anglo-Saxon burial site (Meaney 1964, 89). The burials alluded to may have been of the Iron Age, since the pokers are distinctive of the La Tène II–III period, and are amongst the finest examples known. They have been fully discussed elsewhere (Rodwell 1976c). While it has been presumed that the burials and the pokers were archaeologically associated, this may be an unwarranted assumption: the connection may only have been that they were discovered at the same time.

The Plan of the Earthworks
(Figs. 4, 6 and 10)

Although Chipping Hill was mapped as part of the Tithe Commissioners' survey of Witham in 1839, not a hint of the camp's defences is shown in the relevant fields, even though they were almost entirely intact at this time (Fig. 4A).[12] Likewise, the earthworks — then much

reduced — were largely omitted from the first edition of the Ordnance Survey 1:2500 map of 1874, only the western side being represented. The first attempt at a scaled plan of the camp, albeit crudely executed, was made by Spurrell in 1885, when the earthworks were in a very depleted state, but could nevertheless be traced around almost the entire circuit (Spurrell 1887).[13] A much better plan, of unknown authorship, was published by Allcroft (1908, fig. 117).

Chipping Hill Camp was recorded by D.H. Montgomerie for the Royal Commission on Historical Monuments in 1914, and the published plan accurately shows what then survived of the banks (RCHM 1921, 266).[14] Montgomerie's initial site survey must, however, have been made on an earlier visit to Witham, in *c.* 1911–12, since his plan was first published in Armitage's *Early Norman Castles* (1912, fig. 4).

The revised plan given here, Fig. 10, is largely based on Montgomerie's, but incorporates various pieces of topographical evidence, as well as the results of the excavations described below (pp. 12–25). Past commentators have generally asserted that there were formerly two concentric circuits of sub-circular plan, the western side of the outer defence having been levelled to create an artificial terrace above the river Brain. Moreover, on that same side Spurrell and Allcroft noted two short lengths of bank which linked together the inner and outer enclosures; little notice has been taken of these features.

It has, alternatively, been suggested that the so-called outer bank on the west is no more than a natural terrace of the Brain, with the two circuits of the camp here sharing a common side. Cottrill's excavations, however, demonstrated the presence of both an inner and outer ditch on the western terrace. Moreover, various topographical indicators — such as property boundaries around the north-west side of the camp, and the positions of roads along the northern and eastern sides — point to the likelihood that the outer defences themselves comprised a double line, at least in part (Fig. 10).

On morphological evidence alone, the Chipping Hill earthworks clearly embody more than one phase of construction, and their full plan is still not resolved. The inner circuit appears to be polygonal in outline, with well rounded corners. Its overall dimensions of are *c.* 270 m by 180–220 m, and the area enclosed within the rampart is *c.* 3.5 ha (8.7 acres). The maximum dimensions of the outer circuit are *c.* 380 m in both directions, and the area enclosed is *c.* 10.3 ha (25.5 acres); if a common western side were accepted the area would be reduced to *c.* 9.2 ha (22.7 acres).

No specific archaeological evidence has been recorded concerning entrances through either earthwork. On topographical grounds, it seems likely that the two breaches in the inner circuit are both original, through

Fig. 8. *The north-west corner of the inner earthwork at Chipping Hill, as seen from the north-north-west in 1933; the bank was sectioned here in Cottrill's trench B. (Photo: T.C. Gall).*

Fig. 9. *The west side of the inner earthwork at Chipping Hill, Viewed from the river terrace in 1933. The gravel quarry seen here corresponds to that shown on plan, Fig. 11.*

which the road known as Chipping Hill runs. This same road passes through a presumed original opening in the outer defences, to the south-east, and an early medieval breach to the north-west, associated with the creation of an extra-mural market place. The original northern entrance was probably east of this opening (i.e. nearer to the centre of the north side: Fig. 37). Two further breaches in this circuit are medieval or earlier in origin: Mill Lane (later Guithavon Valley) to the south-west, and Cut Throat Lane leading north-east towards Rivenhall (Fig. 4).

The Excavations of 1933–35

It is now impossible to reconstruct an adequate report on Cottrill's work: the inherent deficiencies here in both the presentation of the data, and their interpretation, are fully recognised. The drawings too are unavoidably Spartan. The sources for this account of the 1930s excavations are principally the site notes, plans and a few photographs deposited by Cottrill in the Colchester and Essex Museum, in 1974;[15] a correspondence file similarly deposited; the texts of two lectures delivered by Cottrill to the Society of Antiquaries;[16] and the glass-plate slides prepared to illustrate those lectures, formerly held in the Society's collection.[17] These accounts are supplemented by the first, and only, published interim report, on the 1933 season (Cottrill 1934); an unofficial account of the same, prepared by one of his local assistants, without consultation with Cottrill (Rowles 1934); and contemporary newspaper reports.[18] Many of the finds have been lost (p. 6), but those that survive, together with old drawings of others, are illustrated and discussed in the appendix, pp. 98–106.

The plans and sections published here have been compiled from originals; only one site notebook has been found, and the amount of information that it has been possible to assemble varies from trench to trench.[19] The excavations of 1933–35 sectioned both the inner and outer earthworks, as well as investigating the ground between the defences, and a small area within the interior of the camp. The order of the work was as follows. The 1933 season began in Temples Field, where trenches A and C were dug across the inner defences, and trench G was begun over the outer ditch. Trenches C1 and L were excavated between the defensive lines, while J and K were opened within the camp (Fig. 11).

In the following year, which was the principal season, the inner defences were again sectioned in trenches B and D, while the outer ditch was further explored in an extension to trench G. Elsewhere, trenches E and F were cut into the outer defences, and trench H was also started (Fig. 10). The 1935 season was short, and solely for the purpose of completing trench H, where a 'hut' site had been partially excavated in the previous season.

Several photographs of the earthworks in Temples Field, taken in 1933, show how impressive the inner circuit still was, particularly around the north-west corner (Figs. 8 and 9). The same photographs also reveal the effects of post-medieval levelling and terracing.

THE INNER DEFENCES *(Figs. 10, 11, 12 and 15)*

The inner defences were sectioned at three points, and also recorded in the sides of a quarry that had been cut into the edge of the river terrace in the early 1900s (Figs. 11 and 12). Trenches A, C and G together formed the only long section through the defences (Fig. 15); trench B sectioned the bank only, and trench D the ditch only. A cross-section of the bank only was studied in the quarry (Fig. 13).

It was demonstrated in trenches A and B that the first bank, composed of fine sandy soil mixed with small stones, was placed directly upon the old ground surface (F1), which it sealed. The same was dramatically revealed in the quarry section. On the south-west side of trench A the old surface was cut by a large pit or posthole 1 m in diameter and 0.5 m deep (F2); this in turn was sealed by the slumping of the first bank (F3). No similarly placed posthole was found in trench B, but a 'slot' 0.7 m wide was observed in the section of the bank revealed in the northern side of the quarry in Temples Field (Fig. 11). These postholes may have held a timber revetment to the front of the rampart (Fig. 14); and, although there was no evidence for this seen in trench B, a rear revetment was indicated by the way in which the tail of the bank stopped against a small mound of turf, F4 (Fig. 12.2; see also p. 23).

Phase 1 of the inner bank may thus have taken the form of a timber-framed rampart, *c.* 4 m wide at the base, with a low turf revetment at the rear. Immediately in front of the posthole of the putative revetment in trench A was a layer of 'burnt earth, wood ash and charcoal' (F5), but whether this represents a burning of the timber revetting in the course of warfare, or simply an act of clearance for the construction of phase 2 cannot be determined on the slender evidence available.

Phase 2 of the bank's construction was a dump rampart of 'sand with some small pebbles', at least 12 m wide at the base (F6), and surviving in 1933 to a height of between 1.5 m and 2.0 m. No constructional features seem to have been associated with this phase. In both trenches A and B it was found that the back of the phase 2 rampart had been cut into; the same was also noted in the section of bank exposed in the modern quarry. There is no ready explanation for this phenomenon, which cannot be interpreted as construction works, or slighting of the defences. Possibly these intrusions into the bank represent no more than small scale gravel quarrying. It was found

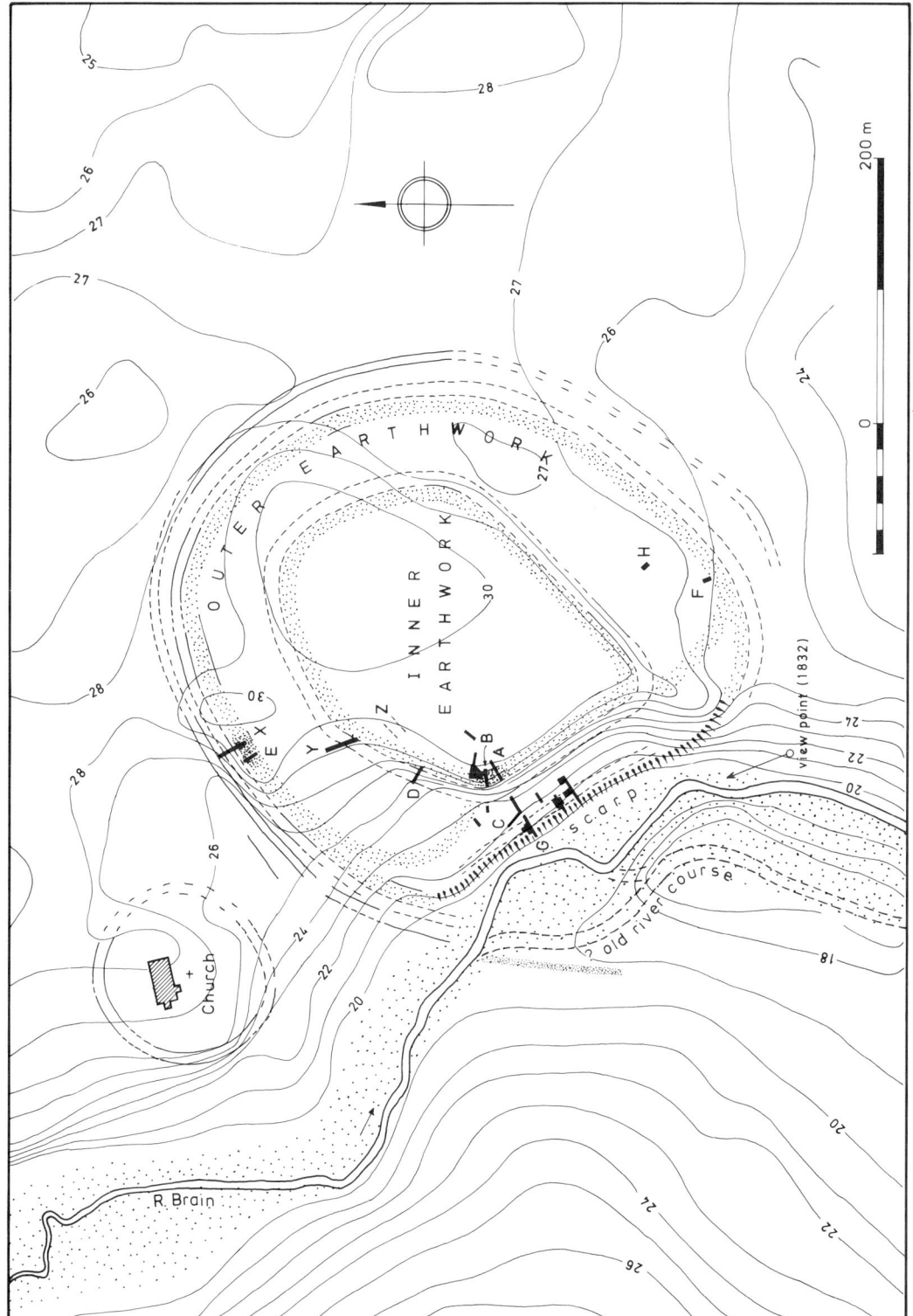

Fig. 10. Reconstructed plan of the landscape contours and earthworks at Chipping Hill, based on a combination of cartographic, field survey and archaeological evidence. Ditches are shown in outline; ramparts are stippled. The positions of the excavation trenches are indicated and the approximate viewpoint of the 1832 illustration (Fig. 3) is marked. Contours in metres above O.D.

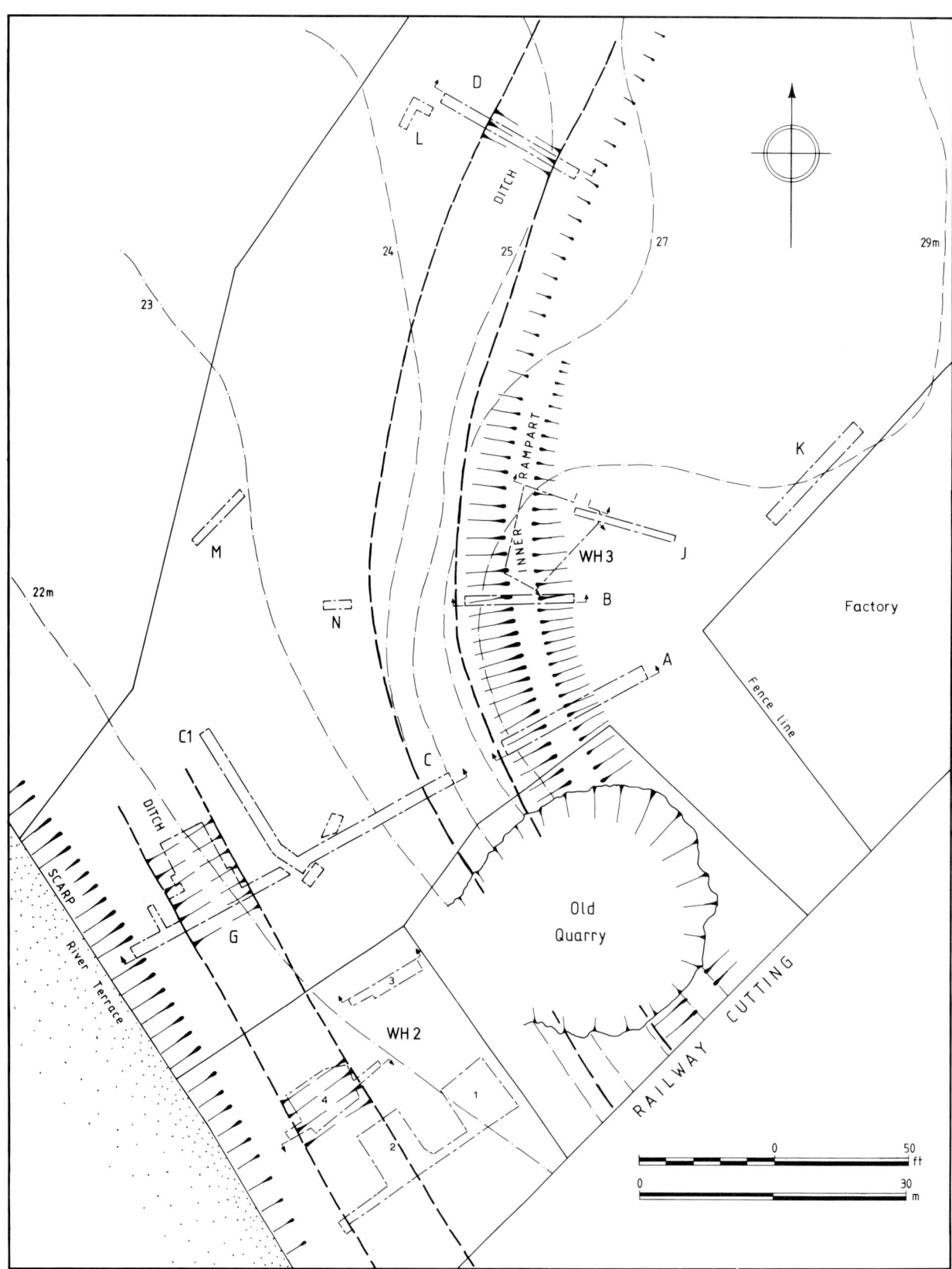

Fig. 11. *Plan of Temples Field, Chipping Hill, in 1933 showing the extant earthworks and archaeological trenches (A-N). The location of the 1988 excavations is also shown (WH2, WH3). Contours in metres O.D.*

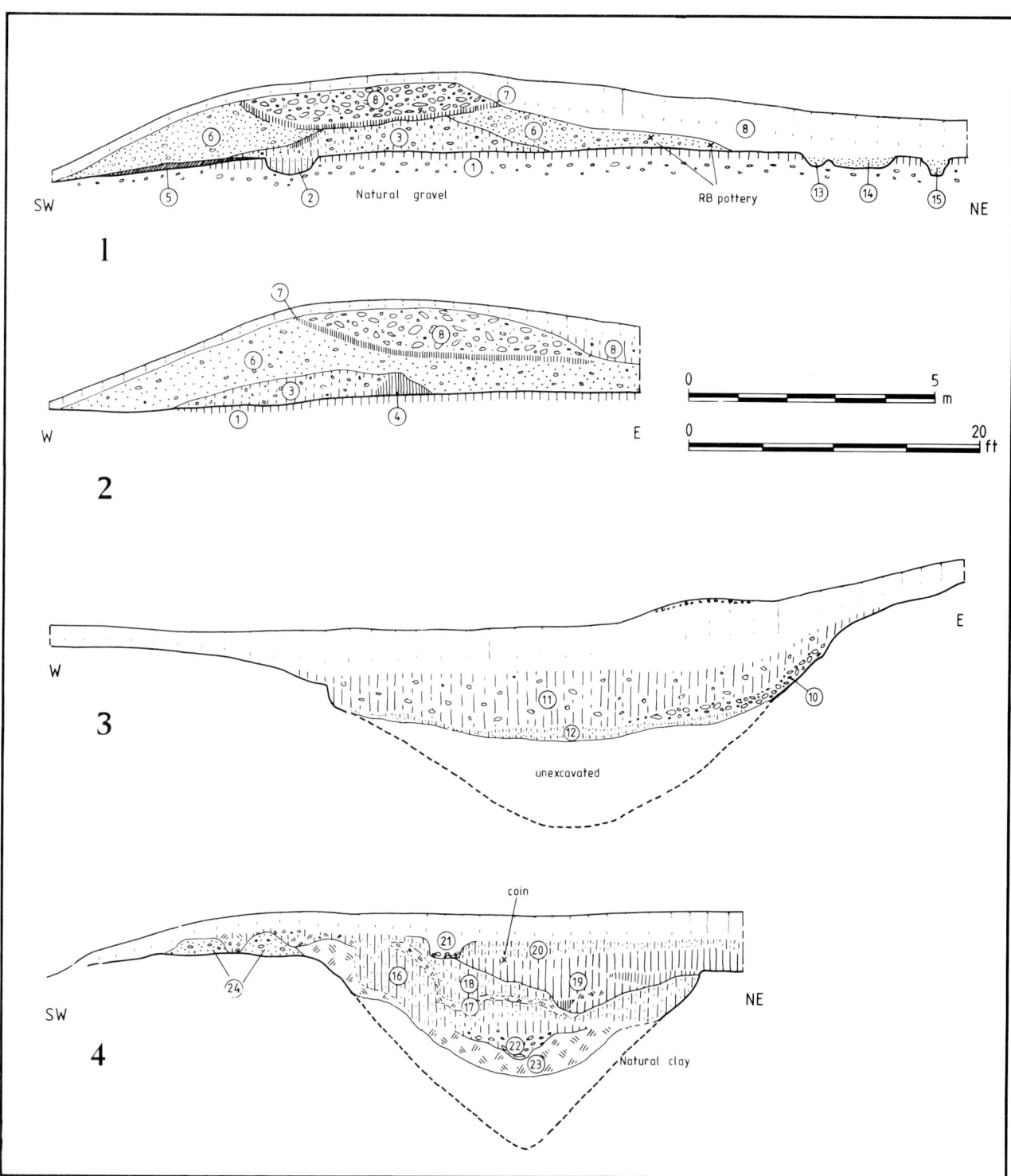

Fig. 12. *Sections through the earthworks in Temples Field, Chipping Hill, 1933. Suggested profiles of incompletely excavated ditches are marked with broken lines. For location plan see Fig. 11. 1. Trench A: south face, reversed. 2. Trench B: south face, reversed. 3. Trench D: north face. 4. Trench G: north face, composite section.*

that these pits or hollows had remained open long enough for a substantial topsoil (F7) to form in them, before being deliberately refilled (F8).

The refilling of these cuts is taken to indicate a reconstruction of the rampart: phase 3. Finally, a shallow scoop (F8), almost certainly a quarry pit, was found to have cut away the inner edges of the phase 2 and phase 3 ramparts in trenches A and B. Regrettably, these trenches were not extended down the slope, and trench C, dug into the level terrace below, failed to locate substantial evidence of a ditch. However, there was a sufficient gap between A and C for the degraded inner ditch to have been entirely missed.

The profile of the slope from the inner rampart down to the river is indicative of artificial terracing, and Strutt's description (1774) gives the impression that this had taken place for agricultural purposes, not too long since (Fig. 15). Terracing must, however, have been carried out before *c.* 1720, since it was clearly, but crudely, shown on Holman's sketch plan (Fig. 6). Moreover, at the east end of trench C a slight dip, F9, was noted in the surface of the natural, filled with lenses of gravel which had entered from the direction of the rampart. These vestigial remains are consistent with a U-shaped ditch associated with the inner rampart, that was later scarped away. It seems likely that this same action not only caused the rampart of the outer earthwork to be entirely removed, but that the surface of the natural gravel was also lowered.

Clear evidence for levelling was revealed in the 1988 excavation (p. 27), and the 1933 photographs show how the profile of the inner defences had been remodelled to such an extent that it had more the appearance of a river terrace than a degraded earthwork. Part of the purpose of the seventeenth-century terracing operation was probably to level out the mess left by repeated quarrying of the river terrace for gravel. Even so, fresh pits, worked from the side, continued to be cut into the terrace well into the present century.[20]

Further to the north-east, trench D located what appeared to be a wide, flat-bottomed ditch, 12 m across, and 2 m deep from the modern ground level (section, Fig. 12.3). Apart from one stoney lens (F10), most of the filling was humic (F11), and the lowest level of silting was described as 'clayey, like natural soil' (F12). Unfortunately, trench D was not extended to link up with the inner rampart. It seems unlikely that this shallow ditch could have obliterated an earlier U-shaped ditch on the same line, and it is posited that Cottrill recorded only the secondary profile, the primary cut having been filled with cleanish gravel was overlooked by the excavators (cf. the true profile recorded in the 1971 excavation, Figs. 17 and 22.4, 5).[21]

No reliable dating evidence was recovered during the excavations for any of the phases of the inner rampart. In the upper levels of the tail of the phase 2 bank (trench A, F6) two sherds of later Roman pottery were

Fig. 13. *South-facing section of the denuded inner west bank, recorded in the side of a quarry in 1933. The buried soil horizon is indicated, and the lip of the partially scarped-away ditch appears to be visible on the left. (Photo: T. C. Gall)*

found (marked on Fig. 12.1), but have since been lost. In this position they are most likely to have been associated with the final scooping away of the back of the rampart: i.e. material trodden into the floor of the quarry pit. Truncated pits of Roman date were recorded in the same trench (F13–15, p. 19). Such slight evidence can only be taken to imply that the final quarry was of Roman or later date. More significantly, the absence of Roman-period artifacts from the bank and ditch points firmly to a pre-Roman date for the inner defences.[22]

Fig. 14. View looking north-east along trench A in 1933. The two buried soil horizons are visible as dark layers towards the base of the bank. In the foreground is a possible posthole or slot that may have held a front revetment. Scale in feet. (Photo: T. C. Gall).

THE OUTER DEFENCES *(Figs. 10, 11, 12 and 15)*

The outer defences were examined at three points, in trenches E, F and G. Trench E, the site of which is now beneath the new Braintree Road (Fig. 10) sectioned only the tail of the outer rampart, yielding no clue as to its construction.[23] An occupation layer said to contain 'Saxon' pottery overlay the tail of the rampart, but in view of the contemporary confusion between Iron Age and Anglo-Saxon ceramics on this site, it is unwise to

base any conclusions on this statement (the pottery cannot now be located).

Overlying the occupation debris was a stoney layer, which was interpreted at the time as material thrown down from the bank; and cut into this was a pit containing sherds of medieval pottery, also no longer extant. This trench was very close to the section cut in 1969 (trench X, p. 20).

There are no surviving plans or sections of trench F, which lay near Collingwood Road, in the garden of what is now number 44 (Fig. 10). This trench is said to have located the edge of the outer ditch, which Cottrill estimated to be at least 6 m wide and 2 m deep.[24]

Trench G continued the long section across Temples Field, begun in trenches A and C. It was positioned to define the anticipated bank of the outer defences, which was supposed to be represented by the scarp slope above the flood plain, shown in Fig. 10. Instead of a bank, however, the trench located what was thought at the time to be an irregular pit (section, Fig. 12.4) containing 'layers of clean, natural-looking sand, clay and gravel' (F16–18). There was a clearly defined secondary fill of 'most dark sandy soil' (F19) in the top of which was found a St Edmund Memorial penny, datable to the early tenth century (p. 106; Fig. 57. Blunt *et al.* 1989, 100–2). This filling material was itself sealed by a 'barren layer of sandy soil' (F20), through which was cut a small circular pit (F21: projected onto the section). This feature was packed with flint pebbles and was interpreted at the time as a hearth, but on the contemporary photographs it has the appearance of being the foundation pad for a large, earthfast post. Interpretation must remain equivocal: in the filling above the pebbles the neck of a Thetford ware pitcher was found (Fig. 54.29), and fragments of a late Roman glass cup (then thought to be Anglo-Saxon) were recovered from 'nearby' (Fig. 55). Beneath all of the sequence just described was an inadequately excavated series of deeper deposits (F22–23), suggestive of the fills of a ditch.

In a letter to Cottrill, Wheeler offered his interpretation of the features.[25] He saw the 'clean, natural-looking' primary fill (F16–18) of the pit as the tail of a bank, and the dark sandy soil (F19) as silt deposited behind it. The bank, he argued, was then deliberately levelled during the tenth century in order to allow for the domestic occupation represented by the hearth (F21). Neither interpretation was satisfactory, and in the light of the 1988 excavation the whole sequence can be re-interpreted.

The section of trench G clearly shows a complex of large features cutting into one another, probably representing a long period of activity. The following sequence is tentatively proposed. The earliest excavated feature appeared to be a U-shaped ditch (F23), but was almost certainly only the secondary filling of a much

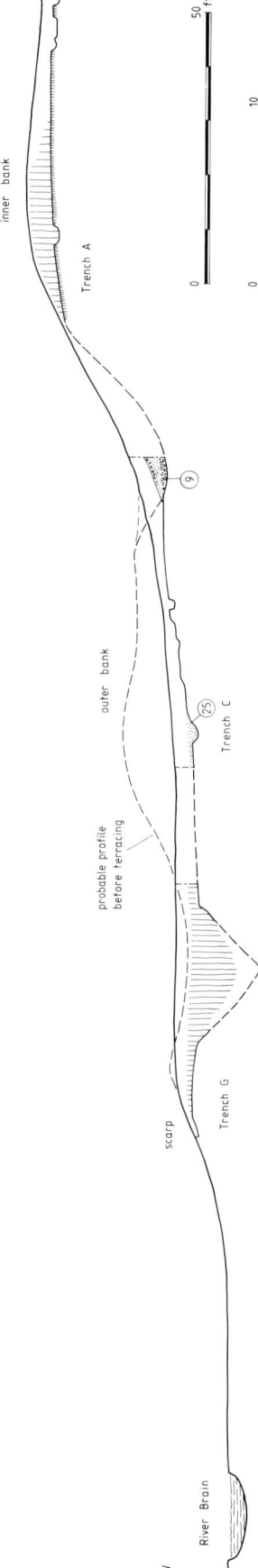

Fig. 15. Composite profile through the earthworks on the south-west side of Chipping Hill Camp (trenches A, C and G), showing the evidence recorded in 1933–34, together with a suggested reconstruction of the ditch profiles and the outer bank as it may have appeared in the seventeenth century, prior to the terrace being levelled.

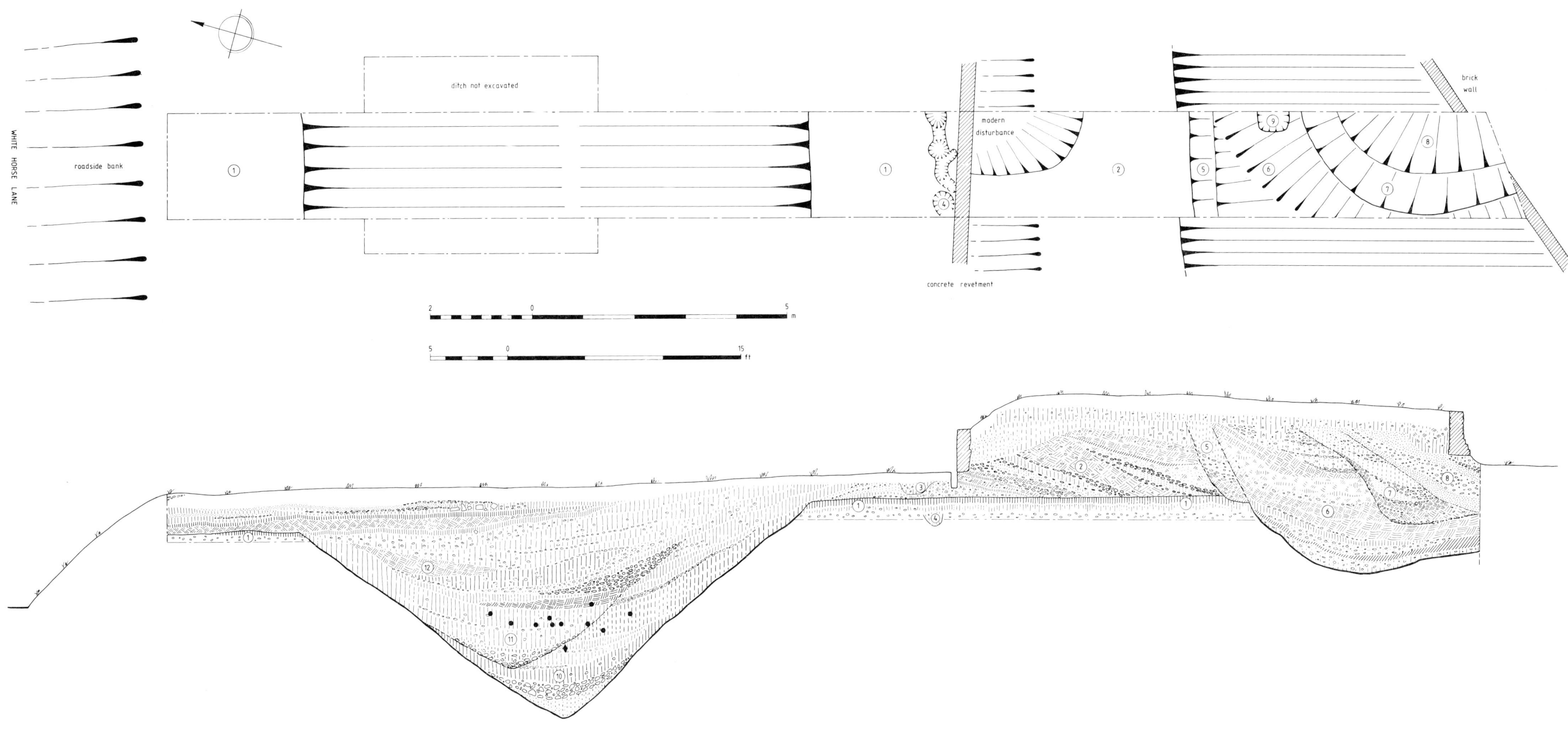

Fig. 16. *Plan and section of trench X, excavated across the outer defences of Chipping Hill Camp in White Horse Lane, 1969. The ten dots marked on the ditch section (on F10) indicate the projected findspots of sherds of twelfth and thirteenth-century pottery. The diamond-shaped symbol (on F10) indicates the findspot of the early Anglo-Saxon perforated sherd.*

deeper V-shaped ditch that was not recognised or fully excavated at the time. The second phase comprised a shallower V-shaped ditch (F16–18, 22). In a third phase, a yet smaller V-shaped ditch (F19) was cut into the top of the earlier deposits. This ditch was filled with dark silt and finally levelled over with a layer of sandy soil (F20) before the hearth pit was dug (F21). Potentially associated with one of the earlier phases are the remains of a truncated outer bank (F24), although these could be prehistoric alluvial deposits (see p. 23). The reconstructed sequence is illustrated on Fig. 22.3.

The dating evidence relevant to the outer defences would appear to be a large quantity of Middle Iron Age pottery (not now specifically identifiable) from the second ditch, a late Roman glass cup from the third ditch phase, the St Edmund Memorial coin from the interface between the final ditch filling and the levelling layer, and the late Saxon (eleventh century) pottery from the 'hearth' pit. The coin may not be regarded as securely sealed, since it was found below sandy soil in which rabbits and moles have doubtless burrowed for centuries; this in turn had been truncated by a major post-medieval levelling operation. The coin might thus have descended from a higher level. A contemporary report referred to 'Norman pottery brought to light in large quantities' in a pit on the outer defences.[26] None of the material has survived for study.

These finds have no bearing on the date of the original, incompletely excavated ditch, other than to suggest that it is not likely to be later than the Middle Iron Age.

TRENCHES IN THE INTERIOR *(Figs. 10, 11, 12 and 15)*

Cottrill excavated an uncertain number of trenches in Temples Field, between the river and the inner defences (Fig. 10: trenches C, L, M and N), and also within those defences (J and K). Trench C provided a typical section through the general stratification of the site between the defences. Below 25 cm of topsoil there was nearly a metre of stoney loam, overlying a darker loam with charcoal; this was interpreted as an 'occupation layer' since it contained much pottery thought at the time to be Anglo-Saxon, but now known certainly to be Iron Age. A beam slot was also reported, and there were several pits (including F25) sealed by this layer. Two of the pits yielded an Iron Age bone comb and a clay loomweight, which at the time were recognised as prehistoric, although no significance was attached to this.[27] Some of the black burnished pottery was also identified in 1934 as being Iron Age.

The excavation's most productive trench in terms of artifacts was trench H, located in a plot to the rear of Church House in Collingwood Road (now the garden of number 61, The Avenue); this lay between the inner and outer defences on the south side of the camp (Fig. 10).

The trench located a large, shallow flat-bottomed feature cut into the natural. Although no detailed plan appears to have survived, its maximum dimensions were 9.25 m by 4.8 m and the feature was filled with 'ash and other debris', including much pottery, several iron objects,[28] and burnt daub with wattle impressions.[29] At the time of excavation, the feature was interpreted as a 'hut floor' of the sunken (*grubenhaus*) type. The pottery recovered was, however, all of Iron Age date, and was accompanied by several Class I potin coins (p. 105). The so-called hut was probably a pit or 'working hollow'.

Three shallow features at the east end of trench A (Fig. 12.1, F13–15) yielded Roman pottery, which was also found overlying the tail of the rampart. The sherds included the complete profile of a vessel that was described as a 'Castor ware beaker' (Cottrill 1934), presumably Nene Valley colour-coated pottery of the third or fourth century.

The Excavations of 1969 and 1971
by B. K. Davison

The examination of the outer and inner lines of defence, carried out in 1969 and 1971, was a response to the proposed realignment of Braintree Road; this involved fresh breaches of both earthwork circuits. The excavations were directed for the (then) Inspectorate of Ancient Monuments, Ministry of Public Building and Works.

The outer defences were sectioned by a single trench (trench X) 25 m long, dug in what were then the gardens of properties fronting southwards on to Chipping Hill Road, and northwards on to White Horse Lane (Figs. 4B and 10). The extent of the excavation was severely restricted by fence-lines, trees and piles of old cars, and there was no opportunity to follow in plan the features located within the trench. The inner defences were sectioned by a single trench (trench Y) 26 m long, dug entirely by machine during actual road construction.

Both these exercises were somewhat hurried operations, with the 1971 section of the inner defences being more of a watching brief than a properly conducted excavation. The following account is therefore brief. The site records and finds have been deposited in the Colchester and Essex Museum.

THE OUTER DEFENCES *(Fig. 16)*

At the time of excavation in 1969, the rampart of the outer defensive circuit on the north survived to a height of 1.4 m, and was 10 m in width, the front and rear faces having been cut back and faced with brick and concrete. The site of the former ditch was a level garden, perched *c.* 1.5 m above the surface of White Horse Lane, which here lay in a hollow-way: while the hollow may have been artificially created to ease the gradient, it is no less likely that this was the site of another ditch forming part of the outer defences (p. 10). The ground levels were further confused by the presence of a late nineteenth-century gravel pit immediately to the west.[30] In the event, the prehistoric and medieval ground surface was found to slope gently down from south to north, at *c.* 27.5 m OD.

The rampart

This was sectioned by a 2 m wide trench (X), dug partly by hand, but using a mechanical digger wherever possible to accelerate the work. The sequence of stratification in the southern part of the rampart was found by machine-digging a narrow slot: thereafter layers were removed by hand. The old ground surface, the southern part of the rampart, and the inner lip of the ditch were excavated entirely by hand (section, Fig. 16).

The rampart was found to have been sited at a slight break in slope, the ground in front of it dropping gently into a shallow valley later occupied by White Horse Lane. The old topsoil horizon (F1) was clearly marked, and there was no obvious truncation of the profile such as would suggest the stripping of turf before constructing the rampart. [31] The only features noted in the buried soil were a series of interconnected hollows (F4), discussed below.

The top of the rampart had evidently been planed off, and the front and rear faces cut back, as a secondary operation. However, some estimate of the original size of the rampart can be made, since the materials used to build it resembled those forming the natural subsoil (that is, bands of sand, sandy gravel and clay), and were presumably obtained from digging the ditch. If all the material obtainable from the ditch was employed to form a rampart 12 m wide, then this would originally have stood some 3 m high. No evidence, in the form of buried turf-lines or stratigraphic unconformities, was found to support more than one period of construction at the front of the rampart.

The tip-lines in the rampart (F2) dipped steeply towards the rear, suggesting that the material had been piled against a frontal revetment which preceded the modern concrete revetting here. The exact location of any original revetment was not clear, the construction of a cow shed having removed much of the evidence. A shallow slot (F3) cut into the front of the rampart (or into collapsed material from it) one metre outside the modern revetting wall appeared to have held posts raking back towards the rampart at an angle of forty-five degrees. A second slot (or series of hollows, F4) was found dug into the subsoil immediately below the first slot, and apparently sealed by the old turf line. This may have been an animal burrow, rather than a structural feature, and the fact that it lay directly below F3 was presumably coincidental.

The two slots were examined with care, in the expectation that they would provide evidence for the frontal revetment inferred from the steepness of the tip-lines in the rampart. In the event, however, no firm conclusion was possible, though in the writer's opinion the balance lies in favour of some form of revetting, probably of timber, cut into the face of the rampart (or into its collapse) at a stage subsequent to its initial construction.

The southern part of the rampart proved to have undergone drastic modification on several occasions. The entire rear portion had been dug away by a large hollow (F5) of unknown size, cut down to a level slightly below the old soil line, leaving the sand and gravels of the rampart standing at an angle of sixty-five degrees. Before this face had time to erode, the hollow was filled again with clays and gravels. This filling was subsequently dug away once more, by a very large hollow (F6) which was cut 1.4 m into the subsoil, again leaving the rear of the rampart standing at sixty-five degrees. This second hollow was in turn refilled, this time with a greater proportion of clay, only to be cut by a third, much smaller feature (F7): only part of this projected into the excavated area, the remainder lying further to the east. This third hollow had apparently been cut at about the same angle as the previous one, but had lain unfilled long enough for the upper part of its edge to erode to an angle of forty-five degrees. The feature was then refilled with clay, sand and gravel before being cut by a fourth hollow (F8), the greater part of which also lay to the east of the area examined.

The purpose of these four consecutive hollows (F5–8) is not clear. No structural remains were associated with any of them, nor was anything found in them to indicate when they were dug. They do not appear to have been quarries, since all except the last was evidently backfilled within a short time with materials similar to those that had been dug out. The two later hollows were clearly only the western parts of features lying substantially outside the trench to the east, and there were indications that the two earlier hollows may have been similar in this respect. This may suggest that the hollows resulted from a series of repeated actions directed at this particular point on the defences. It would be possible to see them as reflecting the repeated insertion and removal of some large structural feature, whether of timber or stone, which rose from the body of the rampart close to the point where the defences crossed the neck of the ridge on which Chipping Hill is set. More than this cannot be inferred from the evidence so far to hand, and any further discussion must be pure speculation. It is noteworthy that similar hollows in the back of the rampart were found in the 1933–35 investigation of the inner defences (see p. 12, where they are interpreted as straightforward quarries).

A single, small pit (F9) cut into the upper part of the rampart contained nineteenth-century pottery.

The ditch *(F10–11)*

This was sectioned by a continuation of the 2 m wide trench cut through the rampart. The upper layers of the filling were removed by machine, the middle and lower layers by hand. The ditch was 10.0 m wide, it had a V-shaped profile, and had been cut to a depth of 3.6 m into the natural gravel and clay.

It was not clear whether there had originally been a berm between ditch and rampart. The twentieth-century damage to the front of the rampart made it uncertain whether the material found resting on the old soil in front of the modern concrete revetment represented the original front of the rampart, or collapse from it on to a berm. Equally, no clear evidence survived for a counterscarp bank. Layers of clay (F12) thrown on to the upper filling of the ditch may have come from cleaning out White Horse Lane, rather than from the destruction of a conterscarp bank.

There were no dateable finds from the lower fills; a single and very small sherd of an early Anglo-Saxon perforated container, found 1.3 m above the bottom of the ditch, is of equivocal value (p. 106). However, medieval pottery recovered from the middle filling of the ditch suggests that there was about 1.5 m of silt in it by the beginning of the thirteenth century.[32]

A further 0.5 m of natural silting resulted in the ditch (F10) becoming filled to the point where it formed a hollow 1.5 m deep. It was then recut (F11) to a depth of 2.8 m below the original ground surface. Pottery recovered from the lower filling of this secondary ditch indicates that the recutting must have taken place some time during the earlier part of the thirteenth century.[33] It is not clear what became of the spoil derived from

digging the second ditch. Layers forming the upper part of the main body of the rampart, and those filling the second of the four hollows later dug into it, were similar to those found in the primary ditch. However, no firm correlation was possible, and the exact stratigraphic relationships of the two successive ditches, the rampart, and the four later hollows dug into it, remain uncertain.

By the eighteenth century the recut ditch was only 1.3 m deep, and by the beginning of the present century it had ceased to be a recognisable feature in the landscape, partly as a result of deliberate tipping.

THE INNER DEFENCES *(Fig. 17)*

At the time of the excavation in 1971, the inner line of defence did not survive as a topographical feature. The location of the defences could thus be determined only approximately on the evidence of Spurrell's plan (1887), distortions in the modern road system, and the results of geophysical prospecting. Unfortunately, these gave conflicting indications, and there was no opportunity to search for the exact line until roadworks started, and *c.* 0.5 m of overburden had been removed from the line of the new road.

A single trench (Y) 0.9 m wide was dug mechanically, within the confines of the new road. In the event, the trench turned out to lie at approximately forty degrees to the line of the inner defences. The cross-section of the ditch exposed in this trench was hurriedly drawn, and the trench immediately refilled. The section shown in Fig. 17 is a true profile, the distortions caused by the obliquity of the trench to the line of the ditch having been corrected.

No trace remained of the inner rampart, nor of the old ground surface below it, the latter at least having been removed by the recent roadworks. The ditch (F13)

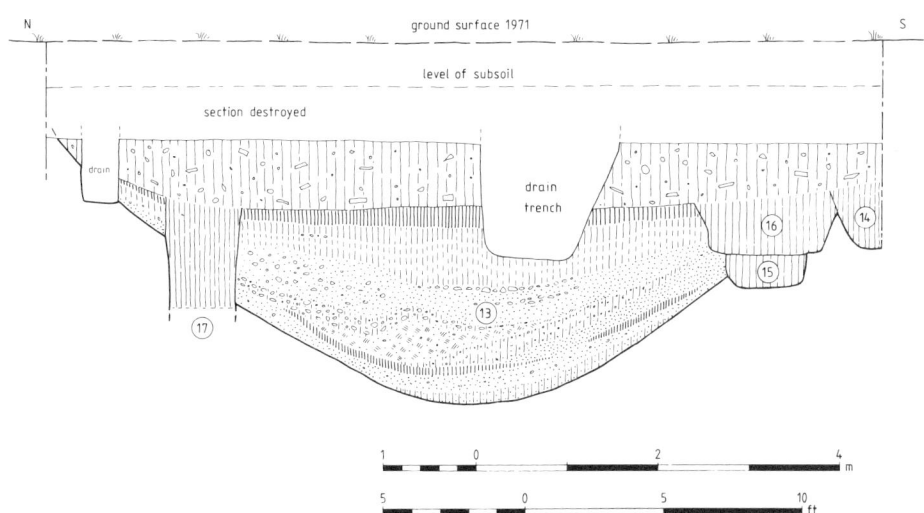

Fig. 17. Section of trench Y through the northern ditch of the inner earthwork, Chipping Hill, 1971. The profile has been replotted to eliminate the distortion caused by the oblique intersection between the excavated trench and the course of the earthwork.

was 10 m wide and must originally have been about 3.6 m deep, being dug 3.3 m into the subsoil. There was a primary filling *c.* 0.5 m deep, over which a topsoil had formed. The subsequent filling was much sandier and stonier than that of the outer ditch, especially in the southern part. This may indicate that the rampart had collapsed gradually into the ditch over a long period of time: certainly it had not been pushed bodily into the ditch. The filling stabilised and became grassed over after 2 m of silt had accumulated, leaving a hollow *c.* 1.4 m deep.

Through this surface four pits had been dug. There were three small rubbish pits (F14–16) near the inner lip of the ditch, and a deeper one — perhaps a well (F17) — near the outer lip. Two sherds of pottery recovered from near the top of the deeper pit (F17) are of late Saxon type.[34] By contrast, five sherds from at least three vessels found in the lower silting of the ditch suggest that the defensive circuit may have been dug in the Early or Middle Iron Age, a date which would not be at variance with its being substantially silted by the late Saxon period.[35] Both ditch and pits disappeared from view as a result of further silting during the seventeenth to nineteenth centuries.

Geophysical prospecting in gardens just inside the northern perimeter of the inner earthwork revealed an anomaly — apparently a large and otherwise unrecorded ditch — on an east-west alignment (marked at Z on Fig. 10).

The Excavations of 1988
by Roland Flook and Owen Bedwin

INTRODUCTION

During the spring and summer of 1988, the opportunity arose for two small rescue excavations on the Chipping Hill earthwork, both in advance of separate housing developments. By coincidence, these involved stretches of earthwork in the same general area as some of Cottrill's trenches (Fig. 11).

In April and May, a substantial ditch was investigated in an area of garden belonging to the house known as 'Saxons' (Figs. 11 and 18; site code WH2). In June and July, an area corresponding to the rear half of the inner bank was examined at the edge of the former Button Factory. The end of Cottrill's trench J was re-located within the 1988 excavation (Fig. 11; site code WH3).

Both excavations were carried out by Essex County Council Archaeology Section, under the direction of Roland Flook. Following his departure from Essex to work in North Wales, this report has been prepared by Owen Bedwin.

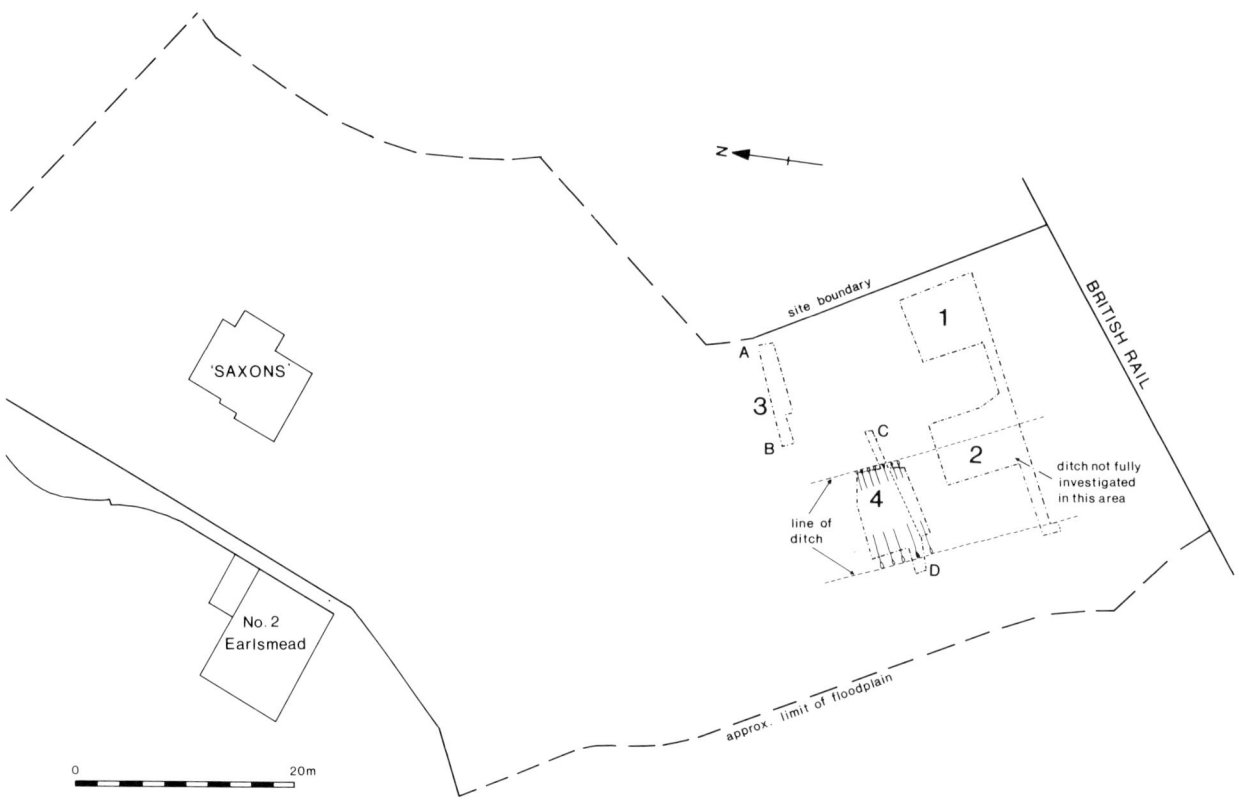

Fig. 18. *General plan of the 1988 excavation at 'Saxons' (site WH2). For location plan see Fig. 11.*

THE EXCAVATIONS

'Saxons' *(Site WH2)*
The area available for excavation had until recently been a plot for vegetable growing, adjacent to the railway line. It was a flat and featureless site, with no indication of the line of the ditch. Four separate trenches were dug (1 to 4, in Figs. 11 and 18) although trenches 1 and 2 were eventually linked up. Trenches 1 and 3 revealed only three shallow scoops (all undated), exemplified by context 128 in Fig. 19 (section AB). Trenches 3 and 4 located a substantial ditch, interpreted as part of the hillfort defences. Because of constraints on the dumping of spoil, the ditch could only be partly excavated in trench 2, but a full-width section was established in trench 4, even though it was not possible to bottom the ditch because of the high water table (Fig. 19, section CD). The ditch was 8.5 m wide at the top, and at least 3.3 m deep (cut at least 2.0 m into the subsoil, which was a slightly gravelly silt). It seems highly likely that this was the same feature located by Cottrill in his trench G, only 20 m away (Fig. 11), even though he clearly did not bottom it (Fig. 12, section 4).

The ditch deposits were mainly silty in character, with a variable amount of small gravel. One point that should be noted is that there was a major change in the ditch fills about halfway down the section, indicated by the thicker line above contexts 84, 61, 54 and 47 (Fig. 19, section CD). Below this line, the fills were clean gravelly silts with few finds; these consisted of the occasional flint flake and small flint-gritted potsherds, of which the only diagnostic piece is probably Late Bronze Age (Fig. 19, context 77). Above the line, deposits were softer and darker, with Middle Iron Age pottery, charcoal and animal bone. Other finds included a potin coin, part of a shale bowl and part of a baked clay loomweight (these Middle Iron Age deposits included contexts 98 and 134, where finds were especially abundant, but which do not appear in section CD). With the benefit of hindsight, it seems likely that Cottrill dug out these upper deposits in his trench G (Fig. 12, section 4), but misinterpreted the much cleaner primary silts as the natural subsoil.

The outer edge of the ditch cut through a number of layers (contexts 88 to 75) of soft, silty material, apparently of alluvial origin. These layers contained a few sherds of flint-gritted pottery, very similar in fabric to the diagnostically Late Bronze Age material. Finally, attention should be drawn to the extensive layers spreading across the top of the ditch (i.e. contexts 123, 124 in section AB; 36, 37, 38 in section CD). These were very uniform and similar to one another; they contained only small pieces of charcoal, burnt clay and coal. The significance of these layers in connection with the recent history of the earthwork is further considered in the discussion.

The Former Button Factory *(Site WH3)*
Although a large area was potentially available for investigation, the substantial brick footings, drains, service trenches and underground fuel tanks of the factory meant that much of the archaeology had been destroyed. Those areas which were free of buildings were covered with tarmac, concrete or rammed gravel, and there was no indication of any surviving bank around the factory perimeter; in short, the whole aspect of the site was highly unpromising.

Because of problems caused by standing buildings, fuel tanks and live electric cables, it was decided to examine a small area, *c.* 9 m by a maximum of 8 m, corresponding to the rear half of the inner rampart (Figs. 11 and 20). The western end of Cottrill's trench J was also re-located. After breaking up a concrete rubble and gravel hard-standing, it became apparent that the bank had survived to a maximum height of 1.2 m (Fig. 21, section AB). The subsoil here was gravel, in contrast to the slightly gravelly silts of the trenches through the hillfort ditch.

A buried soil beneath the bank was clearly visible (context 38 in section AB; context 4 in section CD); this is referred to hereafter as the primary buried soil. It was sealed beneath simple gravel dumps (contexts 46 and 37 in section AB; context 128 in section CD), which constituted the rampart. In section AB, the finer, slightly looser gravel of context 36 is interpreted as material which has weathered or washed down from the top of the rampart (in section CD, context 126 is the equivalent). On top of this had developed a thin, dark grey-brown stone-free layer (context 35), interpreted as a soil and known hereafter as the secondary buried soil. This was then itself sealed by further gravel layers (contexts 31 and 32), indicating a bank considerably broader than the original. Above that were layers of recent origin, connected with the construction of the factory and with the provision of a hard-standing for car parking. In general terms the 1988 section AB is reasonably similar to Cottrill's section in his trench B (Fig 12, section 2), indicating two buried soils and a dump rampart. There is a suggestion, too, in the thickening of context 38 at the rear of the rampart, of turf revetting, also proposed by Cottrill (Fig. 12.2, context 4).

In the stratigraphic sequence indicated in Fig. 21 (especially section AB), there is dating evidence only for the very top (which is modern) and for the primary buried soil, and one or two features at the base of the section. The latest material from the primary buried soil is diagnostically Late Bronze Age, although a few sherds of Grooved Ware were also present. Cut into the gravel subsoil were a number of shallow features (Fig. 20; the sections shown in Fig. 21 are representative). Only two were dateable: slot, context 16 (fill, context 17), containing Late Bronze Age pottery; and a small

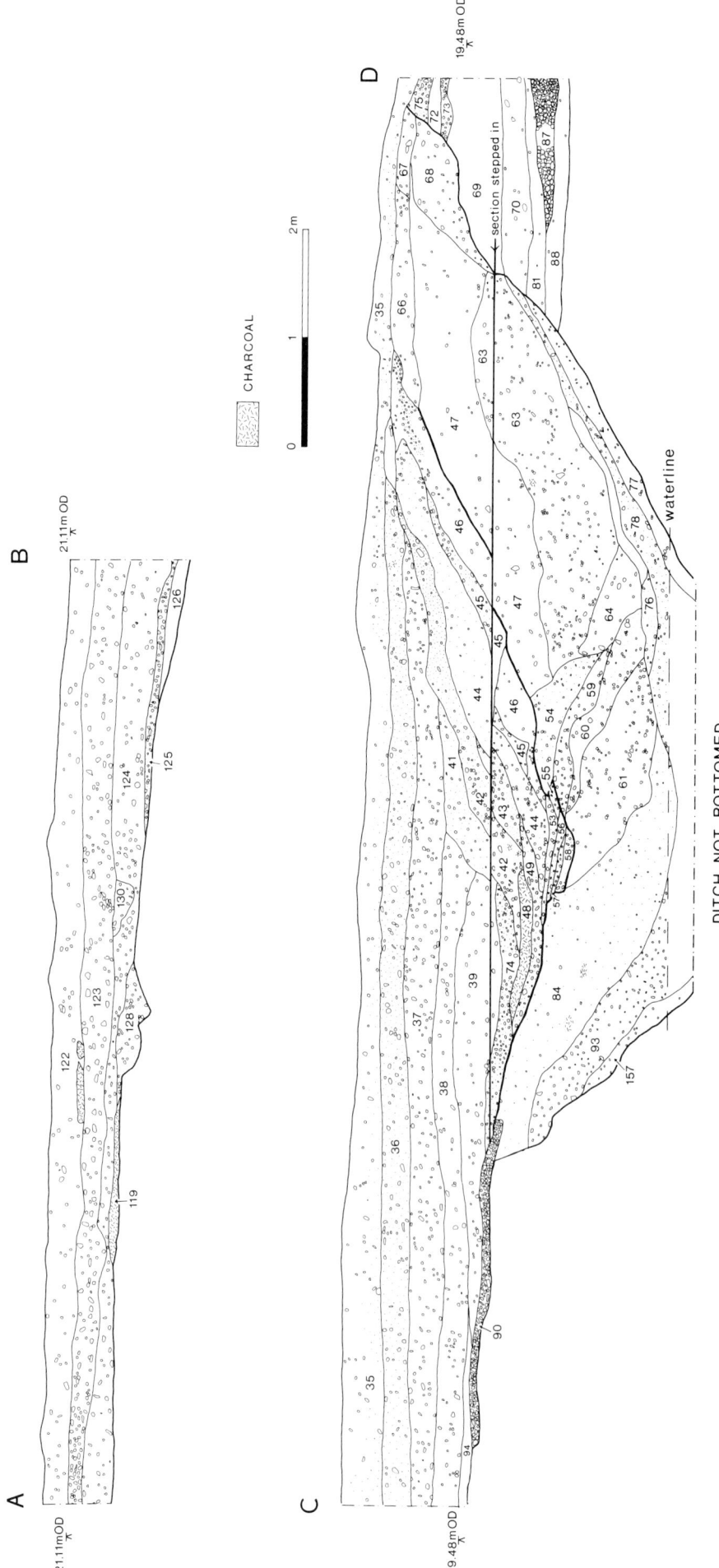

Fig. 19. Sections across the ditch and berm at 'Saxons'. For location of sections see Fig. 18.

A

21.11mOD

B

21.11mOD

126
125
124
123
130
128
122
119

CHARCOAL

0   1   2m

C

19.48mOD

D

19.48mOD

35
66
67
68
69
section stepped in
72
73
75
70
81
87
88
63
47
63
46
77
78
76
waterline
45
47
64
64
59
60
61
55
44
46
54
41
42
53
45
44
56
43
42
49
57
48
39
74
90
84
93
157
37
38
36
35
94

DITCH NOT BOTTOMED

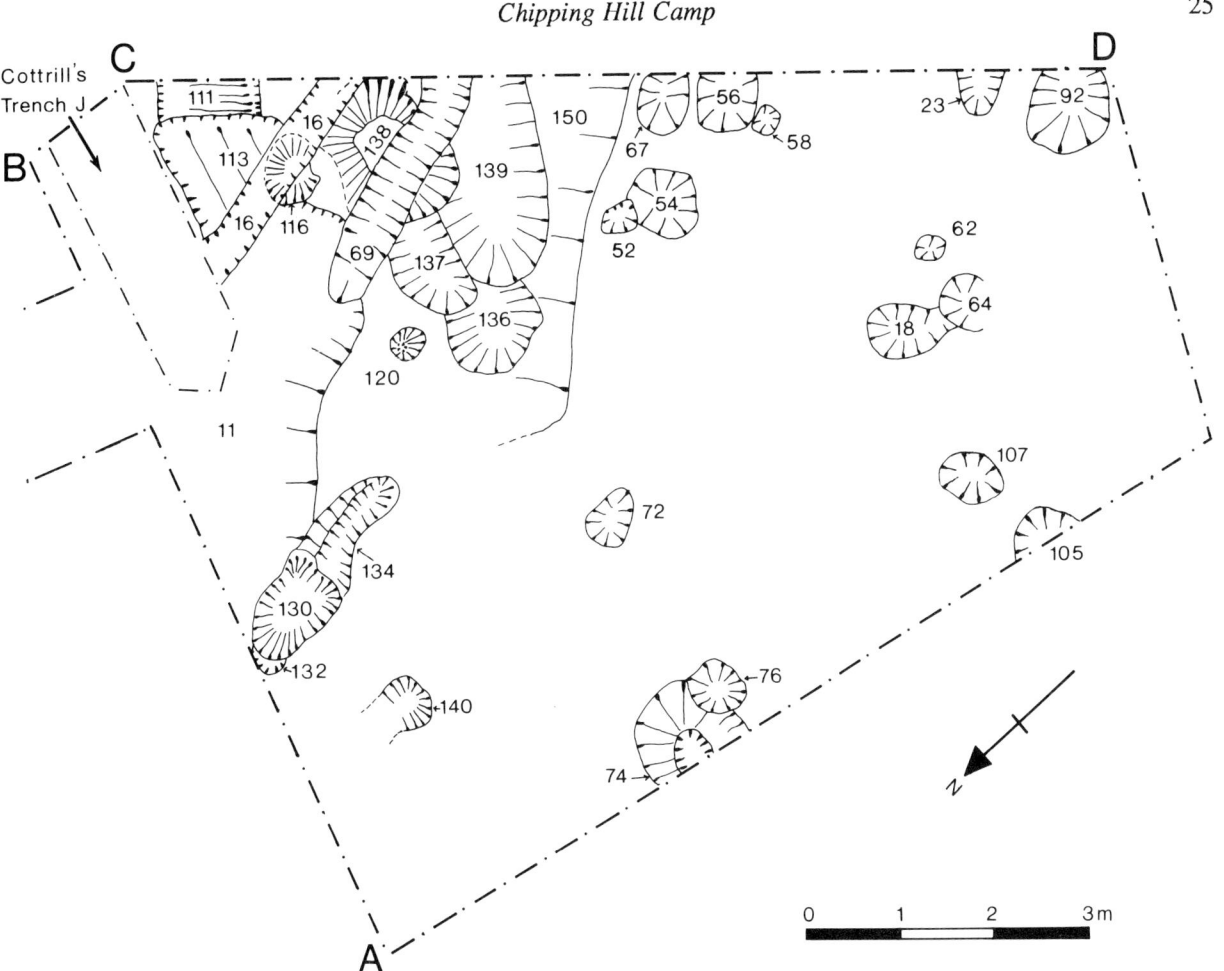

Fig. 20. *General plan of the 1988 excavation at the former Button Factory (site WH3), showing all features cut into the gravel subsoil.*

irregular hollow, context 107, containing Grooved Ware. There is little in the way of apparent pattern in these features, which clearly cannot all be contemporary.

Cottrill recorded no worked flint from his trench J, in spite of the fact that he had over-cut well into the natural subsoil, but from the 1988 excavation trench were recovered 367 struck flints, of which 328 came from the primary buried soil. The range is from the Mesolithic, through the Neolithic, though most belong to the late Neolithic, suggesting a domestic site of that period.

DISCUSSION

This takes the form of a consideration of the local sequence of events established by the 1988 excavations, followed by a comparison of these results with the work of Cottrill and Davison.

The Sequence
The sequence is divided into six phases, as follows.

Phase 1: Mesolithic/Early Neolithic
This is defined by flintwork, there being no features

dated to this phase. There is insufficient material to characterise the nature of the occupation.

Phase 2: Late Neolithic
Most of the flintwork from WH3 belongs to this phase, and is broadly contemporary with the Grooved Ware from the primary buried soil and from the shallow feature, 107 (fill 108). Some of the other features shown in Fig. 20 may also be of this date. Although the excavated area was small, the evidence points to domestic occupation, and is a significant addition to known sites of this period in mid-Essex, the only other being Springfield Lyons, near Chelmsford (Buckley and Hedges 1987a, 3).

Phase 3: Late Bronze Age
In WH3, a sizeable group of Late Bronze Age pottery is the latest material from the primary buried soil: the inner earthwork must therefore be Late Bronze Age, or later. However, by the Middle Iron Age the evidence (below) is that the ditch(es) were being filled in. In the absence of any significant assemblage of Early Iron Age pottery from the 1988 excavations, the likelihood is that

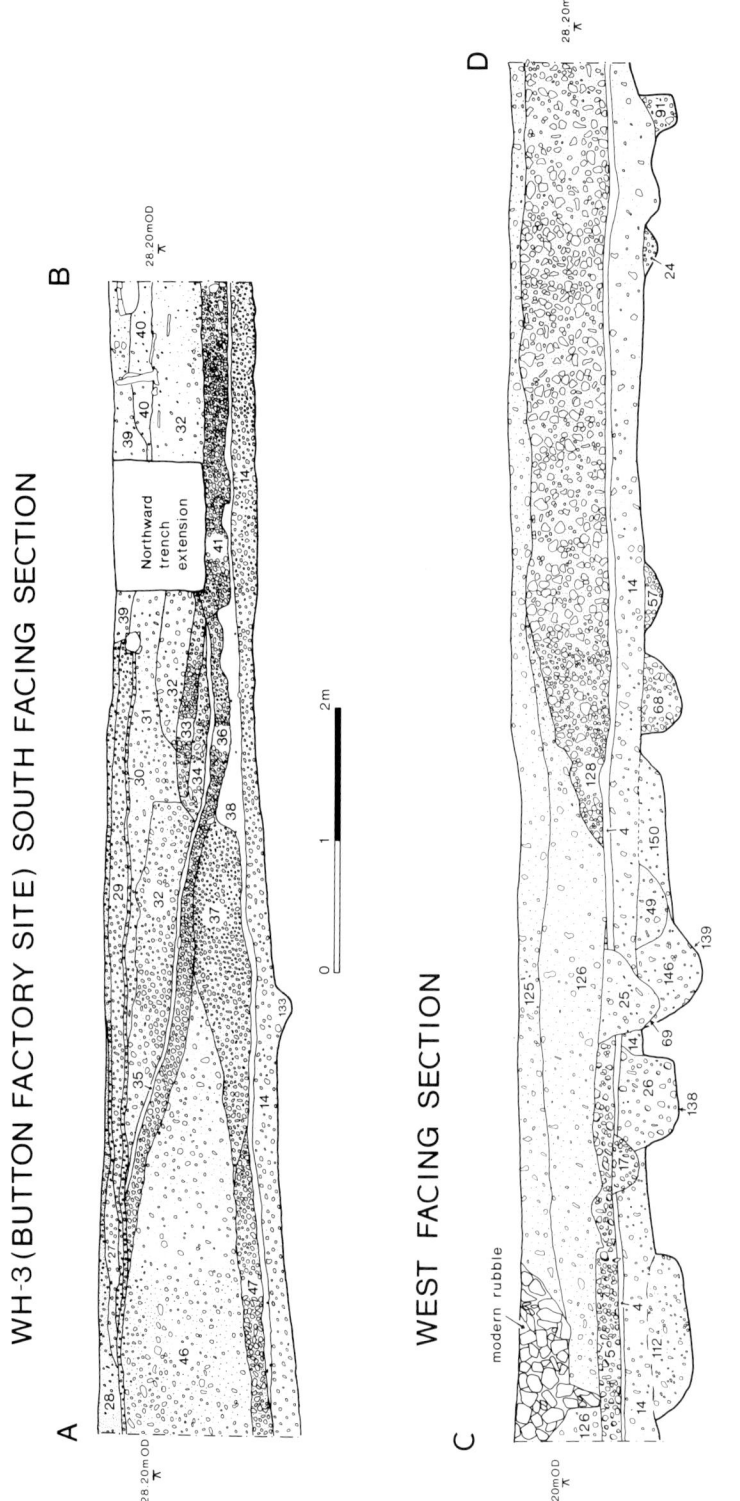

WH-3(BUTTON FACTORY SITE) SOUTH FACING SECTION

WEST FACING SECTION

Fig. 21. Main sections of the excavation at the former Button Factory (site WH3). For location of sections see Fig. 20. AB represents a section through the rear half of the bank (the 'northward extension' was simply a sloping cut for a barrow-run).

the inner defensive circuit was constructed during the Late Bronze Age.

In WH2, the sequence of deposits at the outer edge of the ditch (contexts 88 to 75) contained a few sherds in a flint-gritted fabric compatible with a Late Bronze Age date. A few similar sherds were found in the early ditch silts, including one from context 77 (the primary silt), probably of Late Bronze Age date. However, the amount of pottery here is relatively small compared with that from the primary buried soil in WH3, and the sherds in the ditch may well therefore be residual. The date of the ditch must lie within the Late Bronze Age or Early Iron Age, as by the Middle Iron Age it was almost completely filled in.

It is unfortunate that the number of well dated Late Bronze Age contexts with charred grain is so few and therefore does not add greatly to our information about the agriculture of that period.

Phase 4: Middle Iron Age
Most of the pottery from the 1988 excavations belongs to this phase, and the bulk of it came from the upper levels of the ditch in WH2. This implies a substantial re-cut, into which was dumped considerable quantities of domestic debris during the Middle Iron Age, to the extent that this ditch would largely have disappeared at that time. (Note that, strictly speaking, the re-cut itself cannot be closely dated, only the dumping. Also, what is apparent in Fig. 19 may be only the last of a series of re-cuts.)

The examination of charred grain shows emmer wheat as predominant, with some barley, a pattern recognised from other Middle Iron Age contexts in Essex (eg. Asheldham Camp: Bedwin 1991).

Phase 5: Roman
This is characterised by two virtually complete, though fragmented, *tegulae* lying side by side in a layer just below the topsoil in WH2. Cottrill found Roman material also in his trenches A (through the inner bank) and G.

Phase 6: Post-Medieval
To this phase are assigned the extensive layers seen in WH2, i.e. contexts 123, 124 in section AB, and contexts 36, 37, 38 in section CD. They would seem to correspond very well with the eighteenth-century levelling operations described by Strutt (1774).

Comparison with Earlier Excavations at Chipping Hill
The sequence which has emerged from the 1988 work is broadly compatible with the earlier work of Cottrill, though there are differences of detail. Reconciling the results with Davison's trenches X and Y is more difficult.

As far as the 1933–35 work is concerned, it is only possible to make reliable comparisons with trenches A,

B, C, G and J (Fig. 11). The stratigraphic sequence recorded in Cottrill's trenches A and B through the bank (Fig. 12.1 and 2) fits well with the 1988 rear-half section of the bank (Fig. 21, section AB). A primary and secondary buried soil were identified in both cases, as was some form of turf revetting at the rear of the rampart (context 38 in Fig. 21, AB). It is possible too that the suggestion of a three-phase rampart, derived from the interpretation of Cottrill's section in Fig. 12.1 and 12.2, may be supported by Fig. 21 (AB), with context 37 being the first rampart, and context 46 representing a second rampart. It would, however, be surprising that no soil had developed on the upper surface of context 37, before being buried by 46, unless of course the gap between them was only a few years. An alternative explanation for the difference between contexts 37 and 46 (which amounts merely to a difference of stoniness) might simply be that their materials were quarried at the same time, but from slightly different places. The difference in stoniness would then be a reflection of a variation in subsoil.

There is a marked contrast between the sections by Cottrill, who recorded the ditch in his trench G as cutting only *c.* 1.5 m into the subsoil (Fig. 12.4), and the 1988 section in trench 4, where it was cut at least 2.2 m into the natural (Fig. 19, section CD). This contrast is nevertheless easily explained by Cottrill having mistaken the clean primary silts for natural subsoil. On this basis, the writer would suggest that the 1988 trench 4 and Cottrill's trench G sectioned the same substantial ditch.

The critical question to be answered, then, is whether this is the inner or the outer ditch; and Davison's results on the north-west side of the earthwork are hard to reconcile with the 1933–35 and 1988 evidence on the south-west side. On the face of it Davison's *inner* ditch, measuring *c.* 8 m across at the top (Fig. 17, trench Y), with its Early and Middle Iron Age pottery, would appear to be the more likely candidate. In addition, the probable Late Bronze Age or Early Iron Age date (from WH2) is compatible with the inner bank evidence from WH3. However, if the 1988 ditch is interpreted as the inner one, then there is the major problem of a 35 m gap (or berm) between the bank and ditch, which seems highly improbable.

The alternative explanation, that the 1988 ditch is the outer one, makes far better sense topographically (Fig. 11), but of course has its own major problem in that Davison's outer ditch (Fig. 16, trench X), although the right size, seems to be of medieval origin, unless one assumes that a localised medieval re-cut has largely obliterated the prehistoric evidence here. The writer would suggest that the latter interpretation offers a better rationalisation of the evidence.

It is particularly unfortunate that Cottrill's trench D (Fig. 10) is not more helpful, as it was located midway between Davison's trenches on the north-west and the 1988 work on the south-west. Trench D did locate a substantial feature on the line of the inner ditch (Fig. 12.3), but it was only half the depth of Davison's inner ditch in trench Y. However, given that Cottrill seems to have misinterpreted the primary silts in his trench G as natural, he may well have done the same in trench D.

Other Discoveries at Chipping Hill

Various other archaeological discoveries have been reported from the vicinity of the camp, apart from those relating to the excavations.

1. Roman coins were found when the outer earthwork was being levelled on the south side of the camp, in the *c.* 1690s (p. 8).
2. When the camp was bisected by the London to Colchester railway line in 1844 several inhumation burials, and three iron pokers were found (p. 10).
3. In 1852 F. Chancellor exhibited to the Essex Archaeological Society 'Roman fictile ware found at Witham'.[36] This was probably derived from the railway cutting in 1844: the description may well refer to Iron Age pottery similar to that described below.
4. There is a silver *denarius* of Trajan in Colchester Museum which was possibly found at Avenue Lodge (TL 8204 1504).[37] See also 7 below.
5. In the diary of P. G. Laver, in Colchester Museum, an entry dated 17 February 1930 records the finding of a gold coin of Honorius at Chipping Hill.
6. In the late 1940s J. G. S. Brinson examined an area around the south-east side of the camp and reported a scatter of Romano-British pottery in gardens between The Avenue and Avenue Road, in the area centred on TL 823 150 (Fig. 37).[38]
7. It is said locally that a number of Roman coins were found in the 1930s, when work was carried out at the 'hall' at the north-west end of The Avenue. This may have referred to Church House (adjacent to Avenue Lodge on the west), or to the club premises that were then next to it.[39]
8. A scatter of Romano-British pottery was reported in 1960 from a site close to the centre of the camp, adjacent to the north-west side of the railway line: TL 820 152 (Colchester Museum).
9. In 1933 it was reported that 'treasure and weapons' had been found in digging a gravel pit inside the north-west entrance to the outer earthwork, but by that date the pit had already been infilled and a house built on the site (Rowles 1934, 30).
10. Rowles (1934) also noted that in the old quarry adjoining the 1933–35 excavations (Figs. 10 and 13) 'on its east side near the top are several large stones which appear to have helped to form the breastwork' of the inner rampart. Cottrill commented on these stones in his 1934 lecture.
11. Part of the Deal Cullen Seed Works was redeveloped in 1980, and a watching brief carried out under near-impossible conditions. The site, which lies between the inner and outer earthworks on the north side of the camp (TL 8195 1535), had suffered extensive disturbance in the nineteenth century, as well as more recently, and failed to yield any conclusive results.[40]
12. A small cast bronze figurine of the Virgin and Child was found on the scarp close to the river, at the south-west corner of the camp (TL 819 150), sometime in the 1940s or '50s. The object was seen by M.R. Hull at Colchester Museum, and a fourteenth-century date was suggested. There is a tiny photograph of the figurine in Hull's topographical file. The present whereabouts of the object is unknown.
13. In 1944 M.R. Hull noted the line of the former road from Chipping Hill to Witham Mill, on the west bank of the river, as a band of gravel in a freshly ploughed field[41] (Fig. 4B).

3

The Occupation Sequence at Chipping Hill Camp: an Evaluation

The Prehistoric Fortifications

The excavations of 1933–35, 1969, 1971 and 1988 have clarified certain aspects of the history of this site, but have left other, important questions unanswered. It will be useful at this stage to take stock of the evidence. Chipping Hill Camp has been classified as a 'hillfort': this is somewhat misleading since the site, which is only 30 m above O.D., occupies a modest spur at the entrance to the Brain valley, where it opens from the north side of the much broader valley of the Blackwater. The term 'plateau fort' would be topographically more appropriate.

The site of Chipping Hill Camp was strategically chosen with a view to controlling access from the Blackwater valley into the Brain valley, and the crossing of the latter from the south-west. The defensive strength of the site was towards the west, and its weakest aspect was the north-east. The camp was unrelated to the Roman road, which passed by 0.8 km to the south-east. There are, however, indications in the historic topography of the area to suggest that the local pre-Roman antecedent of this route crossed Chipping Hill (p. 58).

Although none of the gateways to the earthworks has been excavated, it seems probable on topographic and cartographic evidence that there were two principal entrances — north and south — to both circuits.

The presence of Neolithic and Bronze Age domestic-type occupation beside the river crossing was established by the 1988 excavation, demonstrating that the camp was not built on a virgin site. There were also finds of Mesolithic flints. This evidence accords well with the anticipated local settlement pattern. There is now no doubt about the pre-Roman dating of the univallate inner earthwork, enclosing a polygonal space with an area of *c.* 3.5 ha. The plan and sections are characteristic of prehistoric fortification, and the silting of the ditch to the point of stability evidently occurred in the Middle Iron Age. Evidence for the date of construction is insubstantial, but since there are no finds

subsequent to the Late Bronze Age from the buried soil and primary inner rampart, this could well herald a pre-Iron Age origin for the enclosure.

The excavations of 1933–34 and 1988 demonstrated that, towards the west and south sides of the camp, there was considerable domestic occupation of the Middle Iron Age, both within and immediately outside the inner defences. This occupation is not readily reconcilable with the veracity of the earthworks, which must be earlier. The question therefore arises: was there an outer circuit, also of prehistoric date, that fully embraced the Iron Age settlement? There is circumstantial evidence from the 1988 excavation to suggest that there was a prehistoric outer ditch, on the west at least, and that it may have been dug in the Late Bronze Age. There is ample evidence for assigning the intermediate fills, and probably the first recut, to the Middle Iron Age.

The 1930s and 1988 excavations, however, located a ditch on the terrace between the inner camp and the river. It is difficult to see this ditch as relating to the bank of the inner earthwork, since the width of the intervening berm would have varied, and would have been excessively wide at its maximum point (in the order of 30 m). The ditch is more plausibly interpreted as a component of a separate outer prehistoric circuit, which had been virtually levelled by the later Saxon period (if not by the late Roman), and was finally obliterated in the late seventeenth century. In neither of the sections cut on the west side was the bottom of the ditch reached, but it is nevertheless clear from the angles of slope and from the profiles of the silts that the ditch was V-shaped and relatively deep. The evidence is compatible with its having a profile and dimensions similar to those recorded in the 1969 section (trench X). That section, however, failed to supply dating evidence for the earliest phase of the outer earthwork on the north, beyond the fact that it was pre-thirteenth century.

Reconstructed ditch profiles are shown in Fig. 22, but it must be acknowledged that the comparison of such incomplete sections cannot by itself be conclusive,

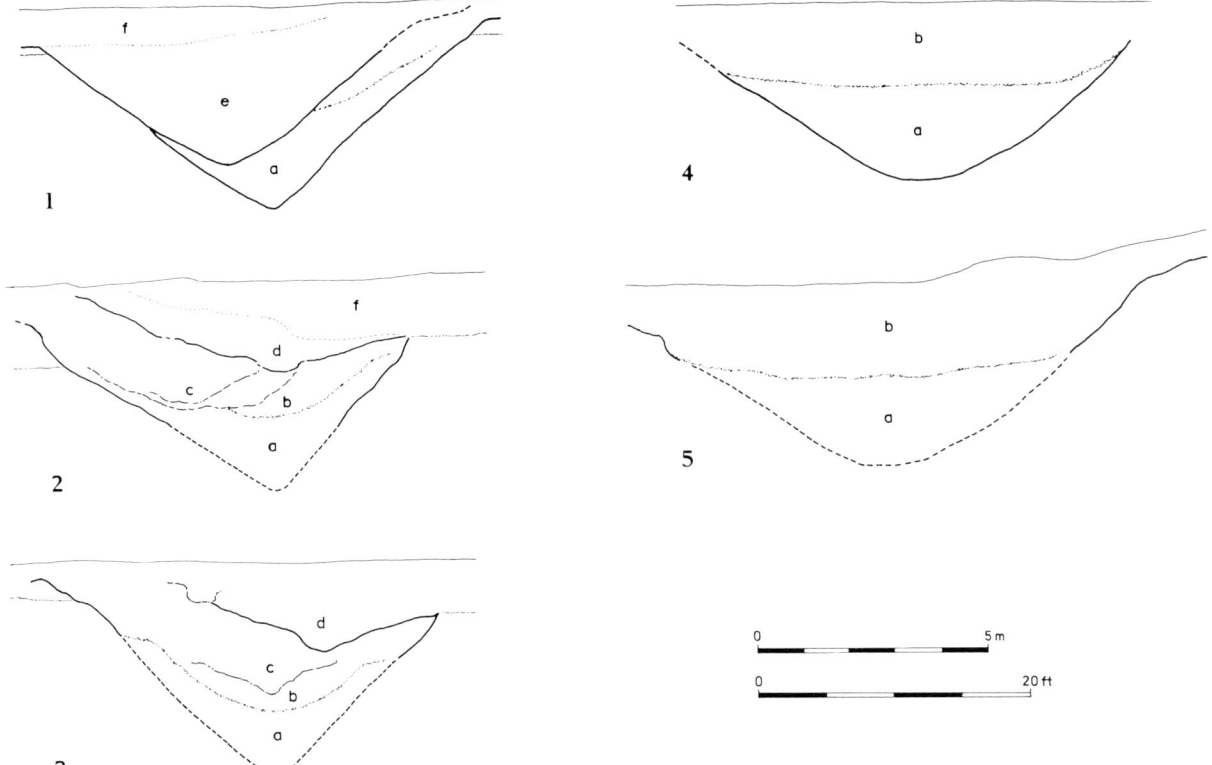

Fig. 22. *Comparative ditch sections of Chipping Hill Camp. In each case the exterior of the earthwork is to the left, and only the principal cuts are shown:* **1.** *Outer ditch, trench X, 1969;* **2.** *Outer ditch, site WH2, 1988;* **3.** *Outer ditch, trench G, 1933;* **4.** *Inner ditch, trench Y, 1971;* **5.** *Inner ditch, trench D, 1934.*
Interpretative key to fills: **a.** *Primary fills of earliest ditch;* **b.** *Secondary fills of earliest ditch;* **c.** *First recut of outer ditch;* **d.** *Second recut of outer ditch;* **e.** *Third recut of outer ditch (trench X only);* **f.** *Post-medieval levelling layers.*

owing to the extent to which extrapolation is necessary. While the sections of the outer ditches on the west and the north may appear superficially to differ, this is probably an illusion caused by the markedly different nature of their respective recuts. It is plain that the north and west sides of the enclosure have not had identical defensive histories, and the confusion is compounded by the likelihood of there being a second outer ditch around most of the camp (excepting the river side), which has never been archaeologically sectioned (p. 10). Thus the outer defence may itself have been bivallate.

The multiplicity of defensive components around the north-west corner is well evidenced by old property boundaries adjoining Moat Farm and White Horse Lane (Fig. 4B): it seems clear that the northern defence once followed a wider sweep towards the river. Indeed, it may be argued that three separate defensive postures are reflected in the evidence here: the outermost line headed directly for the river floodplain; the middle line returned along the scarp edge of the terrace (where it was intercepted by the excavations); and the innermost curled back to clasp the north-west angle of the inner enclosure (Fig. 10). There has undoubtedly been a succession of changes to the plan of the earthworks here, but further speculation on the sequence and dating

is pointless until fresh evidence becomes available. The geophysical evidence for an anomalously aligned ditch within the inner earthwork (Fig. 10, Z) may be relevant.[42]

Morphologically, it is difficult to see how the inner earthwork could have originated at an earlier date than the outer one. First, the two circuits are of roughly similar plan, and more or less concentric. This implies a meaningful relationship, but the significantly different ditch profiles argue against strict contemporaneity. The width of level ground between the circuits varied from less than 20 m on the west, to 45 m on the north and 75 m on the south. These latter distances are too great for the berm of a small multi-vallate earthwork; while at the same time the land enclosed between the circuits was too attenuated to comprise a worthwhile space in its own right.

The available evidence supports — or at least does not conflict with — the hypothesis that both the inner and outer defences originated in the Late Bronze Age, or perhaps the Early Iron Age. If the enclosure was primarily designed to be defensive, it could be argued that the outer earthwork is likely to have been created first, and that the inner was the result of a subsequent modification. By effecting a symmetrical contraction, the defended area was reduced to one-third of its former extent, the strength of the fortification was increased, and whatever structures lay at the nucleus of the site still retained their focal position.

Had the reverse process taken place, involving the enlargement of the earthwork, an eccentric plan is more likely to have been achieved than a concentric one, and less labour would have been involved. Moreover, in such circumstances it would have been unlikely for the inner circuit to have remained intact as a major earthwork.

Two, or perhaps three, structural phases of the inner defences appear to be indicated by the evidence from the rampart sections, but less obviously so by the ditch. The following may be posited from the 1930s and 1988 sections.

(i)   The primary rampart had a front revetment of timber, and a low turf wall at the rear; there was a berm and U-shaped ditch. This may be equated with the 'Poundbury type' of defence (Cunliffe 1978, 248).

(ii) Deposition of burnt material on the berm: while this may represent a phase of destruction, it could equally be no more than a localised activity.

(iii) The rampart was rebuilt, more than doubling its size. This was a 'dump' rampart.

(iv) Slighting and quarrying, followed by restoration of the rampart.

The dating of this sequence must necessarily remain vague: the first phase appears to be Late Bronze Age, and the third belongs broadly to the Middle Iron Age. A few sherds of the latter period were recovered from the 1971 ditch section (trench Y), on the surface of what seems to have been a buried turf-line, not far above the bottom of the ditch. The last rampart phase (iv) need not be prehistoric. Cottrill's trench D seems only to have sectioned the late fills and the Middle Iron Age turf-line over the primary silts below (this line was probably mistaken for a dark silt in the 'bottom' of the ditch).

The outer ditch on the west was recut twice, as revealed in trench G and area WH2. These later cuts were broad and relatively shallow, and both exhibited a slight extra dip at the centre. At least one, and potentially both, belong to the Middle Iron Age. In trench G, the ditches were all found to be sealed by deposits that yielded Roman and late Saxon artifacts. It is particularly unfortunate that the position of the late Roman glass cup in the filling of the third ditch was not adequately recorded; there must remain a slight possibility of a Roman-period or early post-Roman recut. In trench Y the inner ditch was found to have been largely filled by the early Middle Ages, when pits were being dug into it. The scarping away of the back

of the inner rampart, noted in trench A, seems certainly to be of post-Roman date, since this act was responsible for the truncation of several Roman features inside the camp.

The outer ditch on the north, sectioned in trench X, had a different history: whatever its date of construction — which could be anywhere between the Bronze Age and the twelfth century — there was a major recut in the early thirteenth century. This must have been part of a medieval defence which has not yet been encountered elsewhere at Chipping Hill.

Dating the limits and peaks of prehistoric occupation depends upon a gross assessment of the artifacts from the site. Flints provide the earliest evidence, and although many must have been unearthed in the 1930s excavations, they were neither retained nor mentioned in surviving records.[43] The flint collection deriving from the 1988 excavations contains some Mesolithic and early Neolithic artifacts, and a greater quantity of late Neolithic and Beaker material, including pottery. The assemblage is domestic in character.

There is some Late Bronze Age pottery from the excavations, and a few sherds assignable to the Early Iron Age. The bulk of the pottery, however, belongs to the second and earlier first centuries B.C., and thus to the Middle Iron Age. It is regrettable that the assemblages recovered by Cottrill, from trench H in particular, have become dispersed, since they were clearly of significance to the study of Middle Iron Age Essex. Here, coarse, semi-fine and fine pottery vessels were found together, alongside metal objects and potin coins. Burnished footring bowls and curvilinear-decorated pottery, in particular, have rarely been found in central Essex, and their ceramic associations are ill-known. Furthermore, the possible hint of a Dressel 1 amphora fragment being incorporated in the inner defence is tantalising (p. 120, n. 22). The 1988 excavations added a further potin coin and fragment of a shale bowl to the artifact list.

Equally interesting is the fact that none of the pottery from the camp belongs to the 'Belgic' tradition, which is helpful in isolating the immediately pre-Belgic ceramics of the region. The Chipping Hill pottery is comparable to that of the last Middle Iron Age phase at Little Waltham (Drury 1978). Until recently, the period has been poorly represented in the ceramic record from Essex, but several small collections from the Witham area have now begun to fill out the local picture.[44]

It finally remains to mention the three iron fire-pokers of La Tène II-III which were discovered in 1844, in the railway cutting. These are exceptionally fine specimens of their type, and have been previously published (Rodwell 1976c). The circumstances of their discovery are vague, which is particularly to be lamented since it is unclear whether the three pokers were actually found in association with one or more of the skeletons mentioned in the same brief report (Anon. 1844). The pokers are of similar date to most of the other Iron Age artifacts from the site, and this is a period when grave goods, and indeed inhumation burials generally, are very scarce.

Since the pokers are clearly a 'set', and appear to have been in good condition when buried, it is unlikely that they were separate accompaniments to individual interments. Moreover, the presence of the ferrules which secured 'handle' bindings of organic material, demonstrates that the pokers were complete and finished objects when buried, and were not merely bars of iron. Nevertheless, the pokers could still have been buried as a 'hoard' of ironwork, perhaps in ritual association with a multiple inhumation. Since the discovery was made in Temples Field, there is a strong likelihood that the burials were inserted within the ditches, or into the strip of land between the outer and inner defences on the west side of the camp. Inhumation burials, either singly or in small groups, have occasionally been recorded in association with hillforts, as at Uley Bury, Glos. There, a single grave was found on the berm between the ramparts, near to a deposit of two iron currency bars (Saville 1983, 12–13; cf. generally Whimster 1981, esp. 25–31).).

Occupation of the Roman and Anglo-Saxon Periods

A few excavated features, coins, glass and a small amount of pottery of the Roman period indicate occupation within the camp, while other finds from outside it show that settlement extended south-east, towards the Colchester road (p. 28). The immediate post-Roman period is represented by a single find, a fragment of an early Anglo-Saxon perforated vessel, recovered from the 1969 section of the outer ditch (trench X; p. 21).

The later Saxon period, over which there has been much speculative interest in the past, is equally poorly represented: the only find of undoubted tenth-century date is the St Edmund Memorial penny. Unfortunately, its context is archaeologically meaningless, except to say that the outer ditch on the west had been infilled long before the coin's deposition. While there is no specific reason to doubt that this was a genuine site find, one might observe that it was an extraordinarily fortuitous discovery in the circumstances.[45] That there was some late Saxon, or early medieval, occupation overlying the levelled ditch on the river side of the camp is not in doubt, but it cannot be closely dated. In trench G, a pit ('hearth') was found containing pottery probably of the eleventh century, and from nearby came sherds described at the time as 'Norman'. Two sherds of late Saxon pottery were also recovered from a well or pit in trench Y, cut into the silted inner ditch.

No specific evidence has been found to show that any phase of the earthworks is of Anglo-Saxon construction. Indeed, the only excavated ditch for which a Saxon date could be entertained would the undated primary cut of the outer ditch on the north. But since this has a profile matching that of the prehistoric ditch on the west, the case for assigning it hypothetically to the Anglo-Saxon period is weak.

Medieval Occupation

A few sherds of medieval pottery were noted in the 1930s in the upper levels of the site, but little attention was paid to them and no evidence was found for earthwork construction of the period. This contrasts markedly with the results of the 1969 excavation of the northern outer defences, where the fills associated with both phases of the large, V-shaped ditch in trench X yielded medieval pottery (Fig. 16). While there is no doubt that the major recutting of the ditch must belong to a substantial refortification of the site in the first half of the thirteenth century, the dating of the primary cut is somewhat more equivocal.

Twelfth and thirteenth-century pottery was found at a considerable depth, at the junction between the primary and later fills in the original cut. The fact that the sherds were found near to the interface with the recut — which yielded medieval pottery close by, and at the same depth — is slightly disconcerting. Given the extreme paucity of finds from trench X, it is a concidence that medieval pottery should have occurred in the two successive ditch cuts at virtually the same level, and nowhere else. Could the sherds in question in the earlier cut have migrated across the critical boundary in an undetected rabbit burrow?

The complete absence of artifacts in trench X from the rampart, from the series of scoops cut into its back, and from the buried soil horizon beneath, is particularly unhelpful. It may, however, be safely concluded that there was no significant amount of occupation on this part of the site at any period prior to the construction of the earthwork. This is a potential pointer to the early origin of the outer earthwork. Nevertheless, the bank and its associated features are clearly of several periods, and the later phases must be medieval.

It must be admitted that, until fresh evidence is available, there are several alternatives for the origin of outer north ditch for which a plausible case can be argued. It would, for example, be possible to assign a late Saxon date to the earliest phase of the bank and primary ditch. However, in the circumstances, this would be wholly speculative: while one, and almost certainly two, lines of prehistoric fortification at Chipping Hill are not in doubt, no Anglo-Saxon earthwork phase has yet been positively identified anywhere on the site.

The extent, in plan, of the medieval fortification — or

refortification — of the outer earthwork is puzzling. It is tempting to see the two curving sections of bank that link the inner and outer circuits on the west as belonging to this phase, forming two conjoined 'baileys' (Figs. 4B and 46C). While any evidence for the refurbishment of the inner enclosure ditch on the west side would have been destroyed by eighteenth-century terracing, the third phase of the bank recorded in trenches A and B is potentially medieval.[46]

Post-Medieval Usage

There is no indication that the Chipping Hill earthworks served a defensive role after the thirteenth century, or that there was any appreciable amount of occupation within their circuit. The single exception to this was Temple Farm which lay north of the centre of the site. The farm was sold for building development in 1882;

the house itself survives, and is now the property known as The Grange. The Albert, superficially a Victorian railway inn, appears to incorporate some of the farm buildings. The conversion — to what was then known as The Albert Hotel and Railway Inn — presumably took place soon after Witham station was built, in the 1840s.

The early antiquaries showed no interest in Temple Farm, and both Holman and Strutt omitted it from their plans; it was, however, shown on the Chapman and André map of Essex (1777). The ancient importance of Temple Farm is casually revealed in a survey of Witham Manor, taken in 1608, when it was described as the 'site of the aforesaid manor'.[47] Not only was Temple Farm the direct successor to the Templars' manor house here, but it very likely also marked the focus of an early medieval property that was of sufficient importance and status to acquire defences. This was surely a castle (for further discussion, see p. 85).

4

Settlement Outside Chipping Hill Camp

Witham Churchyard and its Enclosure (Fig. 23)

Immediately outside the north-west entrance to Chipping Hill Camp is a forked junction between Church Street and the road named Chipping Hill, and in the intervening angle is a triangular green, the presumed site of the original Witham market. The northern side of the green is delimited by the churchyard which, superficially, appears to be of rectilinear plan, enclosing an area of 0.47 ha (1.16 acres). The vicarage (now private house) adjoins the north-west corner. While three sides of the churchyard are straight, the north boundary is canted and gently curved in part. Just outside the churchyard on the west — and following the natural contour — is a curving drive and garden boundary associated with the (old) vicarage. Reference to the Tithe map of 1839 and the Ordnance Survey plan of 1874 strongly suggests the former continuity of these curving boundaries, with the vicarage house superimposed across the line at a discordant angle (Figs. 23A and 24). It is also noticeable how the Woolpack Inn does not conform to property alignments in Church Street, but is tangential to the churchyard enclosure, and appears to have been built in its ditch.

Approximately half the circumference of a circle *c.* 140 m in diameter was described by boundaries still extant in the early nineteenth century. There was an entrance towards the north, beyond which various boundaries indicate the line of a former track running parallel to Church Street, and lying to the rear of the properties on its west flank. The southern end of the track pointed directly towards the medieval north door of the church, and in the opposite direction, it evidently followed the valley contour for 900 m, before merging with Cressing Road (a continuation of Church Street).

If the earthwork circle is completed on the map, it is found that the southernmost extremity of the enclosure thus defined coincides with a slight change of alignment in the road (and associated property boundaries) from Chipping Hill to Powers Hall End (Fig. 23B). Here also is the entrance to the churchyard, and the path leading

to the medieval south door. There is no explicit cartographic evidence for the completion of the eastern side of the enclosure — a complex of medieval tenements covers the area in question — but subtle hints may be gleaned from changes in boundary alignments. It is also observable that in the late medieval infilling of part of the triangular green, south-east of the church, a gap left between properties appears to mark the site of the enclosure ditch.

Church Street Settlement (Figs. 24 and 25)

Analytical study of the property boundaries to the east and north-east of the churchyard reveals two significant facts. First, the southern end of Church Street has been realigned certainly on one, and probably on two, previous occasions, each time pushing it further west towards the church. Moreover, on topographical grounds, it is clear that Church Street is the successor to the valley-side track (mentioned above) that entered the churchyard enclosure from the north (Fig. 23B). The new street provided a medieval bypass for the churchyard.

Secondly, a small block of properties flanking the street exhibits elements of deliberate planning. The arrangement is reconstructable from boundaries recorded on the 1839 and 1874 maps (Fig. 25A). Church Street, north of the churchyard enclosure, was flanked on both sides by lines of tenement plots with an average depth of 34 m. The principal lateral boundaries are spaced at *c.* 19 m intervals, giving a plot area of slightly less than one-sixth of an acre. Twenty-one such plots are defined, in two blocks (sixteen and five) separated by a cross-street, one arm of which is perpetuated by the present Chalk's Road. The other arm, now a relict landscape feature, led to Chipping Hill mill. The rear boundary of the plots on the east side of Church Street was defined by a water-filled ditch substantial enough to have merited inclusion on the Tithe map.

At the southern end of the development, Church Street opened into the apex of a triangular market place,

34

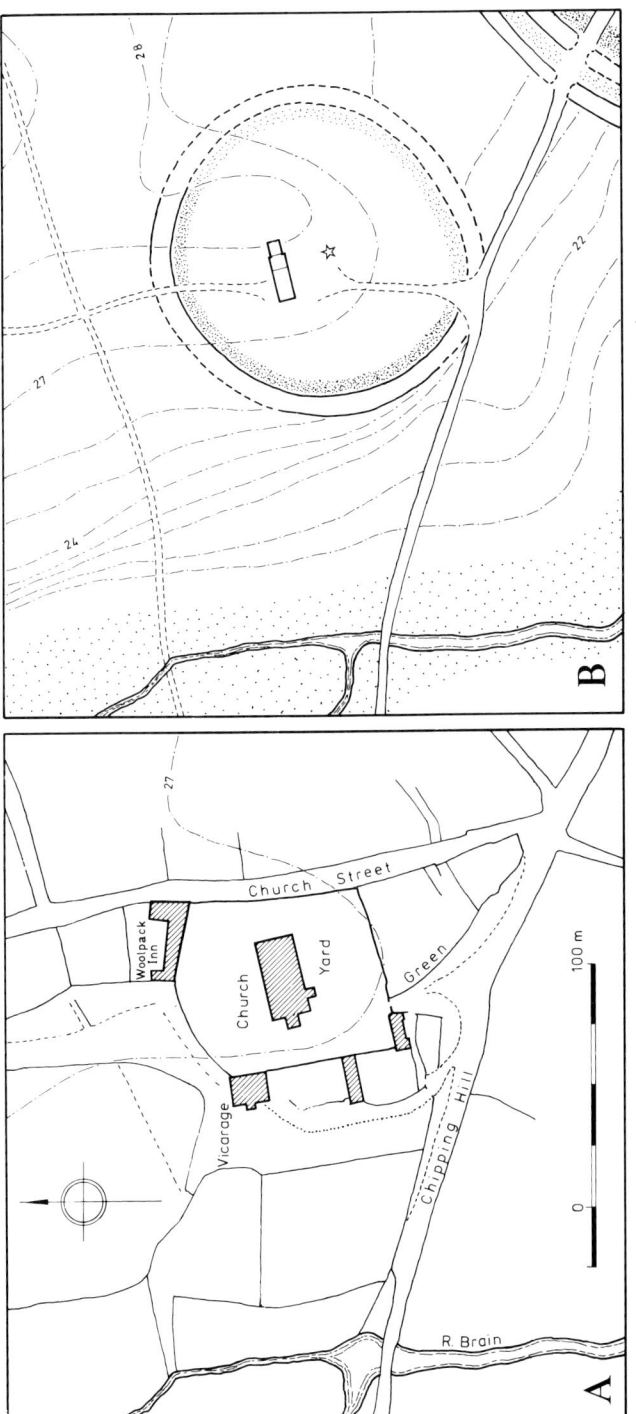

Fig. 23.
*A. Plan of St Nicholas's churchyard, Witham, and its environs, replotted from the Tithe map (1839),
with the addition of detail supplied by the 1874 Ordnance Survey map.
B. Reconstructed plan of the topography of the churchyard in the late Saxon period.
The asterisk marks the approximate centre of both the enclosure and the tongue formed by the 27 m O.D. contour.*

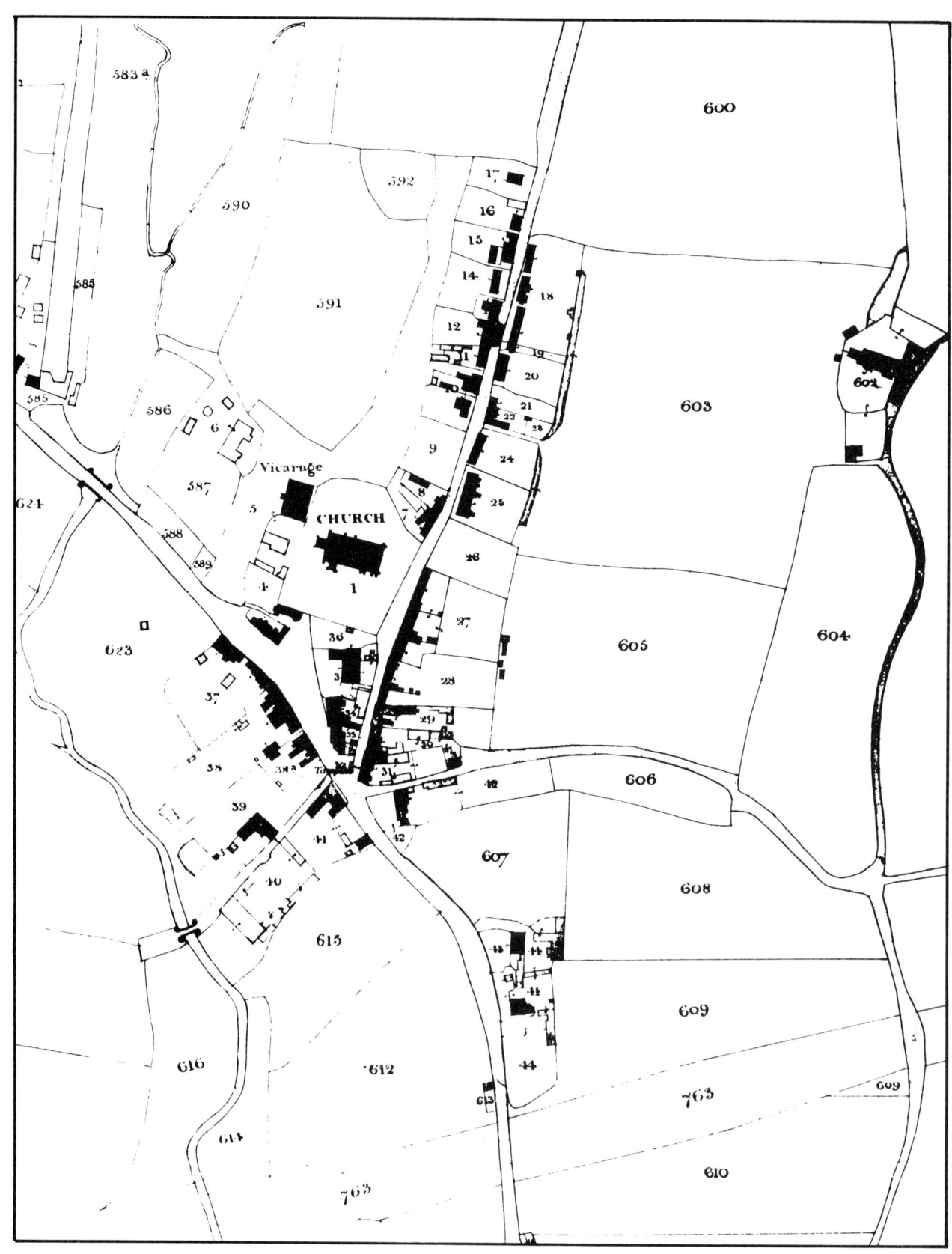

Fig. 24. Plan of the settlement at Chipping Hill according to Witham Tithe map, 1839.
(Reproduced by courtesy of the Essex Record Office).

the plan of which is still recoverable. The base of the triangle lay immediately outside the north-west entrance of Chipping Hill Camp (Fig. 25B). The market place has been infilled, and is now only a continuation of Church Street. The original east flank is discernible amidst the rear boundaries of properties on that side of the street; and the west side is marked by the present churchyard wall.

The Church Street unit would appear to have originated as a small planned medieval development, an adjunct to the Chipping Hill settlement. It is likely to have ante-dated the foundation of the new planned town at Newland Street in 1212 (p. 88). Morphologically, it seems certain that the Chipping Hill development, as well as the street alignment to which it is appendant, is considerably later than the curving churchyard boundary, and that this was no longer an intact enclosure.

The integrity and viability of the churchyard enclosure were negated by the medieval roads and property boundaries on both the east and south sides, and there can be little doubt that what we see here is the relict outline of a pre-medieval earthwork. Specifically, the creation of the market place was responsible for the destruction of a large slice of the enclosure on the east. The formal definition of an essentially rectangular churchyard, fronting on to the new market, must be attributable to the same period.

Beyond this generally stratigraphic and morphological relationship, there is no direct dating evidence for the earthwork enclosure, but two alternative possibilities suggest themselves: an Anglo-Saxon *enceinte*, directly associated with an early church; or a prehistoric earthwork which was conveniently adopted for a new use. The latter seems the more likely, and is discussed further on p. 73.

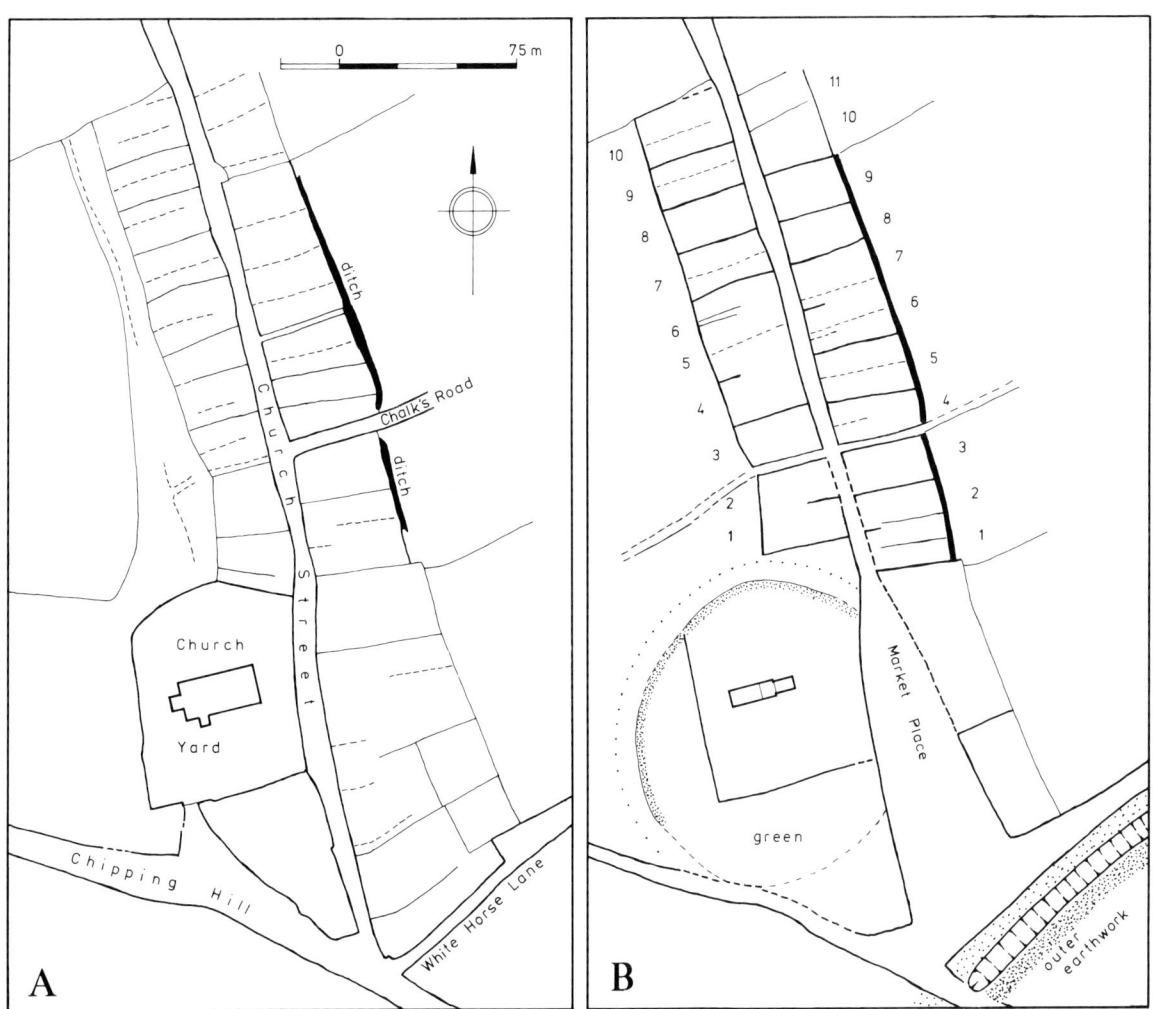

Fig. 25. A. *Plan of Church Street, Witham, replotted from the Tithe map (1839),*
with the addition from detail by the 1874 Ordnance Survey map.
B. *Reconstruction of the medieval planned development and triangular market place at Church Street.*

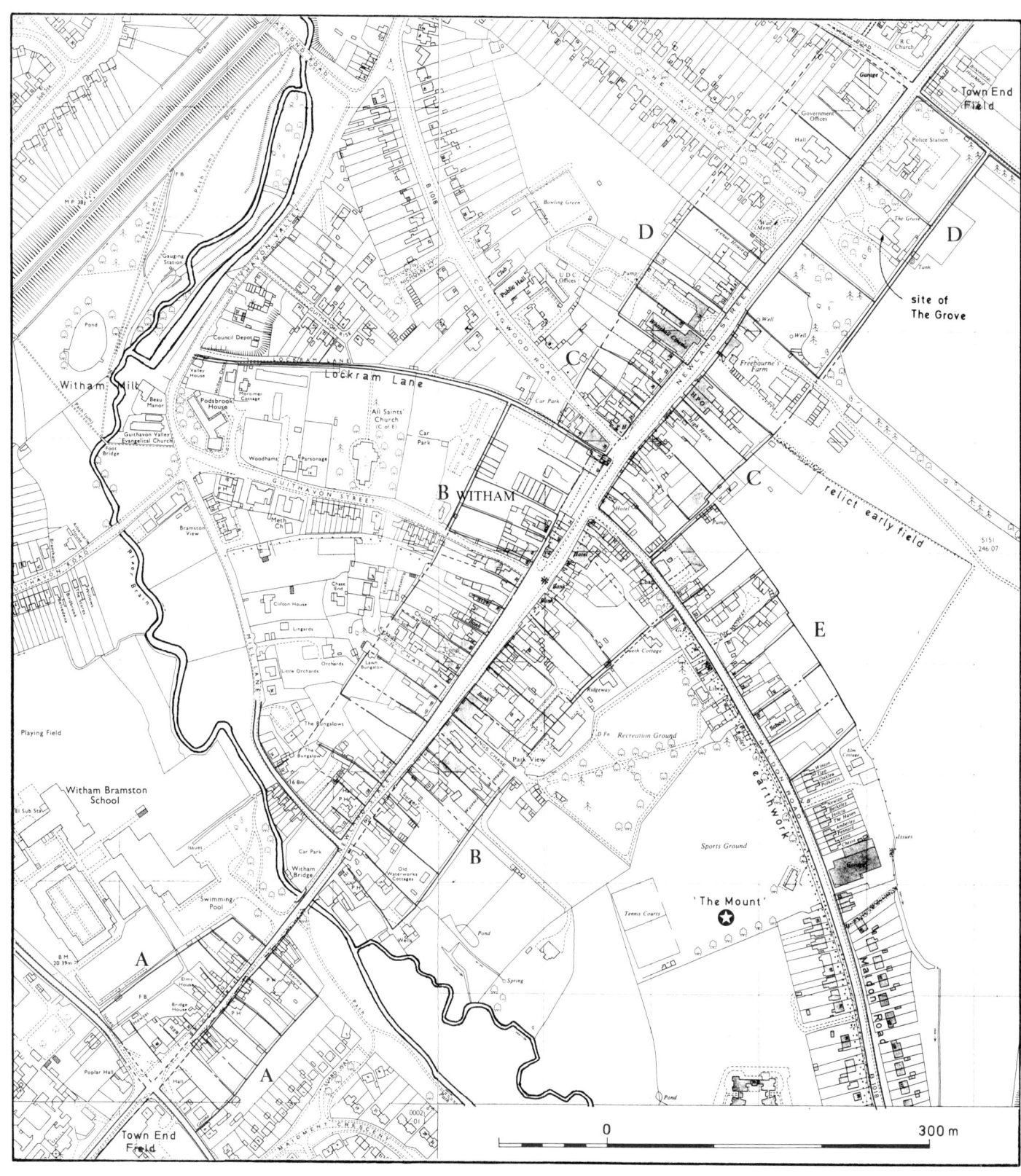

Fig. 26. *The morphology of the medieval planned town at* Wulvesford, *alias* Newland Witham, *showing the full extent of development. The five identified phases of development are lettered A to E. Replotted from the Tithe and 1874 Ordnance Survey maps, on to a modern base map.*

5

Wulvesford and Witham New Town

When the Knights Templar founded their new town, which was to become the core of present-day Witham, they sited it at a place called *Wulvesford*. The name, which is plainly of Anglo-Saxon origin, soon passed out of regular use, and its very existence was overlooked by Reaney (1935; but see below, p. 88). Presumably the name referred to a settlement that was identified with a certain Wulfhere, on the Roman road to Colchester at the fording point of the river Brain. Nothing further is recorded concerning that settlement — which must have been subsumed by the emergent town — but its site may be broadly identified from relict features in the post-medieval landscape.

The New Town of the Knights Templar (Figs. 26 and 27)

The Templars' town was of elementary plan, a single street (Newland Street) lined by a single depth of burgage plots on both flanks. The medieval plan-form was still clearly preserved down to the mid-nineteenth century, when it was recorded on the Tithe map (1839) and the first edition of the Ordnance Survey map (1874). Close inspection, however, reveals a greater complexity in the morphology of this seemingly modest urban development than might be expected.

First, it is evident that there have been no less than five distinct phases of town planning at Witham, and these are represented by discrete groups of burgage plots, as indicated on Fig. 26.

Group A An unequal pair of blocks of small and somewhat irregular plots flanking Bridge Street, south-west of the river crossing. The depth of the plots on the south-east flank averages 60 m and the width 20 m, giving a unit area of one-third of an acre. Plots on the north-west flank were possibly shallower, owing to the presence of a stream which may have formed the rear boundary. The block appears to have comprised eighteen plots in all. In the early modern period this area of Witham was known as Duck End.

Group B North-east of the river crossing, where Newland Street begins, both frontages are lined by well defined burgage plots having a depth of 80 m. These continue north-eastwards to the point where Newland Street fans out into a triangular market place and is intercepted by Maldon Road (entering from the south) and Lockram Lane (from the north).

Group C Beyond Maldon Road and Lockram Lane, Newland Street is flanked by a group of smaller and less well defined plots with the appearance of having been fitted into a constricted space, possibly a former rectangular market area, outside the limits of the original town.

Group D Continuing north-eastwards along Newland Street, we find blocks of large plots with a depth of 85 m and, at least on the south-east flank, there was a back lane servicing these burgages.

Group E On the east flank alone of Maldon Road there appears to have been a fairly regular series of large plots with a depth of *c*. 75 m.

The Wulvesford Enclosure (Fig. 28)

There is nothing to suggest that any of these elements of medieval town planning was accompanied by contemporary defences, but the phase represented by group B seems to have utilised a pre-existing earthwork. This feature is first recorded on the 1839 map as a long, curving boundary on the east side of the Brain, with both ends meeting the river: a large enclosure of pointed oval form seems to be defined, bisected by the Colchester road. In the nineteenth century the northern and southern extremities of this enclosure were still undeveloped and were occupied only by fields, lying beyond the rear boundaries of the medieval burgage plots that were strung across its centre (Fig. 27).

There can be little doubt that the *Wulvesford* enclosure is unrelated to the history of the Templars'

Fig. 27. Plan of Witham town (Newland Street) according to the Tithe map, 1839. (Reproduced by courtesy of the Essex Record Office)

new town — other than by chance association — and is a legacy of an earlier phase of occupation, or defence. The scale and siting of the enclosure seem to imply the latter. Modern development has obliterated virtually all topographical evidence to the north-west of Newland Street; but the line of the defences to the south-east is still clearly defined.

The southern section of the enclosure is marked by Maldon Road, which runs south-east from Newland Street to the river Brain at Saul's Bridge, a distance of 700 m. The road is undoubtedly of medieval origin, being the principal lateral route leading out of the town (to Maldon), although the earliest surving buildings on its frontage are of the seventeenth century.[48] The road occupies the site of the enclosure ditch, with its associated bank on the west.

Close to the town centre, the west flank of Maldon Road is fully built-up, except for a plot next to the former nonconformist chapel, where the bank survives to a height of one metre above pavement level. Halfway between the town centre and the river, on the west side of the road, is a sports ground with a nineteenth-century frontage wall standing on a bank 1.5 m above road level; and on the opposite side there is a marked rise in the level of the front gardens of the villas. Further south still, and close to the river, the villas on the west side of the road are perched on a steep bank, rising more than 2 m above road level. In effect, the road here has become a hollow way.

It is not possible to make a useful assessment of the dimensions of the earthwork since levelling and infilling for tenement plots have taken place at the town end of Maldon Road, while widening and gradient-easing have distorted the picture at the river end. The Tithe map, however, shows Maldon Road when it was a narrow, undeveloped lane, with the tree-lined bank as a prominent feature on its west flank. The bank, capped by a walk, formed part of the perimeter of the grounds of Witham House. Since banks, avenues and walks were not normally depicted on the Witham Tithe map, this feature must have been of considerable prominence in 1839 to merit inclusion.

North of Newland Street nothing remains to be seen of the earthwork, the whole area having been developed for shopping precincts and car parks in the 1960s. The Tithe and later maps, however, show a lane (Lockram

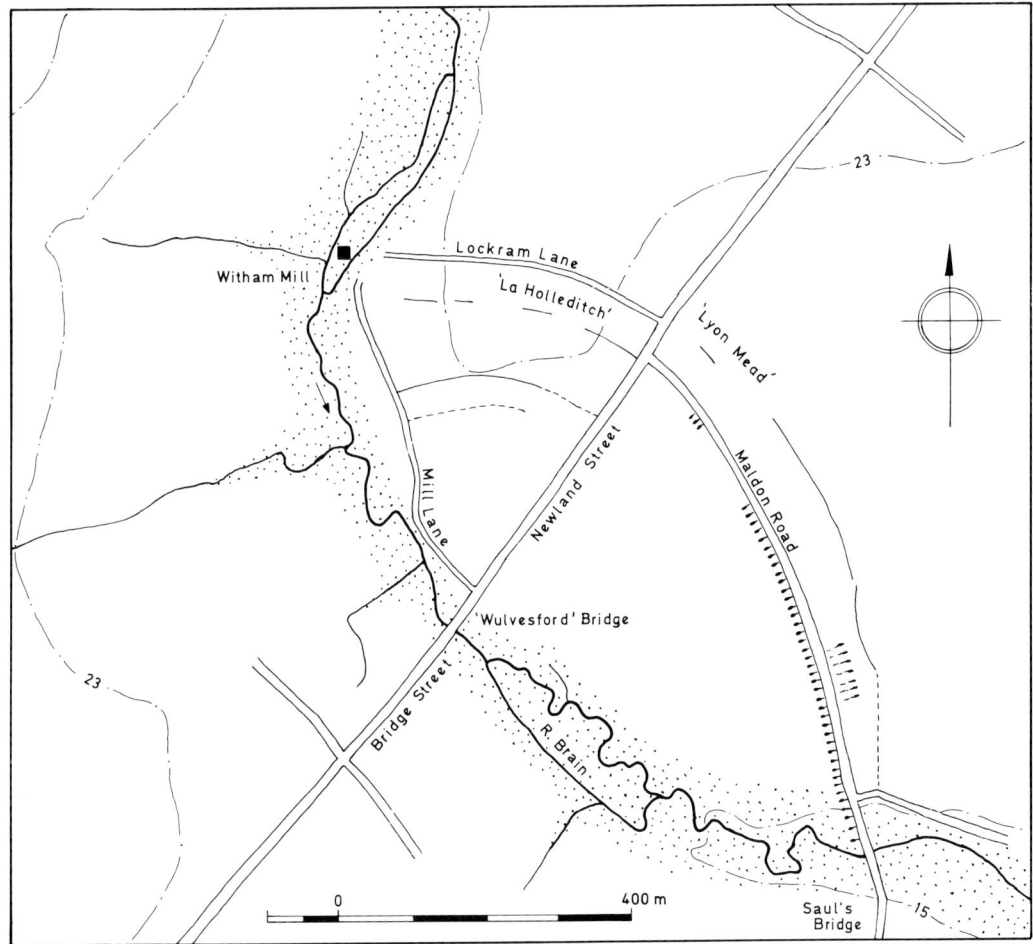

Fig. 28. Plan of the Wulvesford *earthwork, Witham, in relation to major topographical features; stippling indicates the flood plain of the river. Based on surviving field evidence and nineteenth-century maps.*

Lane, alternatively Queen's Street or Church Street) and a curving footpath running north-westwards for 450 m, to meet the river at Witham Mills. All Saints Church, built here on an open-field site in 1842, stands dramatically askew to the modern townscape, having taken its orientation from boundaries that followed the earthwork (Fig. 26).

Lockram Lane and Maldon Road form a distinctly offset junction with Newland Street, which is not convincingly explained in terms of post-medieval street-plan distortion caused by the infilling of the former market place. It seems more likely that Lockram Lane followed the outer perimeter of the earthwork, whereas Maldon Road lay in its ditch. Indeed, there are possible hints in the disposition of boundaries to the north and south of Newland Street that the defences comprised more than a single line of earthworks. That visible traces of the *Wulvesford* earthwork survived as relict features in the medieval and later urban landscape is potentially attested by several documented references. In the early fourteenth century there is a mention of la *Holleditch*[49], and in 1608 of 'a certain hollow' called 'Lyon Mead'.[50] The former was on the north side of Newland Street, somewhere near Lockram Lane; and the latter lay behind the Lion inn, on the south side of Newland Street, just outside the posited line of the enclosure.

The area enclosed by the *Wulvesford* earthwork was *c.* 27 ha (67 acres). There has been no archaeological investigation of the enclosure or of the area contained within it and, apart from medieval pottery found on sites in the town centre, few casual discoveries have been reported. A coin of Constans was found on the north-west side of Newland Street, close to the river crossing, in 1955.[51] Ploughing in an unspecified field in the south-east part of the town in 1844 revealed a Bronze Age cemetery, on land belonging to J. H. Pattisson. Illustrations survive of several of the Deverel Rimbury-type urns that were found (Repton 1854, pl. 9, nos. 1, 3, 8, 9 and 10; also Anon. 1844, 393). Reference to the Tithe Award, 1839, shows that Pattisson owned Witham House and the fields inside the southern end of the *Wulvesford* earthwork, one of which was, significantly, known as Mount Field. The mount itself was still preserved as a feature in the boundary (and was part of a rookery, Fig. 26): almost certainly this was a prehistoric barrow, and circumstantial evidence may be invoked to suggest that the urns were recovered from the site of another ploughed-out Bronze Age barrow on the east bank of the Brain. This does not, however, help with dating the enclosure.

6

Witham Lodge and Ivy Chimneys

Eight hundred metres south-west of the river crossing, alongside the Roman road to Chelmsford (here called Hatfield Road), lies a sixteenth-century house known as Ivy Chimneys; and behind this lay a pair of nineteenth-century cottages, demolished in 1970. They were known as Ivy Chimneys Cottages (Fig. 2). Trenching nearby, in 1849, brought to light quantities of Roman pottery and coins, and cremation urns. Further discoveries led to the relocation of the site in 1937, and then to amateur excavations in 1966–73 (Hull 1963, 201–2). The finds indicated a settlement of some importance, and included circumstantial evidence for a late Roman temple (Frere 1970; Henig *et al.* 1972). Large scale excavations carried out by Essex County Council in 1978–80 not only confirmed the pagan religious nature of the site, but unexpectedly also revealed an early Christian baptistery and possible church (p. 59. Turner 1982; and forthcoming). During building works in the 1960s groups of pottery vessels, apparently associated with Romano-British cremation burials, were encountered, but were hastily destroyed. Scattered inhumations of uncertain date have also been reported.

Witham Lodge Earthwork (Figs. 29 and 30)

Meanwhile, in 1970–72 an adjacent property to Ivy Chimneys — Witham Lodge — and its small park was developed for housing, leading to further unexpected discoveries. First revealed was an Early Iron Age settlement on rising ground to the north-west of Hatfield Road; secondly, sewer trenches dug in 1970 intercepted a parallel pair of major ditches running on an east-west alignment and appearing to pass obliquely under the Roman road. Unfortunately, circumstances permitted no more than the briefest investigation, providing just a tantalising glimpse of a large earthwork enclosure and multi-period settlement alongside the road leading into Witham from the south west. Fuller accounts have been given elsewhere (Brooks and Stokes 1976; Rodwell forthcoming).

Slight traces of earthworks were visible in the remaining parkland, and further evidence for their former course was provided by ponds and by the curving drive to the lodge. Fieldwork and excavation thus established some 450 m of the west side of the Witham Lodge enclosure, together with the south-west corner and, nearby, an entrance in the south side. East of the entrance gap there appeared to be a third ditch outside the others; all three were clearly overlain by Hatfield Road. The re-emergence of the south side of the enclosure on the opposite (south-east) side of the road is marked by oblique property boundaries, a linear hollow in a field and a slight change of alignment in Maltings Lane where it crosses the earthwork.

Continuing east, the south side made use of a slight declivity through which a streamlet runs, towards Howbridge Hall. This side of the enclosure may have followed the declivity all the way to the floodplain of the Brain. Alternatively, if there was a defined east side to the enclosure — as would seem probable — the earthwork probably turned north, approximately along the line of Howbridge Road and Spinks Lane (Fig. 29). There are no earthworks visible in this vicinity, since the whole area of potential interest has been overrun by development.

Nor is there now any field evidence for the earthwork on the north side, since this area too has been engulfed by modern housing estates. Cartographic evidence, however, indicates another natural declivity containing a streamlet, flanked by a series of land boundaries running from the presumed north-west corner of the Witham Lodge enclosure, towards the flood plain of the river. Whatever the precise line of the earthworks, it is clear that the north and south sides were basically pre-determined by a pair of minor side-valleys of the Brain, and that it was on the west side that the principal defensive measures were required, linking the heads of these two valleys. The plan of the earthwork was undoubtedly irregular, although roughly quadrangular, and the minimum area enclosed must have been in the order of 56 ha (140 acres).[52]

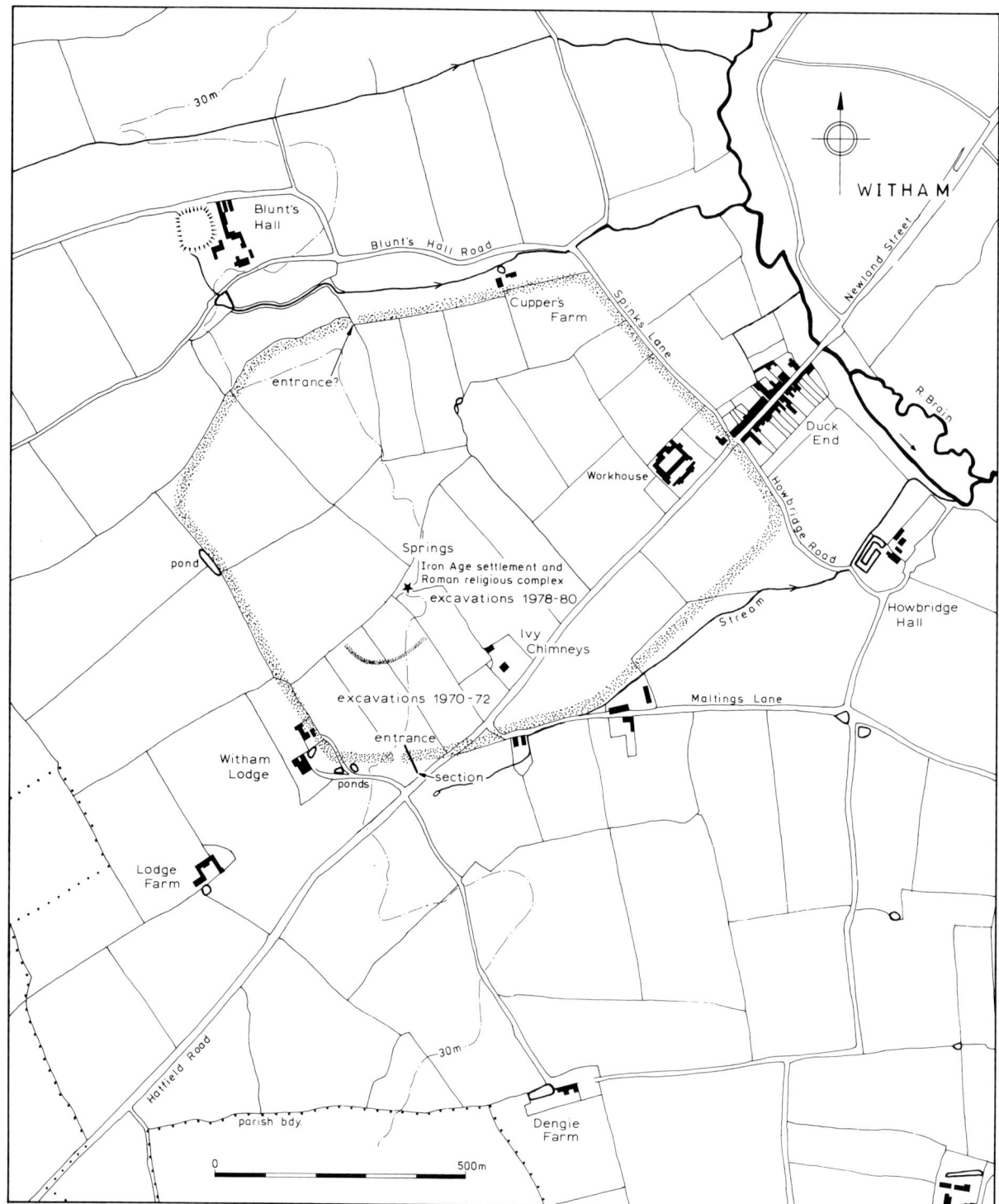

Fig. 29. *The Witham Lodge Earthwork: probable extent of the Iron Age enclosure and Roman religious complex (within a sub-enclosure) in relation to topographical features extant in the eighteenth and early nineteenth centuries. Stippling marks the posited site of the bank. The postion of the section recorded in 1970 through the defences of the south side is indicated.*

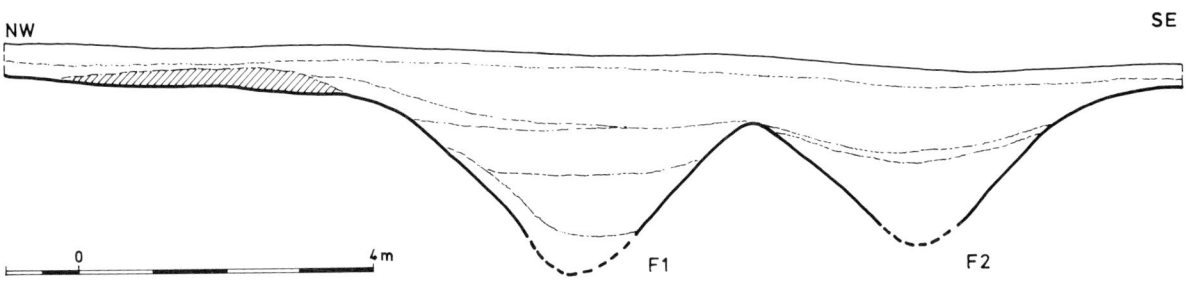

Fig. 30. Simplified section through the Witham Lodge Earthwork, 1970, adjacent to the south entrance.
For position see plan, Fig. 29. The vestigial remains of the bank are hatched.

Observations at the south-west corner of the enclosure established that there had been an internal bank upwards of 3.5 m wide and two, or three, ditches. The first ditch had a slack, V-shaped profile, and its original dimensions were *c.* 5.0 m wide by *c.* 2.8 m deep (Fig. 30). Immediately outside this, with no intervening berm, was a second ditch *c.* 4.6 m wide by *c.* 2.5 m deep. There was a slight inturn to the terminals of the inner ditch at the south entrance. Evidence for a third ditch was noted on the east flank, but insufficient was seen to determine whether this was an entrance work, or another phase of fortification altogether.[53] Nothing can be said with certainty about other entrances to the enclosure, although a likely position for one on the north is topographically indicated.

Direct evidence for dating the Witham Lodge enclosure is slight, since no artifacts have been recovered from the primary earthwork phases. A prehistoric origin is however indicated by two pieces of evidence: first, the inner ditch was half silted by the later Roman period (when debris from the nearby temple site was dumped in it) and, secondly, the London to Colchester road passes obliquely over the levelled southern defences, disregarding the adjacent entrance. Since the road is part of the primary Roman military layout of the AD 40s (or possibly the early 60s), the earthwork cannot be post-conquest. The most likely date for the enclosure is Late Iron Age. It was surrounded by, and clearly related to, an extensive pre-Roman rectilinear field system, parts of which have survived in the landscape into recent times (Fig. 36; p. 58).

There is one small piece of evidence for post-Roman activity at Witham Lodge: a sherd of a late Saxon cooking pot was found beneath a spread of burnt debris on the site of the levelled bank and inner ditch. No occupation site of the Anglo-Saxon period is otherwise known within 1 km. (but see p. 63).

7

Burgate Field Enclosure, Rivenhall End

Heading north-east from Witham, the Colchester road follows approximately the 20 m contour of the Blackwater valley. This is transected by three closely spaced side-streams flowing into the river (Fig. 2). The third and furthest stream from Witham — Cressing Brook — is more substantial than the others, and between it and the second — Burghey (Burgy) Brook — is a naturally defined plateau on which is situated a medieval crossroads (Fig. 31). This intersection forms the nucleus of the hamlet of Rivenhall End. The arrangement represents a modification of a Roman road junction, the north-western arm of which led to the major villa site at Rivenhall Church (Rodwell and Rodwell 1985, 66, fig. 49).

During a programme of research in the 1970s into the history and topography of Rivenhall parish, it became apparent that the hamlet at Rivenhall End developed following the disappearance of a minor Domesday manor, 'Godsalves', the lands of which were confined to the small plateau between Cressing and Burghey brooks. It was further established that the manorial holding was apparently coterminus with a single parcel known from numerous medieval and later references as Burgate Field. No satisfactory explanation for the name could be found in relation to the medieval history of Rivenhall parish, and since Burgate Field both occupies a relatively commanding position and adjoins the boundary with Witham, the possibility that it was connected with a lost *burh* seemed worthy of exploration. The topography and history of Rivenhall End have been generally discussed elsewhere (Rodwell and Rodwell 1985, 179–82; and 1992 forthcoming), and only a summary of the salient evidence need be given here.

First, it must be noted that the evidence for the Burgate Field enclosure is largely historical and cartographic, there having been no archaeological investigation here. Most of the earthwork circuit as well as much the interior of the site has been destroyed, first by the railway line transecting it in the 1840s and, secondly, in more recent years by road building (1960s),

a pipeline (1973), and sundry housing developments.

The earliest reference to the site, in the Domesday Survey, is to a manor and 30 acres, held by a free man in 1066 and by Roger *Deus Salvet Dominas* ('God Save the Ladies') in 1086 (*Rivenhall iv*: Rodwell and Rodwell 1985, 174). In the later Middle Ages the holding was known variously as Godsalves and Goodwins, but with no hint of manorial status. This was clearly lost at an early date, perhaps soon after the conquest, and the holding was absorbed into the manor of Rivenhall Hall, and later became a parcel of Hoo Hall. Godsalves, however, remained readily identifiable as a distinct sub-unit, both physically and tenurially, down to the eighteenth century. It was customarily referred to as a tenement and 30 acres, regardless of the actual size of the holding, which was progressively depleted.

The land parcels associated with Godsalves were *Burgate Field* and *Whaleslond*, for which the earliest reference by name is in 1383. The extent of Burgate Field was then given as 30 acres lying in Faulkbourne parish, and Whaleslond as 5 acres in Rivenhall. Later mentions assign both parcels to Rivenhall. The apparent confusion is explained by the fact that Burgate Field lay at a complicated junction of the parish boundaries of Rivenhall, Witham and Faulkbourne (the last being a detached portion, far from the parent parish: Figs. 31 and 39). Maps since the early eighteenth century have shown a small part of Burgate Field as lying in Faulkbourne parish, and the remainder in Rivenhall.[54] There is reason to believe that parish boundaries in this area have not remained static: several parcels of land elsewhere in the southern extremity of Rivenhall parish were within the jurisdiction of the manor of Witham until recent times, perhaps recalling a tenurial pattern that antedated medieval fragmentation.

It may be noted, *en passant*, that Faulkbourne is generally a problematic parish to understand: it adjoins Witham on the north-west and in plan has the appearance of being a cut-out corner. Yet its parochial morphology is most unusual: it is small and compact and, if one ignores some obvious encroachments, its four sides are seen not only to be remarkably straight but also define a square. Nor was natural topography the determinant, because one corner of the square is severed by the river Brain. It is difficult to envisage circumstances that could have given rise to such a piece of planning in the Anglo-Saxon period, or later. Arguably, Faulkbourne's parochial outline preserves the bounds of a very early (Roman?) estate that was embraced in the *parochia* of Witham minster, and subsequently released again without having suffered fragmentation. Faulkbourne was a separate Domesday manor with a single entry.

Given the strikingly unitary nature of Faulkbourne, it is all the more surprising that there should be a remotely detached portion of the parish, with contorted boundaries, on the east side of Witham, spanning its

junction with Rivenhall parish and including the western abutment of the Burgate Field enclosure (Fig. 39). Moreover, most of the land in this block had been in the hands of the Templars, and fell within the jurisdiction of Witham manor. In view of the demonstrable confusion over the parochial affiliation of at least part of the enclosed site, it is arguable that Burgate Field itself may have acquired an identity with Rivenhall that it did not initially possess. If so, it was a pre-Conquest acquisition, because 'Godsalves' was unequivocally listed as one of the five holdings of *Ruenhale* in the Domesday Survey.

Topographically, if not tenurially, the development of Rivenhall End seems fairly clear, and the Burgate Field enclosure is well defined on an estate map of 1716 (Fig. 31); it occupies the western angle of the crossroads,

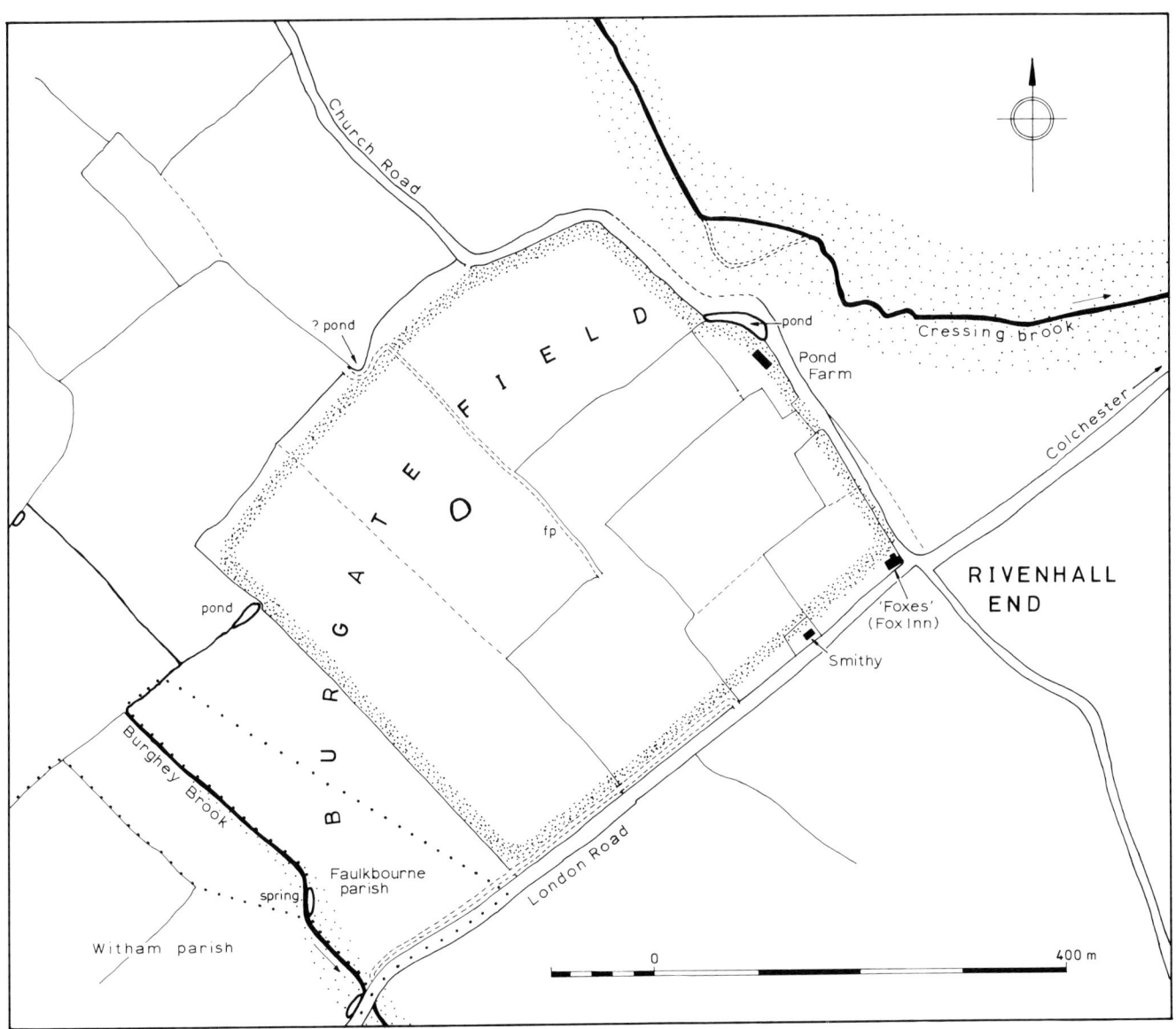

Fig. 31. *The topography of Burgate Field and its environs, Rivenhall End, replotted from maps of 1716 and later. Stippling marks the posited site of the enclosure bank.*

where all evidence for medieval activity is concentrated.[55]

The road from Rivenhall End to the church (Church Road), although basically Roman in origin, has a curious double bend towards its southern end, where it circumvents the north corner of Burgate Field. This is plainly a medieval diversion: the original Roman line would appear to have passed directly through the centre of the field, which was a near-rectangle with sides of *c*. 420 and 460 m. Thus the Burgate Field enclosure straddled the original side road to Rivenhall, while fronting the Colchester road. The cross-sectional dimensions of the earthwork cannot be accurately determined, but the area it enclosed must have been in the order of 18 ha (*c*. 45 acres).

The north-west and south-west sides of the enclosure were marked by field boundaries into modern times, and the latter occupied a natural break of slope. The position of the north entrance was indicated by a kink in the boundary, while an internal track perpetuated the original cross-axis of the enclosure. Exactly where Godsalves' tenement was situated is unknown, but the east corner would seem the most likely, since this was the place occupied by its successor, known as 'Foxes' in the seventeenth century (now the Rivenhall Fox Inn).

The diverted course of Church Road from Rivenhall End evidently followed the north-east ditch of the Burgate Field enclosure, close to the Cressing Brook. The north corner is still marked by a high roadside bank here. Halfway along the north-east side a pond was formed in the hollow of the ditch (perhaps by natural flooding from the brook), and a further kink developed in Church Road, to avoid this obstacle. The first implied reference to the pond is in 1415, when a certain John lived *atte Ponde*. Also dating from the fifteenth century was the substantial timber-framed house with hall and cross-wings, known as Grygges, later Pond Farm. The house stood on the bank, overlooking the ditch and pond; behind it was a croft of *c*. 4 acres.[56] This is the first identifiable encroachment into Burgate Field: others followed in due course, along both the Church Road and London Road frontages, gradually reducing the field from a square to an L-shaped form. A drawing of the north-east front of Pond Farm in 1836 shows how it was perched on the ancient bank, with the ground in front falling rapidly into the silted ditch (Rodwell and Rodwell 1992, forthcoming).

There is no independent dating evidence for the Burgate Field enclosure, although landscape analysis indicates an origin somewhere between the (?later) Roman period and the early Middle Ages: for further discussion see pp. 80–84.

8

Minor Earthworks in Witham Parish

Blunt's Hall Moat (Figs. 32 and 33)

From time to time, antiquaries have commented on the earthworks at Blunt's Hall to the west of Witham town. Here lay the seat of one of two manors entered as *Blundeshala* in the Domesday Survey (Round 1903, 462, 526). The larger manor, to which this site must relate, comprised 21/2 hides and had other substantial assets in 1066. The site of the smaller manor, with half a hide, is uncertain, but must have been to the south (see further, p. 64).

When the site was examined by the Royal Commission on Historical Monuments in 1912 it was classified as a 'homestead moat' having 'a strong inner bank' (RCHM 1921, 265).[57] A survey and small-scale excavations carried out in 1958, as part of the quest for Edward the Elder's *burh*, demonstrated that the sub-rectangular moat and its inner bank enclosed an area *c.* 60 m by 45 m, or 0.27 ha (0.67 acres). At the south-east corner the rampart incorporated a mound, presumably the base for a tower-like structure in timber.[58] Another length of water-filled ditch, presumed to be associated with a subsidiary moated enclosure, lay to the east of the farm buildings.

Artifacts recovered during excavation indicated a twelfth-century date for the earthwork, and its identity as the remains of an adulterine castle was proposed by the excavator. The local historical context for the castle's construction was suggested (Trump 1961). Reference to maps of the manor of Blunt's Hall, dated 1752 and 1812, shows that although the moat had long stood empty of buildings its military origin had not been forgotten: the adjoining parcel was known as 'Casting Bailey(s)'.[59] The buildings of post-medieval Blunt's Hall stood in a separate enclosure to the east of the moat. These are shown in a perspective view on the 1752 map, which also depicts the mound at the south-east corner of the small bailey as a tree-covered motte.

The configuration of the land boundaries adjoining the castle, the position of a pond and stream to the south, and the encircling course taken by Blunt's Hall Road, are together suggestive of a second and much larger enclosure to the south and east of the recognised motte-and-bailey, containing *c.* 2.8 ha (7 acres). This is most plausibly interpreted as an outer bailey, perhaps an addition to an earlier ringwork (Fig. 33.1, 2). The outer bailey appears to have been cut in half by the digging of a straight length of ditch across it, perhaps in the thirteenth century. The purpose was doubtless to create a fashionable moated enclosure for a rebuilt manor house (Fig. 33.3). This moat still houses what is left of the manorial buildings, although Blunt's Hall is now a housing estate. The disused outer bailey appears to have remained as a open space, and was referred to as Bluntshall Green in a rent roll of 1619.[60]

Howbridge Hall Moat (Figs. 32 and 33)

The medieval manor of Howbridge lay to the south of Witham, close to the river Brain. Like Blunt's Hall, *Hobruge* also appears in the Domesday Survey as two separate manors, one with half a hide, the other with 21/2 hides. It was the latter entry that referred to Howbridge Hall:[61] the smaller holding is probably to be equated with Isham's Farm (alias Little Howbridge), the only part of Witham which lay on the east bank of the Blackwater (Fig. 48. Gyford 1985, 11).

The present Howbridge Hall is a late sixteenth-century building, lying within and against one side of a sub-circular enclosure: this is defined for more than half its circuit by the road leading to the hall. Next to the hall, and also within the enclosure, is a tiny rectangular moat, with a causeway entrance at the north-east corner. Overall, the moat measures 60 m by 25 m; and the island defined by it is only 38 m by 12 m. The moat, which still partially survives as a pond, was planned in 1874 by the Ordnance Survey, and was shown in exactly the same form on the Tithe map of 1839. The feature carries little conviction as a medieval moated homestead, and is surely a seventeenth or eighteenth-century garden embellishment.

Adjoining the hall on the north-east is a second

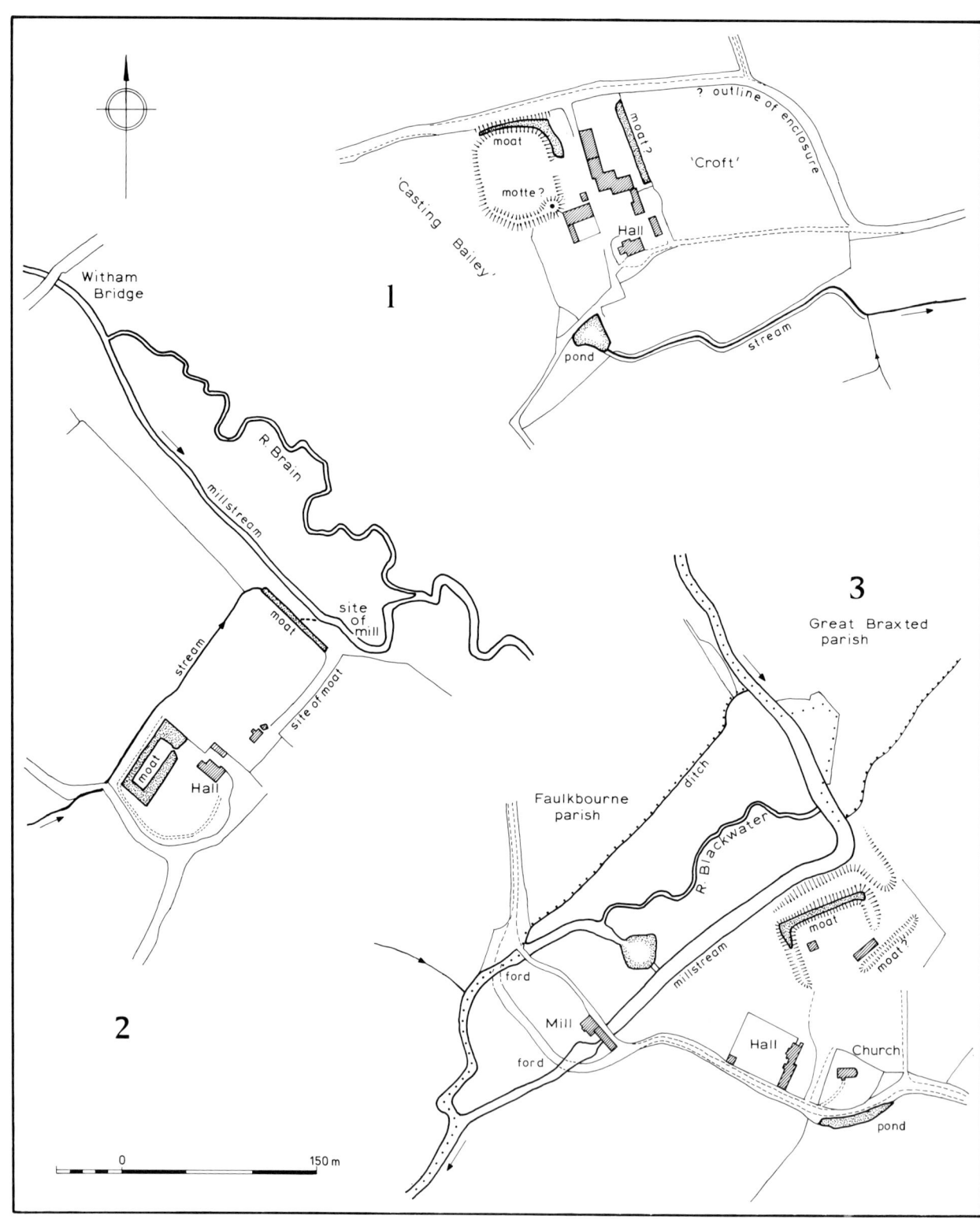

Fig. 32.
1. The topography of Blunt's Hall, Witham, replotted from maps of 1752, 1812 and 1839.
2. The topography of Howbridge Hall, Witham, replotted from the Tithe and 1874 Ordnance Survey Maps.
3. The topography of Little Braxted Hall, replotted from the Tithe and 1874 Ordnance Survey Maps.

enclosure of markedly rectangular outline; it was formerly divided into paddocks, but is now occupied by houses and gardens. This enclosure appears to have been moated, although hitherto unrecognised as such. A good deal of landscaping has taken place, but three sides of the moat are recorded on early maps and are still detectable on the ground. The north-west side is marked by a canalised stream in a boggy hollow. The north-east side is now only a very slight earthwork, but was a water-filled feature in 1874; and the south-east side is still distinctly visible as a hollow.

It is possible that, as at Blunt's Hall, there were two conjoined enclosures at Howbridge. In this case, the nucleus was a sub-circular enclosure adjacent to, and perhaps incorporating, a stream on the north-west: the remainder of the *enceinte* was presumably defined by a ditch, approximately where an encircling road now runs (Fig. 33.4). Attached to this primary enclosure, and on slightly lower ground, was a rectangular moat (Fig. 33.5). The complete site contained 1.2 ha (3 acres). Immediately beyond the moated enclosure is a millstream adjoining the river Brain. The stream itself has now become the main river channel; the position of the former mill is clearly indicated where a loop in the stream formed the bypass. There are no recent records of a mill at Howbridge, and the site was probably abandoned in the Middle Ages. The early origin of the Howbridge mill is, however, attested by its appearance in the Domesday Survey.

Although no archaeological exploration of Howbridge

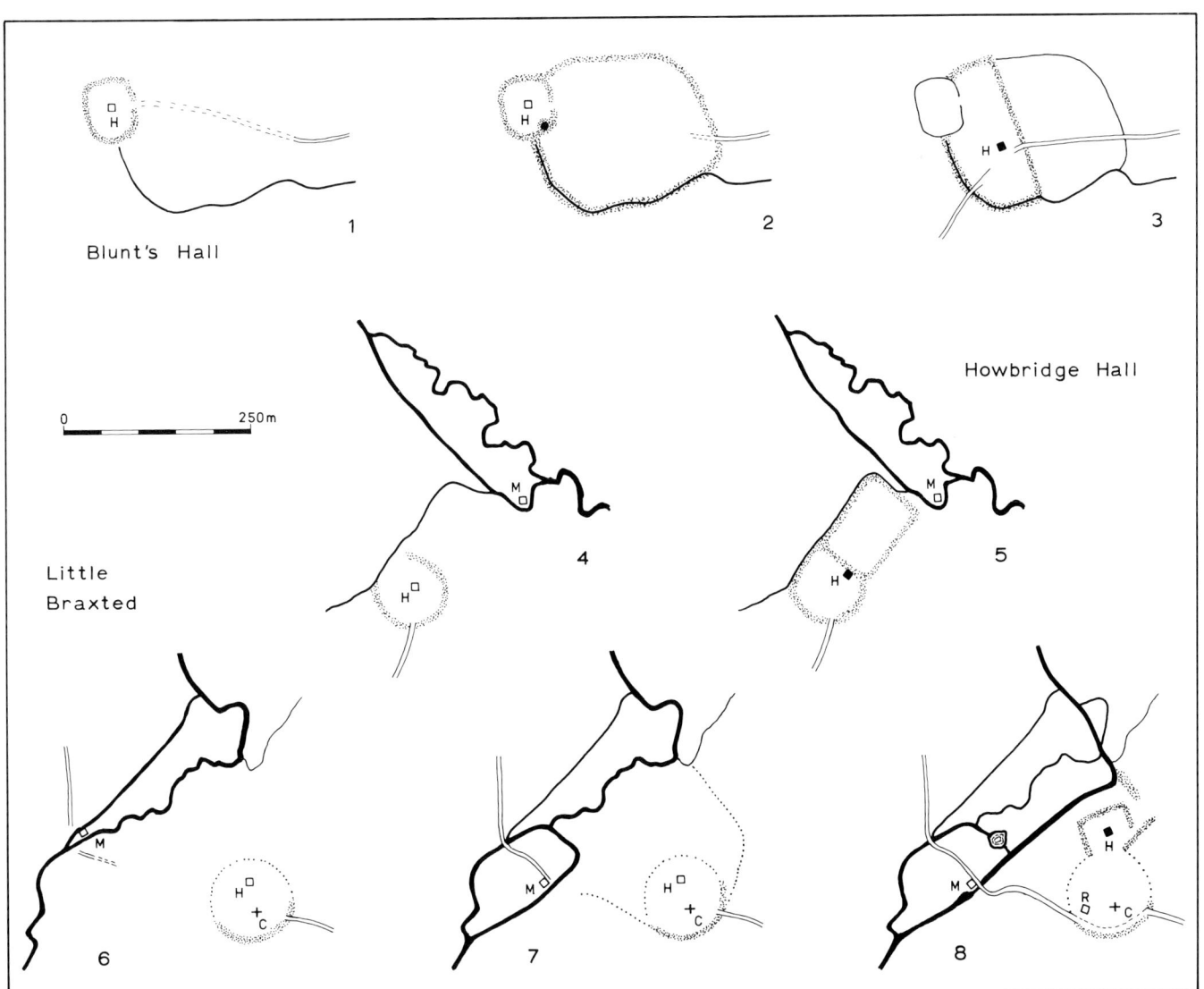

*Fig. 33. Interpretative plans of three moated enclosures and mill complexes. **Blunt's Hall:** 1. Pre-Twelfth century? 2. Twelfth-century castle. 3. Later medieval and post-medieval moated manor. **Howbridge Hall:** 4. Anglo-Saxon or early medieval. 5. Later medieval. **Little Braxted Hall:** 6. Late Anglo-Saxon. 7. Early medieval. 8. Later medieval.*
Key: C. Church; H. Hall; M. Mill; R. Rectory. Open symbols indicate suggested sites of buildings.

Hall has taken place, there is no reason to suspect that the earthworks are other than those of a small medieval moated manor, perhaps with an earlier sub-circular enclosure defining a more ancient nucleus. There is, however, a tantalising reference to a property called 'The Castell' in a will of 1614, but it is not clear whether this referred to any part of the Howbridge Hall site, or to another dwelling on the manorial estate.[62]

The placename, incidentally, provides valuable confirmation of an Anglo-Saxon bridge across the Brain. While it might be assumed that this referred to Witham Bridge, on the main road, the initial placename element *hoh* clearly points to the elevated tongue of land leading down to Saul's Bridge ('bridge by the spur of land': Reaney 1935, 301). Saul's Bridge is at the southernmost tip of the *Wulvesford* enclosure (Fig. 28).

Many comparisons may be made between the moats and enclosures at Blunt's Hall and Howbridge Hall with others in the Witham area. For example, there is another undocumented and unstudied 'castle' earthwork around the hall at White Notley. But most relevant in the present context are the enclosures at Little Braxted Hall, a site immediately outside the Witham parish boundary (Fig. 32.3). Here is an isolated and compact manorial and parochial nucleus, for which an origin in the eleventh (or even the later tenth) century is most likely: the manor and the mill were listed in the Domesday Survey. Although the church itself was not noted by the survey, its priest was: the extant building is of the 'Rivenhall type', and is no later than the eleventh century in origin (Rodwell and Rodwell 1985, 135–8).

It may be argued that Little Braxted Church was built within a circular or sub-circular enclosure also housing the earliest hall (p. 75; Fig. 33.6), and that the resited medieval hall was surrounded by a small, squarish moat which was constructed literally as an adjunct to the church enclosure (Fig. 33.8). A homestead moat of this type is unlikely to have been dug earlier than the thirteenth century. The moated site was effectively abandoned in the seventeenth century, and the present hall lies just west of the church (a house that may in fact have started life as a sixteenth-century rectory, undergoing a change of use when the old timber-framed hall was destroyed by fire). The medieval detached kitchen still stands within the moat, having been converted into a dovecote, perhaps in the seventeenth century. The timber-framed kitchen probably dates from the late fourteenth century (Hewett 1973).

There are, however, topographical indications that the enclosure sequence at Little Braxted was more complex than this and that there was a riverside *enceinte* of D-shaped plan, embracing the hall, church and mill, before the hall itself was separately moated (Fig. 33.7). The area thus conjecturally enclosed was approximately the same as that of the outer 'bailey' at Blunt's Hall (Fig. 33.3).

Powers Hall and Benton Hall Moated Sites

The Witham Tithe map depicts the remains of moats around two other domestic complexes. Both appear to be straightforward rectilinear enclosures, perhaps dating from the thirteenth century. There is no detailed archaeological evidence from either site.

Powers Hall, otherwise known as Little Witham, lies 1.5 km west of Chipping Hill (Fig. 35), and is the site of a Domesday manor with four hides (Round 1903, 514a). A chapel is recorded here, the demise of which presumably occurred in the mid-sixteenth century. The sides of the quadrangular moat measured *c.* 85 m overall. In 1839 only the northern arm and north-east corner remained as a water-filled feature; the west and south sides were marked as boundaries.

Benton Hall lies on the west bank of the Blackwater, 1.8 km south-east of Witham Bridge (Fig. 35), and was recorded in the Domesday Survey as a holding of one hide and 15 acres. It has never aspired to manorial status. The farm buildings appear to have been enclosed within a rectangular moat measuring *c.* 100 m square. Parts of the north, east and west sides were represented as water-filled features on the Tithe map; and the 10 acre field adjoining on the north was known as Church Field in 1839. There is no obvious explanation for this naming, since there was no recorded glebe land in this part of the parish, and no known ecclesiastical site in the neighbourhood. The possibility that this refers to the site of a lost church or chapel at Benton Hall is worth considering.

In view of the fact that Benton Hall lies alongside a mill of undoubted early origin (now called Bluemills), the possibility should not be overlooked of there having been a settlement here which failed to reach manorial status. Indeed, the settlement topography at Benton Hall is closely similar to that at Little Braxted Hall, the centre of a minor manor and tiny parish, 1.75 km up-river (Fig. 32.3; p. 75).

Pondhalton Farm Enclosure (Fig. 34)

A short distance to the south of Howbridge Hall, and on its former demesne land, is Pondhalton (or, corruptly, Pondhaltow) Farm, lying in the south-west angle of a minor crossroads formed by the intersection of Maltings Lane and Howbridge Hall Road. The farm buildings are early twentieth century, and there appears to have been nothing on the site at the time of the Tithe Award, except some ponds. Nevertheless, the interesting placename is clearly not modern and would suggest a derivation from the Halton (*healh-tun*) group, with the descriptive prefix 'Pond'.[63]

Cartographic evidence, from 1839 onward, indicates substantial ponds in the south-east and south-west angles of the crossroads: the former has recently been infilled and built upon, while the latter remains a prominent

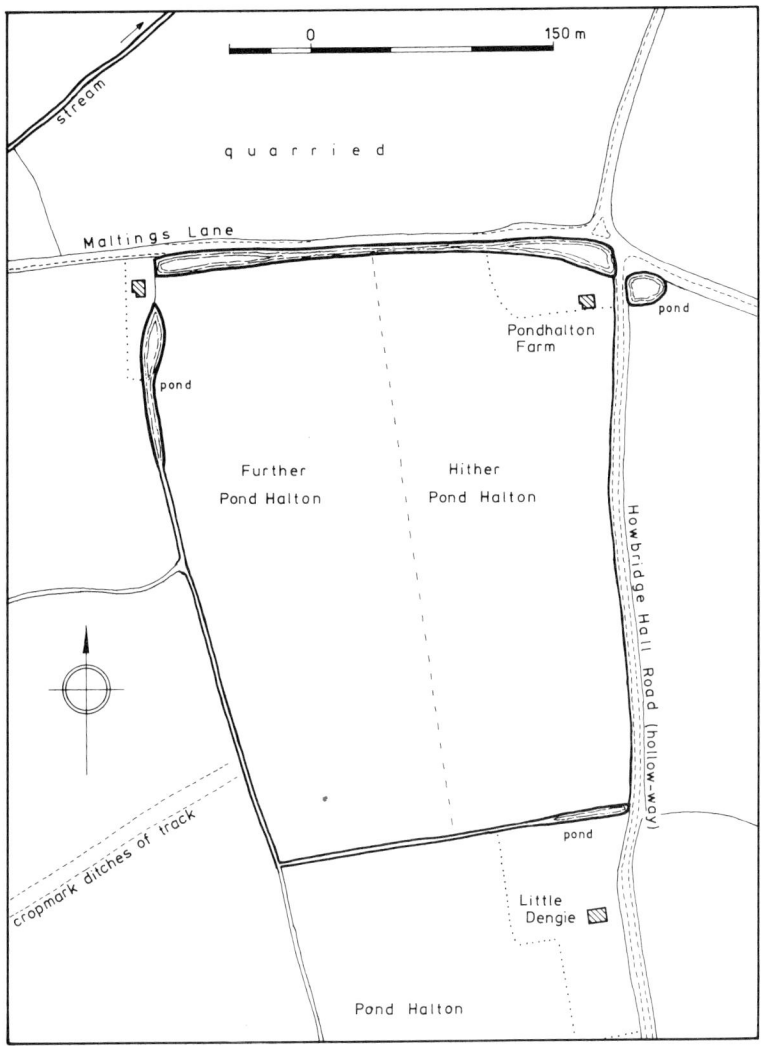

Fig. 34. The topography of the Pondhalton Farm enclosure, Witham. Plotted from fieldwork and the 1874 Ordnance Survey Map.

landscape feature.[64] It is not so much a pond as a length of water-filled roadside ditch. The width, however, which is up to *c.* 7 m, is moat-like and out of all proportion for a road ditch. Further west from the farm, the ditch is now dry and infilled to varying degrees, but is nevertheless a visibly continuous feature for 280 m. This appears to represent the complete northern side of an enclosure. The north-west corner has been encroached upon by a 1930s property.

The northern part of the west side is defined by another elongated pond, while the remainder is no more than a field boundary, and that has been largely expunged in modern times. The east side of the enclosure is marked by a narrow, partly sunken lane (Howbridge Hall Road), which is sited at a natural break of slope. Towards its southern end this lane kinks slightly as it approaches Little Dengie (now called Home Farm), another early twentieth-century creation. Here, alongside the farmyard, a further length of water-

filled ditch is found which could mark the south side of the Pondhalton Farm enclosure.

The enclosure thus defined is a near-rectangle measuring *c.* 330 m by 245 m, and enclosing *c.* 8 ha (20 acres). The corners are markedly angular, even when allowance is made for post-medieval boundary straightening. The site, which occupies a low promontory — presumably the *healh* — on the 23 m contour, is entirely agricultural land, now heavily ploughed. There are no visible traces of an internal bank, not even adjacent to the northern ditch which is so well marked. It would appear most unlikely that there ever was in internal bank. Indeed, Maltings Lane, which bounds the site on the north, is slightly elevated above the adjacent field level, which might indicate that the upcast from the ditch was externally deposited.

The enclosure has been a single parcel since before 1874, but in 1839 it was two fields, aptly known as Hither Pond Halton and Further Pond Halton; the division was probably no older than the eighteenth century. A rectangular field to the south, which belonged to Dengie Farm in 1839, was called Pond Halton, and another field a little to the west was Bean Halton. It is likely that an early settlement, with a 'Halton' name, has disappeared from the rectilinear land-block that contains all these fields. The settlement was probably subordinate to Howbridge Hall. The majority of the demised holding became annexed to Dengie Farm (Fig. 29), but the Pondhalton enclosure alone was taken — or more likely retained — by Howbridge Hall.

No date or obvious function can be suggested for the enclosure, which does not have the appearance of being defensive. It fits perfectly within the more-or-less rectilinear pattern of lanes and fields established over this area in the later Iron Age (p. 58); however, the Pondhalton Farm enclosure could have been created within this morphological framework at any subsequent period. An early date does not seem likely, and possibly the earthwork enclosed no more than a tract of managed medieval woodland. Cropmarks show a pair ditches, defining a former track, approaching the enclosure from the south-west and cutting obliquely across the local field system.[65]

The Warborough Fields

The westernmost extremity of Witham parish — part of the manor of Blunt's Hall — comprises an angular block of fields which projects into Hatfield Peverel parish. On an estate map of 1752, these are shown as three parcels: Lower, Middle and Further Warborough.[66] By 1812, each had been subdivided.[67] The *borough* element of the name presumably referred to an enclosure, or at least to earthworks; and the prefix *war* tends also to be found in association with significant defensive works: eg. War Dykes, Chichester, and War Ditches, Cherry Hinton, Cambs.[68] Warborough is also known as a parish name in Oxfordshire, and is interpreted by Ekwall (1936, 473) to mean 'watch hill'.

Topographically, the location of the Warborough fields evokes interest: they occupy a narrow neck on a ridge formed by the 45 m (150 ft) O.D. contour. The site also marks a discontinuity, or point of junction, in the early field systems between the valleys of the Brain and the Ter (Fig. 36).

The cohesion of the Warborough fields, and their isolation on a projecting limb, demonstrates that there was formerly an identity and significance to the group which is now lost to us. The name occurs too far west to relate to the Witham Lodge enclosure, or to any known medieval settlement, and therefore another archaeological monument of substance may possibly be implied. The area is still farm land, and there should be recoverable archaeological evidence for any former earthworks on this hilltop.

Although strictly outside the area covered by this study, it is relevant to record that to the north-west of the Warborough fields, in Terling parish, there is evidence for another very large earthwork enclosure of unknown date, centred on a farm formerly known as Great Farsley (now Taylor's Farm. Fig. 36). The enclosure, which occupies a west-facing slope adjacent to the river Ter, appears to be of generally similar size, and perhaps form, to that at Witham Lodge. The plan is a rounded sub-rectangle. Part of the earthworks of the north-west side has survived through being incorporated in the boundary of Terling Place Park: the feature is locally known as 'Canewdon Dic' and is marked as such on Ordnance Survey maps.[69] The south-east and north-east sides are delimited by parish and field boundaries; while the river itself could have comprised the south-west side, it seems more likely that the earthwork followed the 30 m contour here and that ploughing has obliterated the evidence. The earliest record of the site on plan is the Terling Tithe map of *c*. 1844.[70]

Although Great Farsley is not recognised as one of the medieval manors of Terling, the name is nevertheless manorial in origin and can be traced back to the twelfth century, to the family of Gilbert Falceillon (Reaney 1935, 297). The enclosure itself is undoubtedly earlier in date, and an inspired guess would place it late in the prehistoric era.

9

The Development of Prehistoric and Roman Settlement in the Witham Area

It is clear from the foregoing chapters that the Witham area has been important for settlement at least since the Late Bronze Age, and that both banks of the river Brain have seen intensive activity. This has not been confined to the usual straggling 'occupation belt' that is now seen as commonplace along the terraces of most Essex rivers, but includes a series of defensive earthworks starting at the water's edge and stretching back into the hinterland in opposing directions. It is undoubtedly Witham's position at a major crossing of the Brain, not far from its confluence with the Blackwater, that has given rise to so much activity. Unfortunately, the abundant archaeological evidence has for the mostpart lain undetected, and has now largely been lost through development.

It is difficult to believe that Witham half a century ago was only a small market town, set in a recognisably rural landscape (Fig. 35): today, new roads, housing estates and factories have obliterated more than 7 sq km of historic landscape, and expansion relentlessly continues in all directions. The death knell for historic Witham was sounded in the early 1840s, when the Eastern Counties Railway was built. Not only did this cut a huge swathe through Chipping Hill Camp, but Witham station was also constructed at its very centre. A single archaeological discovery was reported at the time: the La Tène II-III iron pokers (p. 10). The only previously reported find from the parish was that of Roman coins, around the turn of the eighteenth century (p. 8).

The railway facilitated ready access to London, and inevitably Witham grew. A railway yard, warehouses and a hotel were all constructed inside Chipping Hill Camp, followed by housing in the 1880s. But development did not begin to take a seriously damaging grip on the town before the 1930s; and even so, it was not until the 1960s — when Witham was designated as a housing 'overspill' area for Greater London — that expansion, and with it terminal destruction, proceeded on an exponential scale. Removal of the East Coast traffic from the town centre was facilitated by the construction of the A12 bypass, to the south (Fig. 2).

Very little fieldwork, archaeological excavation or methodical observation has taken place during these decades of development: we have witnessed a saga of lost opportunities. Even Chipping Hill Camp, Witham's only well known monument — and one that has commanded antiquarian interest for three hundred years — has never received statutory protection (despite calls for it to be Scheduled, in 1914 and 1936) and was finally obliterated as a field monument in 1988. Most of the sites described in this volume are archaeologically inaccessible and, deficient as the present evidence may be, it is unlikely to be augmented to any notable extent in the foreseeable future. It is therefore considered timely to attempt an overall assessment of the historical geography and archaeology of Witham.

Later Prehistoric Settlement

THE NATURE AND LOCAL CONTEXT OF THE EVIDENCE

Aerial photography and archaeological fieldwork conducted over the past twenty-five years have revealed a more-or-less continuous settlement zone along the brickearth and gravel terraces of the rivers and many of the lesser waterways in central Essex. The rate of discovery has been dramatic (Priddy and Buckley 1987). The Blackwater valley has been particularly productive of evidence for ring-ditches, enclosed settlements and field systems, ranging in date from Bronze Age to late Roman. Although more ephemeral, evidence of Neolithic activity and early Anglo-Saxon settlement is increasingly coming to light. Wherever large-scale excavations have taken place — and on some smaller investigations too — a long history of site occupation has been established.

Although the precise focus of settlement at any one location may shift from period to period, there is little doubt that a continuous thread of occupation was maintained, and individual site identities preserved over very long timescales. The number of instances where medieval village nuclei, manor houses, or historically significant farms, lie in close juxta-position to sites of Roman and earlier ancestry is sufficiently impressive for coincidence to be an unacceptable explanation. The force of this argument is greatly strengthened when it can be demonstrated that large tracts of ancient field systems are still preserved around these nuclei, as relict features in modern landscapes. The very fact that it has never been found necessary to enclose, or re-enclose, the vast majority of the Essex rural landscape since the Roman period bears eloquent testimony to the abiding maintenance of agriculture and land management systems.

Investigations of several sites in the Witham area have established the veracity of this argument, particularly in the adjacent parishes of Rivenhall and Kelvedon. At the former, it has been shown how a typical medieval manor-church complex developed out of a Roman villa (Rodwell and Rodwell 1985); and at the latter a small medieval town grew out of a minor Roman one (Rodwell, K., 1988). In both instances the archaeological deposits of pre-medieval date had been severely eroded by prolonged and intensive agriculture; and an accurate assessment of the nature and longevity of occupation would have been impossible through small-scale operations.

A side effect deriving from the degradation of sites through agriculture is the emergence of cropmarks. Seemingly endless chains of these have been discovered along the accessible stretches of the Blackwater valley, both above and below Witham, but the crucial area around the confluence of the Blackwater and the Brain is now a write-off for aerial archaeology. In any case, the terraces here are mainly of brickearth, which is notorious for its failure to generate clear cropmarks even on a site with major archaeological features. Nevertheless, there is no reason to suppose that the pattern of multi-period settlements, ceremonial and religious foci, cemeteries and field systems that characterises the wider environs of Witham should not continue, unseen, beneath a brickearth blanket, topped with sprawling housing and industrial estates. Not only does the circumstantial evidence cumulatively support such a contention, but it also points to an intensification of activity around this ancient crossing point of the Brain valley: hence the remarkable cluster of earthwork enclosures described in this report.

NEOLITHIC AND BRONZE AGE
SETTLEMENT AND DEFENCE

Little can be elucidated about Neolithic and earlier Bronze Age activity at Witham: flints and sherds of pottery indicative of domestic occupation have been recovered during excavations at Chipping Hill and Ivy Chimneys. Whether there was a substantial enclosure at this early date at Chipping Hill remains to be seen: such

a discovery would occasion no surprise. There is a miscellany of evidence for prehistoric burial sites in the area: a barrow cemetery is presumably represented by the several ring-ditches recorded through aerial photography on the east side of Witham, in Barn Field, now a factory site (Fig. 2, no. 4). At least one barrow lay in Mount Field, just south of the town (Fig. 2, no. 5).

Between these two sites — and severed by the *Wulvesford* enclosure ditch — lay a field known at least since 1608 as 'Pottlids'; this was an unusual but evocative post-medieval description for barrows that were still upstanding as earthworks (Fig. 2, no. 7. Reaney 1935, 616; Field 1972, 172). On the east bank of the Brain at Chipping Hill, immediately south-east of the churchyard enclosure, yet more barrows are potentially indicated by the field-name Mount Meadow (Fig. 2, no. 8). In all, a considerable concentration of barrows in the angle between the Brain and Blackwater seems to be implied by field names and other evidence.

Despite the thorough destruction of barrows in Essex through agricultural activity, it is interesting how many field names recall their former presence: in addition to the three Witham names (Mount Field, Mount Meadow, and Pottlids) three further local examples may be mentioned. A field known as The Lowes on the west bank of the Blackwater at Rivenhall End has recently been shown to contain a ploughed-out long barrow, a henge and at least two round barrows (Buckley *et al.* 1988, fig. 2). A little further upriver, at the junction of the Kelvedon-Feering-Inworth parish boundaries is a late Roman and early Anglo-Saxon cemetery in Barrow Field and Barrow Hills (Rodwell, K. 1988, 136). Finally, in the valley of the Cressing Brook, east of Rivenhall Church, are Great and Little Barrow Fields, where grave goods from a prestigious early Roman burial were recovered in 1839 (Rodwell and Rodwell 1985, 32–3).

A Late Bronze Age cremation cemetery discovered in Mount Field in the mid-nineteenth century was presumably associated with the barrow(s) here (Fig. 2, no. 5; p. 42). The presence of a settlement of the same period has now been firmly established at Chipping Hill, and with it is associated the first phase of earthwork defence. If, as has been argued, both circuits originated — but not contemporaneously — in the Late Bronze Age, the early importance of settlement at this river crossing becomes apparent. Chipping Hill Camp began as a univallate plateau fort, and the outer circuit probably marks the first phase of construction, enclosing an area of *c.* 10.3 ha (p. 30). The site may be compared with other riverside enclosures, such as that at Cassington Mill, Oxon. (5.3 ha. Benson and Miles 1974, 84–7).

It is particularly unfortunate that there are no firm indications as to whether the enclosure around Witham

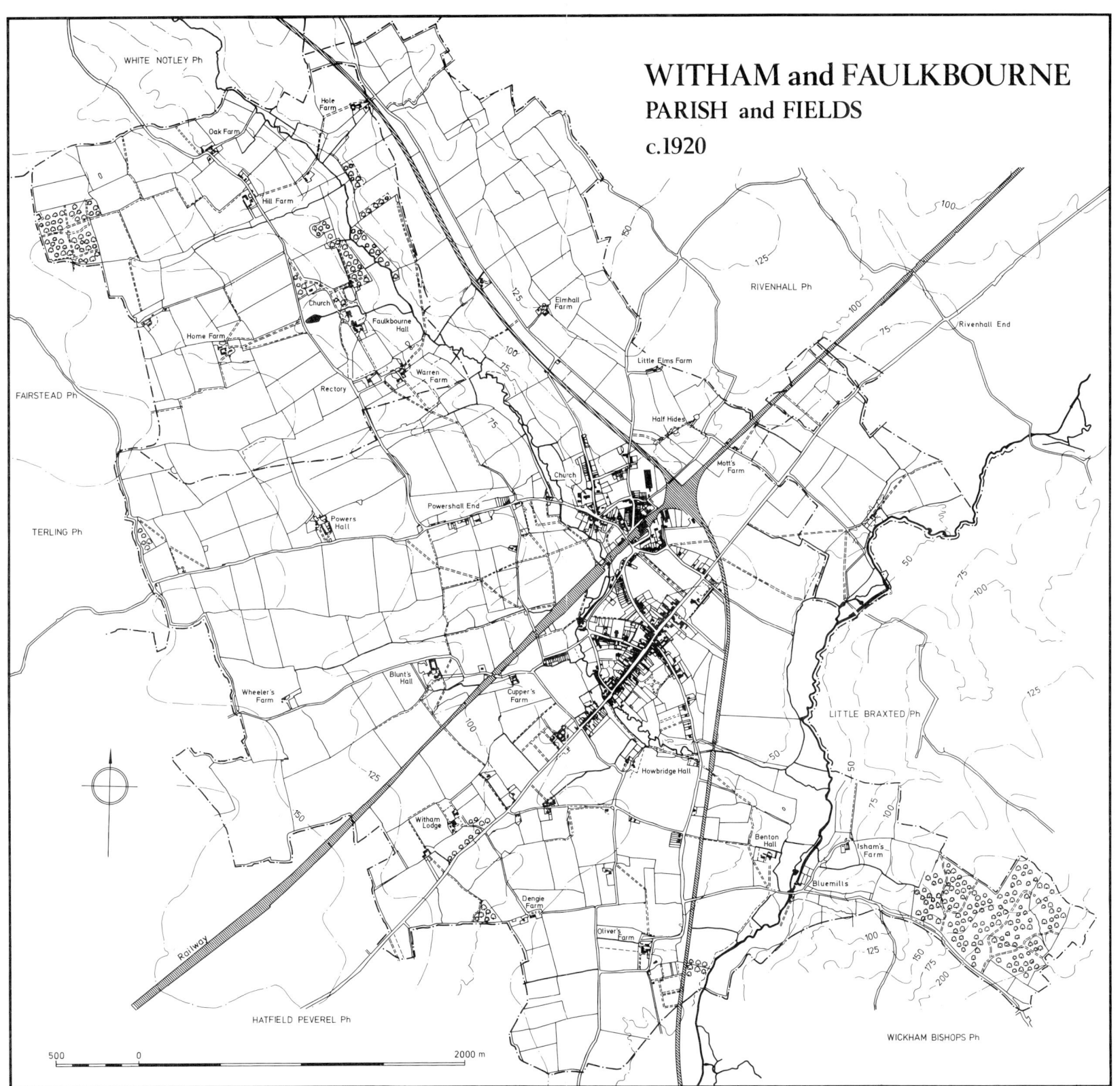

WITHAM and FAULKBOURNE

PARISH and FIELDS

c.1920

WHITE NOTLEY Ph

Hole Farm

Oak Farm

Hill Farm

Church

Home Farm

Faulkbourne Hall

FAIRSTEAD Ph

Warren Farm

Rectory

TERLING Ph

Powers Hall

Powershall End

Elmhall Farm

RIVENHALL Ph

Little Elms Farm

Rivenhall End

Half Hides

Mott's Farm

Church

Wheeler's Farm

Blunt's Hall

Cupper's Farm

Howbridge Hall

LITTLE BRAXTED Ph

Witham Lodge

Benton Hall

Isham's Farm

Bluemills

Dengie Farm

Oliver's Farm

Railway

HATFIELD PEVEREL Ph

WICKHAM BISHOPS Ph

500   0   2000 m

Fig. 35. *Map of Witham and Faulkbourne parishes, c. 1920. This essentially depicts the late nineteenth-century topography of the area, when Chipping Hill and Newland Street (Witham town) were still separate entities, but just beginning to coalesce. Based on the 1924 Ordnance Survey 1:10,560 plan; contours in feet above O.D.*

Fig. 36. *Elements of the relict pre-Roman landscape south-west of Witham, between the rivers Brain and Ter, compiled from early maps and fieldwork. The Roman road from London to Colchester, probably built in the AD 40s, is seen here slicing across the Iron Age fields and enclosures as dramatically as did the railway of the 1840s (Fig. 35). Contours in metres above O.D.*

churchyard is prehistoric or later in origin. But given its location on a river terrace, with Chipping Hill Camp alongside and a string of barrows downstream on the same bank, the former is more likely, with the presumption of a Neolithic or Bronze Age date. Large circular and sub-circular enclosures are not infrequently recognised as cropmarks in river valleys, and many appear to have had religious or ceremonial functions (cf. Priddy and Buckley 1987, 50–3). The Witham Church enclosure has a maximum diameter of *c.* 140 m; a fragment of a circle of similar dimension, apparently associated with a henge monument, has recently been observed alongside the river Blackwater at Rivenhall End, only 3 km distant (Buckley *et al.* 1988, fig. 2). In terms of size, the Witham circle ranks closely with the Devil's Quoits henge monument at Stanton Harcourt, Oxon. (Grimes 1960, 140–69); comparison may also be made with the similar sized South Circle, and the smaller Church Henge, at Knowlton, Dorset (RCHM 1975, 114–5). This last site is discussed further on p. 75.

Chipping Hill Camp and the Middle Iron Age

Early Iron Age settlement is ceramically attested at Witham Lodge and Ivy Chimneys (Turner 1982; and forthcoming), and a few sherds of the period have been found at Chipping Hill, but nothing is known about the condition or use of the earthworks at this period. It was, however, in the Middle Iron Age that the process of enclosure began at Ivy Chimneys, where a timber palisade was constructed around the core of the site, including a pond or spring which was later to become the focus of a Roman religious complex. At the same time, on the opposite bank of the Brain, 1.3 km to the north-east, the outer defensive earthwork was recut at Chipping Hill.

Chipping Hill Camp in the Middle Iron Age may be compared to two other Essex 'hillforts', both of roughly sub-rectangular plan and occupying riverside locations. Uphall Camp, situated on the east bank of the river Roding at Ilford, is by far the largest monument of this class in Essex, enclosing an area of *c.* 18.5 ha. It is univallate and recent excavations have demonstrated that it dates from the Middle Iron Age (Greenwood 1989). There was contemporary internal occupation, and the finds include class I potin coins. The second site is Wallbury Camp, on the east bank of the river Stort at Great Hallingbury. This is a bivallate construction with an enclosed area of *c.* 12.5 ha.; the excavations of 1959–60 are unpublished and dating is uncertain within the Early or Middle Iron Age (Rodwell 1976a, 189–90).

The 3.5 ha inner earthwork at Chipping Hill has been assigned to the Late Bronze Age and, it is argued, to a secondary construction phase (p. 30). It is not clear whether the Middle Iron Age finds from its ditch relate

to a period of recutting, or merely occupation. This smaller and more readily defensible *enceinte* is comparable in size to several other fortifications in Essex. Asheldham Camp, a largely destroyed site lying alongside Asheldham Brook, is situated in the centre of the Dengie peninsula, 21 km south-east of Witham (Rodwell 1976a, 182–3). There the univallate plateau fort of rounded polygonal plan, enclosing *c.* 3.5 ha, is believed to belong primarily to the Middle Iron Age (Bedwin 1991).

Although somewhat smaller than Witham, Weald Park Camp (enclosing *c.* 1.5 ha) is of comparative interest, and bears an almost identical, if fortuitous, topographical relationship to the London-Colchester Roman road, being bypassed at a distance of 1.5 km. It is 31 km south-west of Witham, near Brentwood (Fig. 1). Weald Park Camp is a univallate plateau fort occupying a spur of land overlooking the confluence of several streams that supply the Ingrebourne River (Rodwell 1976a, 184–5). Archaeologically, the site is unexplored. Like Witham, both Asheldham Camp and Weald Park Camp appear to have had a pair of opposed entrances, and to have been built astride a prehistoric route. It may be noted, *en passant*, that Asheldham Camp has yielded Bronze Age artifacts and thus, like Witham, it may be an older enclosure than has generally been supposed.

A consistent feature of the excavations at Chipping Hill has been their failure to yield artifacts datable to the latest (Belgic) phase of the Iron Age, or to the early Roman period. The high status of Chipping Hill as a settlement in the Middle Iron Age is attested not only by the earthen defences, but also by the discovery of the probable hoard of three La Tène II-III iron fire pokers, the finest specimens so far known from Britain (p. 98; Rodwell 1976c). The fragment of a shale bowl, and possible evidence for a Dressel 1 amphora accord with such a status. The recovery of four or five potin coins establishes settlement up to, or beyond, the middle decades of the first century B.C, but the lack of both struck bronze coins and the ubiquitous local 'Belgic' pottery indicates abandonment before the beginning of the first century A.D. The ceramic evidence from Asheldham Camp supports a similar history (Bedwin 1991).

Witham Lodge and the Late Iron Age

The London-to-Colchester road at Witham — an early Roman military imposition — is demonstrably not directly on the site of a prehistoric track, as has sometimes been supposed. Three pieces of evidence make this clear. First, the road ignores Chipping Hill Camp and the river crossing, bypassing them at a distance of 0.4 km. Secondly, the road cuts across the earthwork at Witham Lodge, destroying its defensive capability and ignoring a nearby entrance (Fig. 2). Thirdly, an ancient field system on the west side of the Brain valley is diagonally bisected by the Colchester road, and its integrity compromised in the process (Fig. 36). We shall return to this field system, but first it is necessary to consider the Witham Lodge earthwork.

Apart from the certainty of a pre-Roman dating, there is little evidence for when the earthwork was built. The irregularly polygonal plan enclosing a slight spur, with a long-lived Iron Age settlement at the centre, certainly suggests a late prehistoric date. But whether it should be assigned to the Middle or to the Late Iron Age is less easy to determine. The apparent magnitude of the area enclosed — at least 56 ha (p. 43) — would accord better with a late date, and thus follow in succession to the Chipping Hill Camp. The excavations at Ivy Chimneys have demonstrated that the settlement itself was enclosed with a ditch, and that there was continuing occupation from the Early Iron Age onward (Turner 1982, 3).

Witham Lodge earthwork probably belongs to a class of large enclosures constructed in the final decades before the Roman conquest: it is not, however, in the same defensive league as major works such as Wheathampstead, Herts., or Dyke Hills, Oxon. (cf. Cunliffe 1978, fig. 13.29). The scale of its rampart and ditches could never have been that impressive, and the sections at Witham (Fig. 30) bear favourable comparison with some of the minor dykes at Sheepen, Colchester (eg. ditch IB or ditch II, in Region 5: Hawkes and Hull 1947, figs. 30 and 31), while the plan is reminiscent of the phase 2 enclosure at Stanwick, Yorks. (Wheeler 1954, fig. 2). The Witham Lodge ditches are considerably smaller in scale than those at Chipping Hill (Fig. 22).

EARLY FIELD SYSYTEMS

Excavations and topographical studies of several areas of central Essex have separately demonstrated that the river valleys and their hinterlands were laid out at an early date with field systems and trackways of roughly rectilinear plan. Elements of these systems are relict in the modern landscape (Rodwell 1978a; Drury and Rodwell 1980). In many places it is readily observable that a particular system is pre-medieval, and in certain fortuitous cases an important stratigraphic relationship with an early Roman road has survived. Thus at Little Waltham (Drury 1978, fig. 74), Chelmsford (Drury 1988, fig. 85), Braintree (Drury 1976, fig. 49) and Rivenhall (Rodwell and Rodwell 1985, figs. 49 and 50) the pre-Roman origin of these systems has been archaeologically established. A later Iron Age date is generally indicated. Other, more rigidly rectilinear layouts have been associated with Roman land management, as in the Dengie peninsula, and on

Thameside (Drury and Rodwell 1978, fig. 1; 1980, fig. 22). The Essex evidence is part of a wider phenomenon recorded throughout East Anglia (Williamson 1986; 1987).

With this growing body of evidence from the surrounding area, it is apposite to examine the historic landscape patterns around Witham itself, and in particular to see whether they bear any stratigraphic or spatial relationship to the earthwork enclosures. The earliest available maps (eighteenth and nineteenth century) and other sources of topographical evidence have been studied and collated, and the usual techniques and criteria for landscape analysis applied. It is apparent that there are two strikingly different relationships between the Colchester road and its adjacent field systems.

As a generalisation, lanes and field boundaries to the north-east of Witham tend to meet the main road at right-angles, or nearly so, whereas those to the south-west converge upon it at oblique angles (Fig. 35). Looked at another way, the former group is axially related to the road, while the latter seems to have been planned without regard to its existence. The second group, however, is not only internally cohesive but also displays an intimate relationship to the Witham Lodge earthwork. The impressive pattern of earthwork, fields and lanes on the west side of the valley containing the Blackwater-Brain confluence appears to have been laid out to take full advantage of the local topography.

The Roman military road boldly slices across this system at an angle of forty-five degrees, destroying the integrity of former boundaries (eg. A-A and B-B on Fig. 36) and clipping the corners off fields (eg. at C on Fig. 36). This is precisely comparable to the evidence recorded at Chelmsford, where the same Roman road intercepted a field system in the Can valley (Drury 1988, fig 85); or at Little Waltham, where another early military road took a diagonal course through Iron Age fields in the Chelmer valley (Drury 1978, fig. 74). Express relationships have similarly been observed in East Anglia (Williamson 1986, 242–5; figs. 1 and 2).

Hints of a relative chronology between the Witham Lodge earthwork and the surrounding field system may be gained from the presence of several fragments of boundary ditch, demonstrated by excavation to be of Iron Age origin, which lie within the enclosure but nevertheless relate to the axes of the external fields (eg. D on Fig. 36). Logically, the field system is the older element, with the enclosure superimposed upon it. The undated enclosure at Great Farsley may have had a similar stratigraphic relationship.

No such relationship can, however, be demonstrated between Chipping Hill Camp and its hinterland. If anything can be deduced from topographical relationships, it is that the camp is the most ancient feature in the landscape, converged upon by tracks from various directions. An early prehistoric river crossing was undoubtedly the ultimate originator of this convergence. East of Witham it is not easy to determine the age of the dominant field system in relation to the Colchester road: the two elements appear to go together, and it is arguable that the valley slope from Witham to Kelvedon was replanned with fields and farmsteads in the Roman period. On the other hand, it must be remembered that this stretch of the military road follows the natural 'grain' of the topography, and may thus have run smoothly through an Iron Age agrarian landscape. Only excavation can determine the sequence.

The Roman Period

It is commonplace in Essex to find that settlements established in the Iron Age continued in occupation to the end of the Roman period, or beyond. The focus of settlement was not, however, necessarily rooted to one spot, but tended to shift both with the passage of time, and external influences. In two villages adjacent to Witham — Rivenhall and Kelvedon — this process has been studied in detail, through excavation (Rodwell and Rodwell 1985; Rodwell, K. 1988). Small-scale excavations and casual finds from other adjacent villages provide circumstantial evidence for similarly attenuated settlement histories: eg. Little Braxted and Cressing.[71] With such ample local analogues there is every likelihood of a broadly similar sequence having obtained at Witham itself.

Although in the early Roman period the Witham Lodge earthwork was destroyed as a defensible enclosure, the settlement it housed (centred on Ivy Chimneys) continued to thrive. Whether the community here was primarily agriculturally based, either in the Iron Age or in the Roman period, is uncertain but perhaps doubtful. The archaeological evidence seems to point more emphatically to religious and funerary use. Fuller consideration of the social and economic role of the Ivy Chimneys complex must await the publication of the full excavation report (Turner forthcoming): further comment would be premature.

There is no evidence for Roman military activity at Witham and indeed none would be expected, since there were first-century forts at Chelmsford and Kelvedon.

IVY CHIMNEYS RELIGIOUS COMPLEX

The focal interest of the site was evidently water, in the form of springs and a boggy hollow, later re-formed into a pond. The evidence all points to this being a minor Celtic rural sanctuary which became a Roman roadside temple. Considerable effort appears to have been expended in defining the boundaries of the late Roman site, through ditch digging: the maintenance of a clearly defined *temenos* was a characteristic feature of public temple complexes. That the Witham temple served a public function (albeit probably maintained by private enterprise, as part of a profit-making venture) can hardly be doubted in view of its close proximity to one of the principal routes through Roman Britain. Witham was ideally sited to become one of the lesser posting stations (*mutationes*) on the London-to-Colchester route.

The beginnings of a chain of posting stations and associated religious complexes along that route can now be glimpsed. At Chelmsford, 13 km south-west of Witham, there was a small Roman town (*Caesaromagus*) with a *mansio* and, on the outskirts, a religious complex where a late Roman octagonal temple has been excavated (Drury 1972, 13–28; Wickenden 1992). To the north-east of Witham the nearest substantial roadside settlement — potentially another *mutatio* — was at Kelvedon (*Canonium*), 7.5 km distant (Rodwell, K., 1988, 55–6). The next site was probably at Marks Tey, a further 7.5 km towards Colchester; this was a major junction, where the *Verulamium*-to-Colchester road merged with the London road. Here, various Roman bronze objects, suggestive of votive deposition, were found in the nineteenth century.[72]

Three of the above-mentioned sites — Chelmsford, Witham and Kelvedon — together with Rivenhall End and Brentwood (13 km south-west of Chelmsford; Fig. 1), have yielded evidence of late Roman Christianity.[73] At Colchester itself a fourth-century church and major Roman-Christian cemetery have been investigated immediately outside the town (Crummy 1990), another probable basilican church has been identified within the walls (Crummy 1984, 70), and the potential reuse of the former temple of the imperial cult as a church has been considered (Drury 1984, 33–4). These recent finds and observations constitute a significant element in the rapidly growing corpus of material indicative of late Roman Christianity in south-east Britain (Thomas 1981, esp. ch. 5).

A remarkable site, potentially of great relevance to the study of late Roman Christianity in central Essex, has recently been discovered not far from the Chelmsford road at Boreham, 7 km south-west of Witham. Here, beside a spring at the head of a minor, wooded valley, an aisled apsidal building has been excavated. At first claimed as a villa, the excavator later favoured interpretation as a *principia*, the administrative centre of an imperial estate. The plan, however, is strikingly reminiscent of a late Roman religious building, and its location alongside a secluded water-source evokes particular interest. Indeed, it may be no coincidence that the site is still isolated, wooded and known as 'The Grove'.[74] The remarkable building may be identifiable as a short-naved basilican church with westward orientation and an attached northern baptistery. As yet unparalleled in Roman Britain, this structure finds many analogues elsewhere in the empire.

Fig. 37. *The principal elements of the Iron Age (black) and Roman (brown) topography of the Witham area. Contours in metres above O.D.*

The excavated evidence for a late Roman baptistery at Witham demonstrates the continued importance of, and religious veneration attached to, the natural springs at Ivy Chimneys. It will later be argued that this veneration continued long after the formal end of the Roman period (p. 62). The indications are that late Roman Christianity in Essex was both ubiquitous and organised. ˙

A VILLA AT WITHAM OR FAULKBOURNE?

Turning now to Chipping Hill, we find that no great quantity of Roman material has been reported from within the earthwork circuits, and its dearth was specifically noted when the railway cutting was made, if credence is to be placed on Coller's account (p. 10). The new military road seems to have exerted a magnetic influence on settlement, drawing it away from the old enclosure (much later, the foundation of the medieval 'new town' was simply a restatement of this process).

During the building of an industrial estate in 1937 on Step Field, beside the Colchester road, finds of 'Belgic' and Roman pottery were reported (Fig. 2, no. 2). These are ill-recorded, although some sherds of third and fourth-century date are in the Colchester and Essex Museum.[75] Since there is also a general scatter of Roman pottery through gardens of The Avenue and Avenue Road it seems clear that the Roman settlement straggled between Chipping Hill and the main road (p. 28). The few finds and features reported from within the southern side of the camp may mark the extremity of settlement in the Roman period (Fig. 37).

This hardly constitutes compelling evidence for a villa or other high-status settlement at Witham: a sprawling farmstead would seem more likely. Additional factors, however, need to be taken into consideration. Two well attested finds of late Roman date point to the presence of occupation on a higher social level than that of a common farmstead: viz. a fourth-century glass cup (p. 105) and a gold coin of Honorius (A.D. 393–423; p. 10). In 1975 there was an unconfirmed local report that a hypocaust was exposed (and hastily covered up again) on a building site near to the north-west corner of the camp. A bathhouse here, alongside the river, would not

be unreasonable, and in this connection it may be recalled that a considerable amount of Roman brick has been reused in the fabric of the nearby parish church (Hull 1963, 201). This material was presumably robbed from a masonry structure not too far distant, and the possibility of discovering a Roman building in the churchyard or vicarage grounds should not be overlooked.[76]

On the basis of regional distribution, a villa at Witham would not be surprising, and the principal house would probably have lain in the secluded Brain valley, but not within or immediately adjacent to Chipping Hill Camp. If the circular enclosure around Witham churchyard is an early prehistoric monument (p. 57), it is unlikely that a Roman villa lay within that either, and a site might be sought elsewhere in the vicinity. This could possibly be as far afield as Faulkbourne Park, 1.5 km to the north-west, on the opposite side of the Brain valley. There is a persistent local tradition that remains of a 'Roman villa' have been discovered near Faulkbourne Hall.[77] The adjacent parish church also contains Roman brick and tile in its walls, but these are distinctly different in fabric from those at Witham church.

On balance, Faulkbourne in the Roman period is more likely to have been an entirely separate settlement from Witham, giving rise to the late Saxon manor centred on the Hall; the remarkably rectilinear and precisely defined parish could well equate with a Roman tenurial unit (Fig. 39). No useful purpose can be served by further speculation until the nucleus of a high-status Romano-British site in the lower Brain valley is located.[78]

The general insecurity of the countryside in the final years of Roman rule, and beyond, precipitated the contraction of many sprawling roadside settlements, and the abandonment of others. It therefore comes as no surprise to find that Step Field and other minor Roman sites in the area withered away, and were not succeeded by known medieval settlements. In any case, if the Step Field site were only a subsidiary component of a large Roman estate that had its focus in the lower Brain valley, the former's demise during the process of late or post-Roman contraction would be readily explicable.

10

Anglo-Saxon Witham

Post-Roman Developments

It has long been evident that over a considerable part of Essex, particularly in the central region, there is no clear-cut line of division between the Roman period and the Anglo-Saxon. Large settlements, and particularly cemeteries, typical of the pagan period are scarcely known.[79] Instead, small quantities of finds, and occasional burials, of types commonly associated with Germanic settlement tend to be found in close juxtaposition with long established Roman occupation sites. This is exemplified by fifth and sixth-century occupation on parts of the villa complex at Rivenhall (Rodwell and Rodwell 1985, 74–5), and within the Roman small town at Heybridge, near Maldon (Drury and Wickenden 1982). The small town at Kelvedon has yielded early post-Roman finds (Welch 1989), and nearby is the combined late Roman and early Anglo-Saxon cemetery on the Kelvedon-Feering-Inworth parish boundary (p. 76; Rodwell, K., 1988, 136–7). Lesser Roman sites in the area, such as Cressing, have yielded occasional artifacts or sherds of grass-tempered pottery attributable to the fifth to seventh centuries.[80] So too at Witham: a single sherd of an Anglo-Saxon perforated vessel has been found at Chipping Hill (p. 106).

Other sites, including Ivy Chimneys and Chelmsford, have yielded structural evidence or stratigraphic sequences indicative of continued activity in the fifth century, or beyond. Diagnostic pottery is, however, absent and the demise of coinage in the late fourth century deprives us of the most commonly employed dating tools. In the early 1970s it began to be appreciated that, in broad terms, the local economy in Essex entered a virtually aceramic phase in the fifth century, which continued until the ninth-to-eleventh centuries (depending on settlement status and location). Unfortunately, insufficient material evidence precludes an authoritative discussion of the sequence of events at the two major sites in Witham, but circumstantial evidence, coupled with retrospective projection from the eleventh century, allows some insights to be gained.

THE FATE OF IVY CHIMNEYS

It is an instinctive reaction to assert that the site was abandoned and lost from view long before the Middle Ages. No manorial nucleus is known to have developed here, there is nothing to suggest that an Anglo-Saxon chapel ever occupied the site, and superficially there appear to be no grounds for adumbrating any form of post-Roman survival (at least beyond the early to mid-fifth century). But is the case against survival really as simple as that? Consideration of the on-site archaeological evidence relating to the demise of the Ivy Chimneys religious complex will doubtedless be embodied in the forthcoming excavation report. There are, however, strict limits even to the most optimistic of expectations that can be entertained for a site that was razed, robbed and ploughed centuries ago, built upon in the nineteenth century, and looted in modern times.

The material evidence on the site comprises only part of the story: the wider context provides the rest. Careful examination of the medieval and later history of the area around Witham Lodge and Ivy Chimneys suggests that the Roman religious complex may perhaps not have been lost and forgotten in the fifth century. First, as a matter of general principle, it is worth stating that there must always be a strong presumption that an ancient religious focus, with both pagan and Christian associations, alongside a continuously plied thoroughfare, would have received local veneration for centuries after its formal and organised usage ceased. Religious superstition is an abiding force.

The veneration of the *genius loci* at a ruined site has always been common practice throughout Europe. The nature of the religious observances once attached to a particular site is to a large extent immaterial, and it should be recalled that there was, and still is, no clear dividing line in provincial religion between pagan and Christian. The total loss from folk memory of ancient religious foci is a very slow process. Even when organised practices may have ceased centuries earlier, and the buildings fallen into a state of utter dereliction, the *locus* retains an aura of sanctity which is respected by the local populace, while travellers and pilgrims still visit periodically. That remains as true today as it was in the Middle Ages.

The 'end' of the Ivy Chimneys Roman site must be assessed against this wider perspective. Some specific examples will serve to illumine and reinforce the concept just enunciated. First, Bede recounts how, in the 590s, Queen Bertha of Kent resorted to 'an old church, built in honour of Saint Martin during the Roman occupation of Britain' in Canterbury to pray. Even after nearly two centuries of pagan disruption, neither the building nor its purpose had been forgotten.[81] Second, the isolated late Roman temple at Pagans Hill, Somerset, was visited for centuries after its presumed demise: the evidence for this continued veneration came not only from finds of medieval pottery on the floor of the *cella*, but more importantly from the fortuitous discovery of a well shaft that remained open into the Middle Ages, and into which some remarkable items were dropped (Rahtz *et al.* 1958; Rahtz and Watts 1971, 201). A recent reassessment of Pagans Hill — and in particular its post-Roman history — is of wide-ranging interest and relevance to heavily robbed and seemingly 'abandoned' sites such as Ivy Chimneys. Speaking of the early fifth century, Rahtz and Watts (1989, 361) conclude, 'It can no longer be taken for granted ... that the temple itself or its complex was deserted. Indeed there is no doubt that the temple was largely intact in the seventh century, as it clearly was several hundred years later ... Likewise it cannot be assumed that the surrounding countryside was depopulated and neglected in the fifth century and later, despite the elusiveness of its archaeology. Similarly, the total failure of Roman Christianity cannot be assumed.' The same stance has been taken by other writers in recent years, including, Morris (1989), Thomas (1981) and Rodwell (1980).

Third, at Lullingstone, Kent, the Roman villa — which embodied a Christian house-chapel — was presumed to have been abandoned in the fifth century, but the sanctity of the site was certainly not forgotten, and sometime in the Anglo-Saxon period a chapel was built on the ruins of a mausoleum in the villa's cemetery (Meates 1979). It was not until the eighteenth century that the last vestiges of the chapel disappeared from view. Finally, there are innumerable instances of devotional acts still being carried out amongst the ruins of medieval churches, and at holy wells. In nearly all such cases, the volume of archaeological evidence that could be recovered by conventional excavation techniques — and, more specifically, its intelligibility — would be minimal.

Turning now to the specific problem of Witham, this is best approached by working backwards from the present. The Roman settlement area was fragmented by medieval and later property boundaries, and it is interesting to observe that the religious nucleus lay in the corner of a field belonging to a property called Ivy Chimneys, to the rear of the house (Fig. 29). By contrast, the remainder of the Roman settlement had been abandoned to wasteland, known as the 'Moors', at least since the fifteenth century.[82]

The name 'Ivy Chimneys' provides a potentially valuable clue, although unfortunately its antiquity is unknown: its first recorded appearance is in the eighteenth century. The name was applied both to a sixteenth-century timber-framed house (with eighteenth-century refurbishment) built near to the road frontage, and to two small fields adjoining (8 1/2 acres in all).[83] 'Ivy Chimneys' is a topographical appellation, and not the kind of name that would have been applied descriptively to a Georgian residence. What, therefore, were the *ivy chimneys* that distinguished this place?

There can be little doubt that the name referred originally to the ruins of former buildings, clad with ivy: the association with chimneys recalls a series of tall fragments, silhouetted against the skyline. Two explanations suggest themselves: the more obvious is the literal one. There could have been a medieval timber-framed house in the vicinity that was abandoned and fell into decay, leaving one or more great brick chimney stacks still standing. Until quite recent times (1960s) this was not an unfamiliar sight in Essex. Alternatively, the name could be an allusion to the ruins of ancient and perhaps non-domestic buildings, still surviving as a visible monument into late medieval or post-medieval times. On balance, this is perhaps less likely, since the acute shortage of stone in Essex has always induced the pillage of ruined masonry for church and road building. For a Roman structure to have survived, it is virtually a *sine qua non* that it must have been in use in the Middle Ages. Nevertheless, local names incorporating the element *ivy* can refer to Roman remains (cf. Field 1976, 115), and the possibility of survival should not be dismissed out of hand.

Whichever explanation is preferred, it carries the implication that there was a notable ruin standing somewhere on the Ivy Chimneys site in the post-medieval period. By chance, the identity of that building may be recoverable. It was possibly a property called 'Breche House' in the reign of Henry VIII (Reaney 1935, 616). Exactly where this stood is uncertain but it was evidently set back from the main road, on or close to the Roman site, which was adjoined on the west by Little Breach Field and Great Breach Field. The location of these is first shown on maps of Blunt's Hall manor, 1752 and 1812,[84] and in 1803 they were listed as part of the Ivy Chimneys estate. The same maps indicate that the Roman site itself was then waste land, incapable of cultivation and, typically in such a situation, was named Upper Moors and Lower Moors.[85]

The 1752 and 1812 estate maps show the extent of

Blunt's Hall manor in its terminally depleted state, with the Roman site straddling the boundary between Blunt's Hall demesne lands and those of two of its derivative holdings, Ivy Chimneys and Cupper's Farm. Morphologically, it is clear that Ivy Chimneys, Cupper's Farm (first mentioned in the early sixteenth century: Reaney 1935, 301), Witham Lodge (previously White Gate Farm) and other minor holdings were all carved out of Blunt's Hall, arguably during the sixteenth and seventeenth centuries.[86] But Breche House was certainly a more ancient component of the parent estate, and belonged to a medieval stratum of sub-holdings. Breche House fell into demise before Ivy Chimneys appears in the historical record: there is no overlap of the names. In view of this, the close physical proximity of the two holdings, and the fact that Great and Little Breach fields were part of the Ivy Chimneys estate, surely there was a connection. In other words, circumstantial and topographical evidence invites the suggestion that Breche House was the antecedent of Ivy Chimneys.

The move from the Roman site to a more convenient and better drained location on the road frontage presumably took place in the early sixteenth century, when Ivy Chimneys house was built. Although incapable of proof, we may even suggest that the 'ivy chimneys' were the ruins of Breche House. If that argument is accepted, there is a corollary: the Roman settlement had a medieval successor. The antiquity of Breche House is, of course, unknown, but there is every likelihood that it had stood for some hundreds of years prior to its demise; it was last heard of in the fifteenth century.[87] The intervening gap between the sub-Roman and medieval periods can only be filled conjecturally, using circumstantial evidence. Since the area under discussion was all part of Blunt's Hall manor in the early Middle Ages, it is not unreasonable to argue that Breche House may have descended from one of the hitherto unidentified sub-holdings of Blunt's Hall at Domesday.

In the Middle Ages, the two minor lateral valleys of the Brain, that had once broadly defined the north and south sides of the Witham Lodge earthwork, housed the seats of the manors of Blunt's Hall and Howbridge Hall (p. 49), with the Roman road evidently forming the boundary between them.[88] The Domesday Survey makes it clear that Blunt's Hall in the eleventh century was not the insignifcant holding that it became towards the end of the Middle Ages. Indeed, the entry records two separate manors and their respective lands (Round 1903, 462, 526). The larger manor, with its 2 1/2 hides, was centred on Blunt's Hall moated site (p. 49); attached to this was a sokeman and his sub-holding of 15 acres. Could not Breche House have been that sub-holding?

An alternative would be to seek the ancestry of Breche House, in the lesser of the two Blunt's Hall manors, which currently lacks firm identifcation on the

ground. Domesday records that as comprising half a hide, which had been held by a free woman in 1066, but by 1086 had been subsumed within the demesne lands of Count Eustace of Boulogne. The value of the property had fallen from 20 shillings to ten. Clearly, this holding was on the wane, and nothing further is heard of the manor thereafter.[89]

Whatever the precise historical and tenurial sequence, there remains a plausible case for equating a minor Anglo-Saxon and medieval holding with the Ivy Chimneys estate. This would give meaning not only to the name but also to the small quantity of late Saxon and medieval pottery found on and about the site.

On a broader front, it is worth observing that Roman religious complexes in rural settings were not, in general, overlain by substantial Anglo-Saxon and medieval manor houses, or churches, to the same extent that villa sites frequently were. The explanation for this is probably to be found in tenurial history. Roman religious foci were generally components of, or adjuncts to, substantial estates: they were not centres of secular power and authority in themselves, but villas were. As a result of detailed landscape studies in several areas, including Rivenhall and Kelvedon, an interesting and potentially informative picture of settlement succession is now beginning to emerge. Continuity of the identity and physical integrity of major Roman tenurial units into the post-Roman period may be responsible for the appearance of manor houses and churches on villas and other sites with an adminsitrative importance, and *not* on farmsteads, temples and subsidiary components of estates.

THE REOCCUPATION OF CHIPPING HILL CAMP

While the post-Roman history of the Ivy Chimneys site reflects progressive demise, that of Chipping Hill is quite the reverse. Although the nucleus of the late Roman settlement (villa?) almost certainly lay outside the abandoned Iron Age camp, the possibility of a late fourth or fifth-century retreat back into the old *enceinte* needs to be considered (for late Roman finds see pp. 61). Hypothetical though it must remain, if this happened it could logically have set in train events which determined the physical development and morphology of Witham over the next seven or eight centuries. The prospect of elucidating such a major slice of Witham's undocumented history, however sketchily, must justify the construction of a model.

The reoccupation of abandoned Iron Age and Roman enclosures in the early post-Roman period is a well known phenomenon, and it is surely no coincidence that the important early medieval royal manor of Chipping Witham (or Witham Magna) was centred at Chipping Hill, where power and authority had anciently resided within the impressive earthwork. In the Anglo-Saxon divisions of the shire, Witham was a hundredal centre, and no more obvious meeting place for the hundred-moot, or *gemot*, could be suggested than the prominent earthwork on Chipping Hill. A possible alternative site has been proposed, a formerly distinctive 'mound' on the vicarage manor, next to the church (Christy 1928, 184–5). The mound — which was extant in Christy's day — was presumably part of the west side of the earthwork forming the circular enclosure within which the church and vicarage were built (p. 74).

In seeking the derivation of the placename 'Witham', Reaney (1935, 299) found some difficulty, concluding 'it is just possible that the first element is OE *wiht*, "curve, bend"'. He related this to the adjacent bend in the river Brain, but topographically that is a fairly insignificant feature, hardly worthy of lending its identity to a royal hundred. Reaney dismissed out of hand as 'inconsistent' the form *Witanham*, which occurs in the *Anglo-Saxon Chronicle* (ms D, *sub anno* 913), and is the second earliest rendering of the name. Ekwall, on the other hand, considered the possibility of a personal name, 'Wita's or Witta's *ham*'. He also offered 'the *ham* of the *wita* or councillor' (Ekwall 1936, 502). Considering that Witham was the regular meeting place of the Anglo-Saxon hundredal council, deriving the placename from that or an allied governmental function may seem preferable to other, more tortuous explanations.

The manor of Chipping Witham, along with the hundred, was held by the king at the conquest, and the entry in the Domesday Survey shows that it was large, populous and prosperous (Round 1903, 428–9). A modest town is surely implied. There was, however, no suggestion that Witham was then, or had been, a borough (only two are mentioned in Domesday for the whole of Essex: Colchester and Maldon). The first occurrence of the title *burgh* is in later medieval documents.

The use of 'Withambury' as a specific name for Chipping Hill Camp is of uncertain age; Reaney (1935) makes no mention of it, and all references found by the present writer are connected with antiquarian scholarship of the nineteenth century. Conceivably, the name was recovered from genuine local usage, but equally likely it was coined by antiquaries who were anxious to promote the identification of the camp with Edward the Elder's *burh*. Names ending in *-bury* are common in Essex, both in their application to earthworks (eg. Danbury, Wallbury, Pitchbury) and to early manorial complexes; some are straightforwardly compounded with *bury* as a suffix to the usual name of the parish (eg. Pleshey*bury*, Feering*bury*, Hatfield *Bury*). Whatever the derivation of 'Withambury', it provides no explicit evidence for the presence of a Saxon royal *burh*.

While there is generally little difficulty in establishing the focal points of the larger, and some of the smaller, early medieval manors in the Witham area — their sites remained unchanged for many centuries — the notable exception is the manor of Witham itself. The problem arises in consequence of the king having granted this estate to the Knights Templar in 1147 (p. 85). Thenceforth, the principal manorial functions were exercised from Cressing Temple, and not from a manor house on the spot. Nevertheless, there must have been a manorial complex in Witham from which a bailiff and other officials managed the estate, on behalf of the king prior to 1147, and on behalf of the Templars after that date.

The manorial offices must have been at Chipping Hill, but contemporary evidence for their site in the early Middle Ages is lacking. The sitation has become further confused by the post-medieval use of the title 'manor house' for two other buildings in Witham. In the eighteenth century a mansion in the town centre, on the south side of Newland Street, was called the Manor House (Morant 1748, 106), without historical precedent. More interesting is the Old Manor House at Chipping Hill, a fifteenth-century dwelling of some quality lying to the south of the parish church.[90] The pattern of property boundaries and land ownerships here suggests that this house, like several others at Chipping Hill, was built as a prosperous merchant's residence on a relatively small plot of land. Certainly, the post-medieval manorial estate was never farmed from here.[91]

By far the most likely place for the medieval manorial buildings was inside Chipping Hill Camp, and here Temple Farm is the only known occupation site (p. 33; Fig. 4). There is no reason to doubt that the name is genuine and that this was the farm from which the Templars managed their lands in the core of Witham. The existing house, now re-named The Grange, appears to be seventeenth century in date. The whole of the fortification was known as 'Temple Hill' in the seventeenth century and 'Temples' in the early eighteenth (p. 8). The manorial survey of 1608, when referring to Temple Farm as 'the site of the aforesaid manor', would seem to clinch the identity (p. 33).

Church Origins

The origin of the parish church of St Nicholas is problematic. It stands within a circular enclosure (p. 34) on a low knoll just above the spring-line, 150 m north-west of the outer defences of Chipping Hill Camp. The earliest surviving reference to the building is of the twelfth century, and the oldest visible fabric is possibly late Norman; there is much recycled Roman material in the structure (RCHM 1921, 263–5). The church was substantially rebuilt and enlarged from *c.* 1330 in consequence of Witham's prosperity in the later Middle Ages. The irregularities of the plan are, however, archaeologically revealing and the outline of the nave —

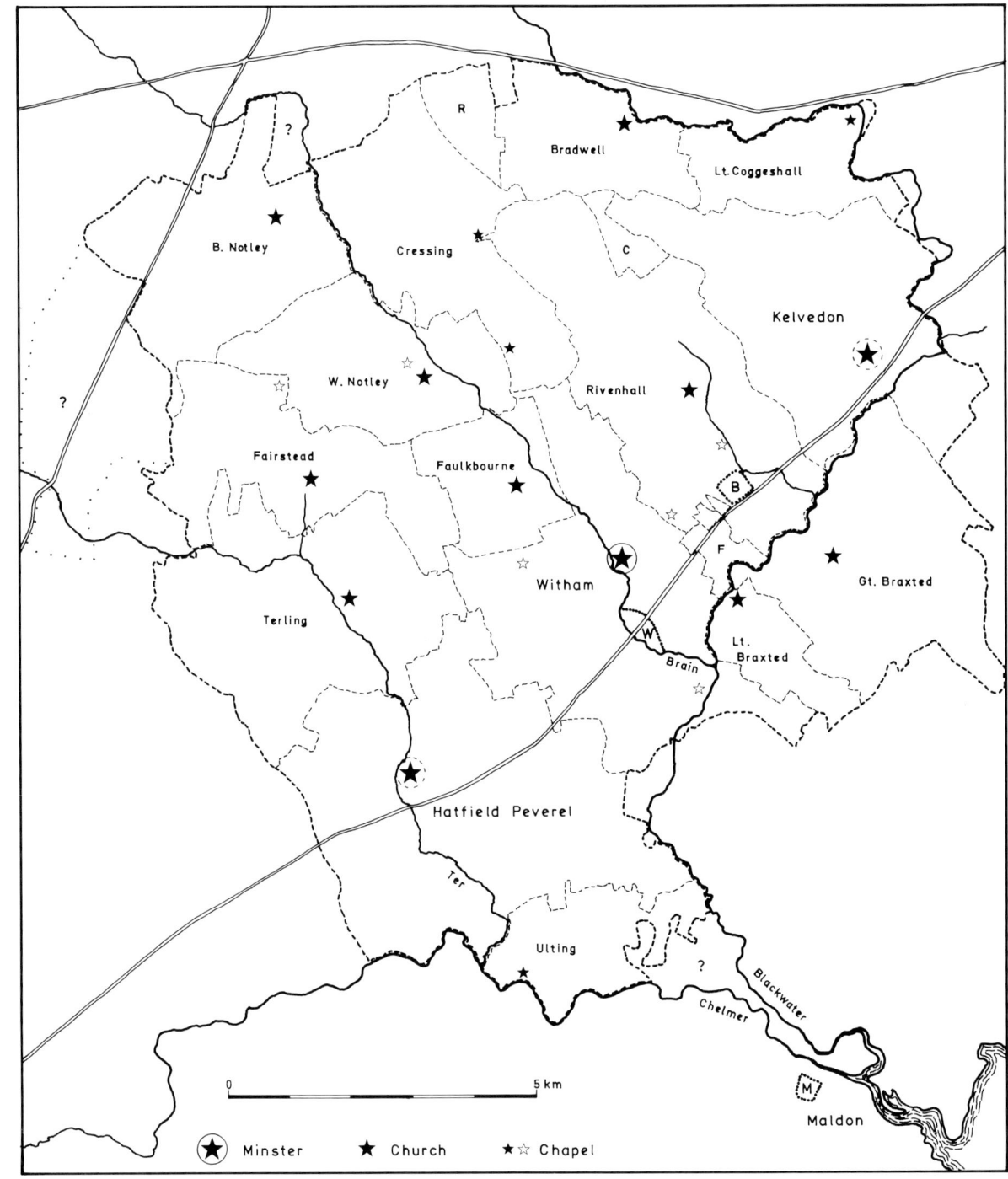

Fig. 38. *Map of Witham Hundred and its constituent parishes, based on Tithe map evidence, and Chapman and André's* Map of Essex *(1777). Ecclesiastical sites are markds and their possible eleventh-century ranking is indicated: head minster (Witham); lesser minsters; proprietary churches becoming parochial; lesser churches and chapels, including some failed sites. The three suggested burghal earthworks are also inidicated: B. Burgate Field (Rivenhall End); M. Maldon; W. Wulvesford (Witham). Other initial letters indicate detached portions of parishes (Cressing, Faulkbourne and Rivenhall).*

a parallelogram — is more indicative of an Anglo-Saxon building than a Norman one. Despite the lack of explicit documentation, there can be no serious doubt either that Witham possessed a substantial pre-conquest church, or that this is its site. Churches were very rarely noted on the Essex Domesday circuit, and no significance attaches to the lack of a reference to one at Witham.

THE CASE FOR A MINSTER CHURCH

Short of carrying out a major campaign of archaeological excavation in the church and graveyard, it will not be possible to establish a date for the origin of a church or cemetery here, or to elucidate the complex structural sequence of the present building. Morphological and circumstantial evidence, however, may be advanced to refine the possible chronological bracket for the church's foundation. Its topographical position is also of signal importance. The first point to note is that Witham does not exhibit the intimate juxta-positioning of hall-and-church, so typical of proprietary foundations in Essex. In the majority of the surrounding parishes, this is the norm: Faulkbourne, White Notley, Rivenhall, Little Braxted, Terling, Fairstead, etc (Fig. 38).

If Witham manor house lay inside the ancient camp — as has been argued — it was admittedly not at a great remove from the church, but the two elements were nevertheless territorially distinct and separated by earthworks. Spatially and topographically, the arrangement at Witham could support interpretation as a market place with minster church immediately outside the gates of an enclosed royal residence; but more evidence would be needed to confirm such a hypothesis.

Although the parochial geography of central Essex was probably formalised during the course of the eleventh century, the churches themselves had in many cases already been founded as proprietary adjuncts to the principal manors in the tenth century. Archaeological studies have demonstrated this sequence at Rivenhall (Rodwell and Rodwell 1985, 85–91, 121–4), and the wider phenomenon has been explored by Richard Morris (1989, ch. 6). At the same time, other, seemingly modest parish churches owed their origins to a wholly different set of circumstances: they were the relics, or sometimes the products, of the pre-conquest minster system (for the most recent consideration of this development, see Blair 1988b). Local parochial anomalies often betray the non-proprietary origin of these churches. Witham is surely a case in point.

If the origins of St Nicholas's Church lay in a proprietary chapel, appendant to the manor of Witham, its logical place would have been inside the earthworks, close to Temple Farm. The separation of the two elements implies a different origin, and royal ownership supplies the clue. Ecclesiastical foundations on major royal estates did not follow the proprietary model, with the result that the secular and religious centres were often distinctly separate in the physical sense.

A second set of circumstances may also be considered: Witham church was placed at the ancient focus of not only the parish, but also the hundred (Fig. 38). Here was a road junction, a river crossing and a meeting place. Witham was, moreover, a royal estate of considerable extent: Faulkbourne manor seems somehow to have become detached by the middle of the eleventh century, acquiring its own parochial status (Fig. 39).[92] Cressing was not severed until much later, its Norman church being only a chapel-of-ease to Witham (p. 85; Hope 1984).

A detailed study of the development of Cressing would be valuable from several distinct points of view, but that cannot be embarked upon here. However, it is worth briefly noting that the manor was not separately recorded in the Domesday Survey, and is believed to have been subsumed under Witham (Hope 1984, 30). The first recorded mention of Cressing does not occur until 1136–37, when the manor and the advowson of the church were granted by Stephen's queen, Matilda, to the Knights Templar (p. 85; Fowler 1907, 177). Assessing the extent of the manor of Cressing is fraught with difficulty, and even establishing the site of the twelfth-century manor house and church is not straightforward. First, there are two ancient foci within the parish, both of which have claims to be early manorial centres (and, incidentally, both are on Roman sites). Secondly, the configuration of the recorded parish bounds, especially between Cressing and Rivenhall, leaves little room for doubt that there were complex tenurial arrangements and boundary changes in the early Middle Ages.

The large moated enclosure and medieval barns at Cressing Temple mark the site of the preceptory of 1136–37: logically, this should also be the site of the pre-Templars' manor. The earliest description of the buildings is contained in an Inquisition of 1309, when it was noted that there was a chapel with a cemetery attached to it. Although not explicitly recorded as such, this was evidently Great Cressing, in contra-distinction to Little Cressing which was first mentioned by name in 1338 (Fowler 1907, 177). Little Cressing, with its parish church of All Saints, lies further north, and is hard against the boundary with Rivenhall. Indeed, a small tongue of Rivenhall land penetrates right up to the churchyard boundary (Fig. 39). A demonstrative connection between the northern end of Rivenhall parish and Cressing is indicated. Moreover, since there was formerly a substantial, detached parcel of Cressing land to the east of Rivenhall, it seems clear that the latter parish underwent considerable enlargement in a northerly direction; this occurred in or before the thirteenth century (Rodwell and Rodwell 1992, forthcoming).

Although there is now no manorial focus associated with Cressing church, it seems likely that there was formerly one. Immediately south of the church clear cropmark evidence of a large moated enclosure has been recorded. All Saints may therefore have been part of a hall-church complex, and indeed there is a *post hoc* record of its foundation in the eleventh century by Elphelmus de Gore. Here, the latinized Old English name, Aelfhelm, does not necessarily indicate a pre-conquest foundation (Hope 1984, 30, 38). Excavation has demonstrated that Cressing church is eleventh-century, or earlier, in origin.

In sum, the evidence is not inconsistent with the hypothesis that within the Domesday royal manor of Witham there were several estates with their own chapels, two of these being retrospectively identifiable as Great and Little Cressing. Another was probably Bereman's *Stow*, which is discussed below (p. 69). Across the river, at the manorial nucleus of Powers Hall (alias Little Witham) — and still within the ecclesiastical parish of Witham — was another proprietary chapel which failed to reach parochial status (Morant 1768). Yet another chapel may have existed at Benton Hall, in the south-east part of the parish (p. 52).

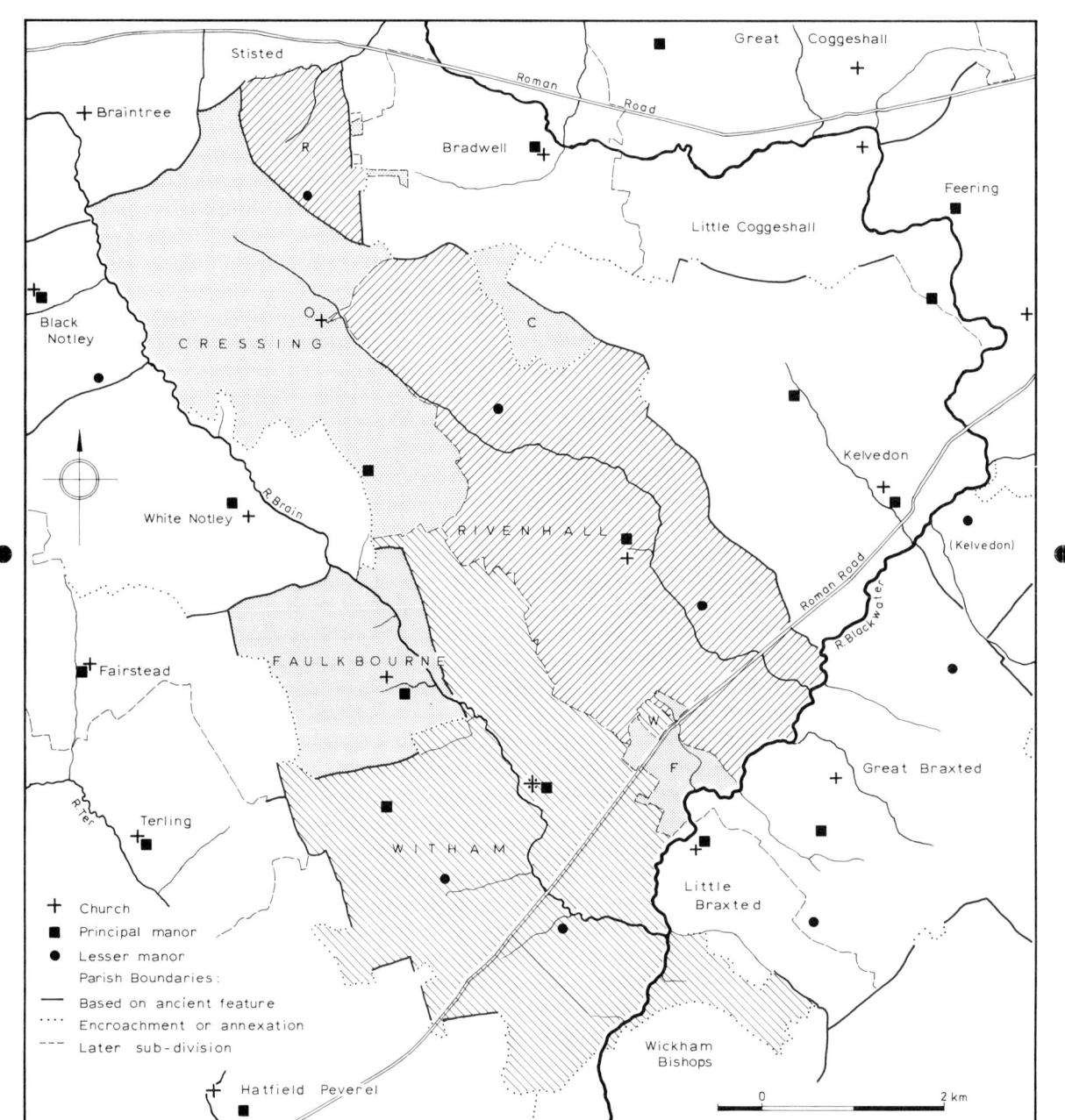

Fig. 39. *The morphology of parishes and their boundaries in the Witham area. Detached portions of Witham, Faulkbourne, Cressing and Rivenhall are indicated with similar shading to the parent parish.*

Even though there is no explicitly corroborative evidence from such sources as wills and charters, Witham must logically have been a minster parish, the breaking up of which is evidenced by the foundation of satellite churches — with their own graveyards and glebe — in the tenth and eleventh centuries. Cressing was, arguably, the last church to be released from the minster's grip, and evidence may also be glimpsed of several other satellite chapels that fell into demise. It may not be too hazardous even to suggest the possible extent of the *parochia* of Witham minster.

Witham Hundred (or Half-Hundred, as it was often known) was a small and relatively compact unit, basically comprising the land between (and including) the valley of the Ter on the west and the broad sweep of the middle Blackwater on the east (Fig. 38). In the case of the latter, the river itself formed the boundary on the north-east, but its valley was included on the south-east. Within the hundred, lie two anciently important foci — Witham and Kelvedon — both being substantial Roman settlements in origin, on the Colchester road. Witham is situated at the centre, on the Brain, and Kelvedon is at the eastern extremity, on the Blackwater. On the opposite, (western) edge of the hundred is Hatfield Peverel, lying on the Ter; this last is a very large parish embracing a complex of manors. Kelvedon and Hatfield, like Witham, do not exhibit intimate church-hall relationships, and in both cases the church stands alone. Kelvedon Hall, curiously, is not only isolated and well removed from the church, but is (now) just within Great Braxted parish; the manor of Church Hall, Kelvedon, is a good deal closer. At Hatfield the capital manor, also isolated, is called Hatfield Bury, and that may itself have a significance yet to be fully appreciated.

Without digressing further into parochial histories, the following model may be offered for ecclesiastical provision in the Witham Hundred in the late Saxon period. Witham was the head minster of the hundred, and there were two lesser minsters, at Kelvedon and Hatfield; between them lay a series of proprietary churches attached to the more important individual manors. Some of these later churches became parochial, while other remained as private manorial chapels, generally disappearing in or before the sixteenth century.

Finally, note should be taken of the interesting pattern of ecclesiastical land ownership on the north-east side of Witham. The parish's post-medieval glebe was in several distinct blocks (Fig. 40). One block was contiguous with the church and vicarage and was situated between the river Brain and Cressing Road (which leads from Chipping Hill to Braintree). Just across the river to the west lay another block, together with a single parcel: the separation of these may have resulted from the creation, on ecclesiastical land, of a small post-medieval estate known as Witham Place.

Three other blocks of Witham Glebe were distinctly separate and lay further east, interlocking with Rivenhall glebe and detached parcels of Faulkbourne land. On the west edge of this combined ecclesiastical block a lost and wholly undocumented church or chapel is indicated by the field name Bereman's *Stowe*.[93] The placename element *stowe* is normally a pointer to a pre-conquest religious site; it is rarely found in Essex.[94] Bereman's was once an independant holding, in Rivenhall parish, and there are frequent mentions of it from 1588 onward.[95] This may well be an example of a chapel belonging to one of the lesser medieval estates becoming lost at an early date; even the secular component itself did not survive as a significant unit into post-medieval times.

In the midst of this complexity lay Rivenhall rectory. More remarkable is the fact that both the rectory and the glebe were significantly distanced from Rivenhall church (by 1.5 km), and two parcels of Witham glebe actually lay within Rivenhall parish, and adjoined its rectory. The arrangement is attested as early as 1185, the date of the first surviving land grant mentioning a rector of Rivenhall (Lees 1935, 4). The disposition of glebe lands was probably long established by this time, since the parish church was already a substantial structure by the late tenth century, and would not have been without an endowment of land. There is thus little doubt that Rivenhall's glebe land was not provided by the manor, but was carved out of the once-large ecclesiastical estate at Witham.

The final sizeable parcel of Witham glebe was an irregular plot in Vicarage Wood, on the border of Rivenhall parish, where it was effectively part of the adjoining Rivenhall Wood (or Thicks). The jagged-edged plan of the parcel suggests that what remained in 1762, when it was first mapped, was only the rump of a larger unit that had been assarted from all directions. In this connection it is interesting to note that two large parcels — both known as Church Field, and totalling 43 1/2 acres — lay immediately north-west of Vicarage Wood (Fig. 40).[96] Another long-lost ecclesiastical association is presumably recalled here.

Witham Vicarage's holding of glebe in 1762 was completed by three tiny parcels, two of meadow on the banks of the Blackwater,[97] and one a little to the south of Vicarage Wood. The stranding of this last plot — of exactly one acre in extent — presumably resulted from the fragmentation of ancient woodland holdings. The plot's retention as part of Witham glebe until the nineteenth century may have been occasioned by the presence of an occupied tenement here, the possession of which was retained by the church long after surrounding land had passed into secular hands.

Possibly analogous to this was the isolated plot of three-quarters of an acre of Rivenhall glebe close to Hoo Hall and amidst its fields (Fig. 40). There is no

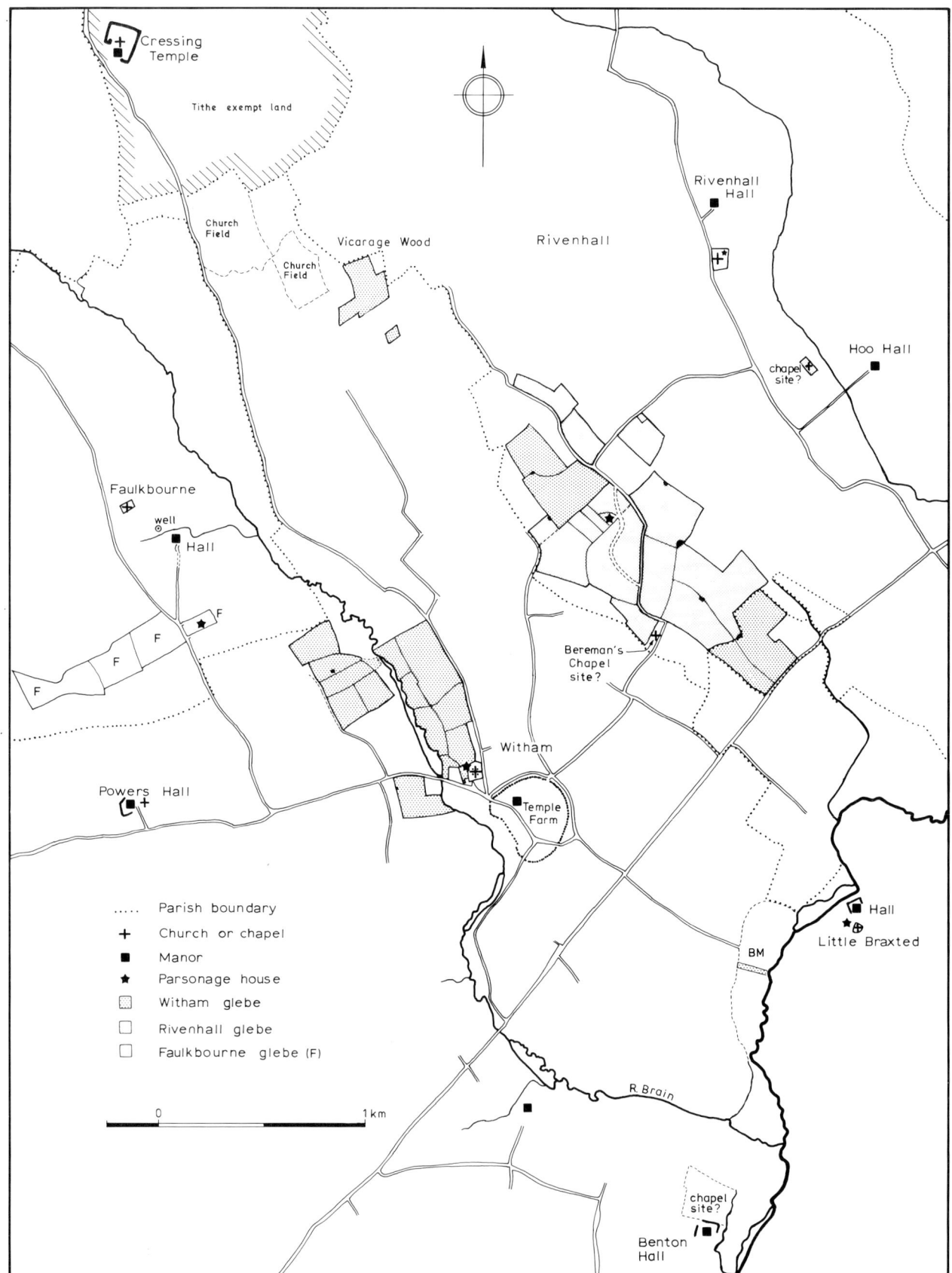

Fig. 40. *Map of ecclesiastical property in Witham, Rivenhall and Faulkbourne. Based on glebe plans of 1762 and 1732, and the 1838 Tithe map, respectively. Other related sites have been added. BM — Broad Mead.*

record of any building on this plot, although there can be little doubt that there must have been one. Arguably, this is the site not of a domestic property but of an early and undocumented proprietary chapel attached to Hoo Hall (Rodwell and Rodwell 1992, forthcoming). This site may be compared to that of Bereman's Stow, although in the case of Hoo Hall the manor has survived intact into modern times.

A detailed study of the early history of church property in Witham, Rivenhall, Faulkbourne and Cressing is urgently needed. There is an additional complication in that Witham vicarage, unusually for a parsonage, enjoyed the status of manor; its origins are obscure (the nucleus of the vicarage manor was locally called Hogg End). It has been argued elsewhere that a large ecclesiastical estate lay at Witham, which was progressively fragmented to provide individual endowments to a variety of churches and monastic houses in the twelfth and thirteenth centuries (Rodwell and Rodwell 1992, forthcoming). Faulkbourne glebe (271/2 acres) may have been part of this estate too: it comprised a string of four parcels across the southern end of the parish.[98] Between the two principal blocks of Witham (and Rivenhall) glebe lay a corridor of land that formed part of King Stephen's grant of *c.* 1147 of the manor of Witham to the Knights Templar. They already held the adjoining manor of Cressing.

There can be little doubt that Witham minster was a royal foundation, originally endowed with a sizeable block of land that stretched from the high, wooded claylands (Rivenhall Wood), across the fertile brickearth and gravel terraces, to the meadows of the Brain valley. The provision of glebe for Rivenhall and Faulkbourne would have become a necessity when the churches of these places were established as independent units, and were no longer proprietary adjuncts to the manors of Rivenhall Hall and Faulkbourne Hall, respectively. The transmutation, which took place sometime before 1185, is undatable but is most likely to have occurred in the late tenth or early eleventh century.

Glebe for the new satellite parishes would naturally have been pared from the extremities of the minster estate. This contrasts with the cutting of a swathe through the agricultural lands at its centre, an act that must be attributed to the Templars. Since they had acquired the advowson of Witham from the king, and installed a vicar, they were in a position to carve further holdings out of the former minster land, thus completing the fragmentation of the ancient estate. The Tithe Awards for Witham, Cressing and Rivenhall parishes record a curious phenomenon: certain blocks of land that had formerly been held by the Templars were, even in the nineteenth century, exempt from all tithes. This exemption was not general to all former Templar lands in the area, and may have been linked to the original extent of the manor of Cressing, and thus to the terms

upon which the Templars were granted their primary holding in this area.[99]

While most of the foregoing discussion necessarily relates to the post-conquest period, it provides essential insights into the likely status and wealth of the Anglo-Saxon church at Witham. The remaining problem concerns the date of foundation of the minster: the extreme limits can be set around the mid-seventh century and the early tenth century. Very little is known of tenth-century and earlier ecclesiastical provision in Essex, a county sadly deficient in pre-conquest charters. All that can be said is that since Witham occupies a nodal point in the county it is more likely to have seen the foundation of a minster on the royal vill here at an earlier rather than a later date (although re-foundation may have been necessary after the Viking interlude). It would come as no surprise if the history of Witham church were eventually to be taken back, through the medium of archaeology, to the seventh century.

THE PLAN OF ST NICHOLAS'S CHURCH AND ITS SIGNIFICANCE *(Fig. 41)*

With the posited historical background in mind, a closer examination of St Nicholas's Church may help our enquiry. The first point to note is the north-east to south-west orientation of the church: the deviation from a 'correct' liturgical axis is twelve degrees. In general terms, such a deviation is likely to betray Anglo-Saxon origins, since there was a marked tendency for Norman church builders to seek a liturgically correct orientation, whenever the lie of the land permitted. Other evidence is needed to reinforce this argument.

Clearly discernible in plan are the elements of an Anglo-Saxon building — nave and chancel, both with skewed angles — to which fourteenth-century aisles and a tower have been added, together with still later accretions (Fig. 41.1). A consistent error of four degrees was introduced in laying out both the nave and the chancel, another occurrence that is common in pre-conquest building, but rare in Norman work: for a local example see the late Saxon church of St Mary, Chickney (RCHM 1916, 62). Although the Witham chancel has been enlarged and now exhibits a stereotyped medieval plan, it may be assumed that this cell was originally more-or-less square: though whether there was an eastern apse is indeterminable without excavation.

The junction between nave and chancel is archaeologically revealing, since the former element is now narrower than the latter, instead of the reverse which would be expected. Clearly, the chancel derived its present width from having its medieval north and south walls built immediately outside the earlier ones, another common phenomenon. Originally, the chancel was inset from the nave by half a wall's thickness on

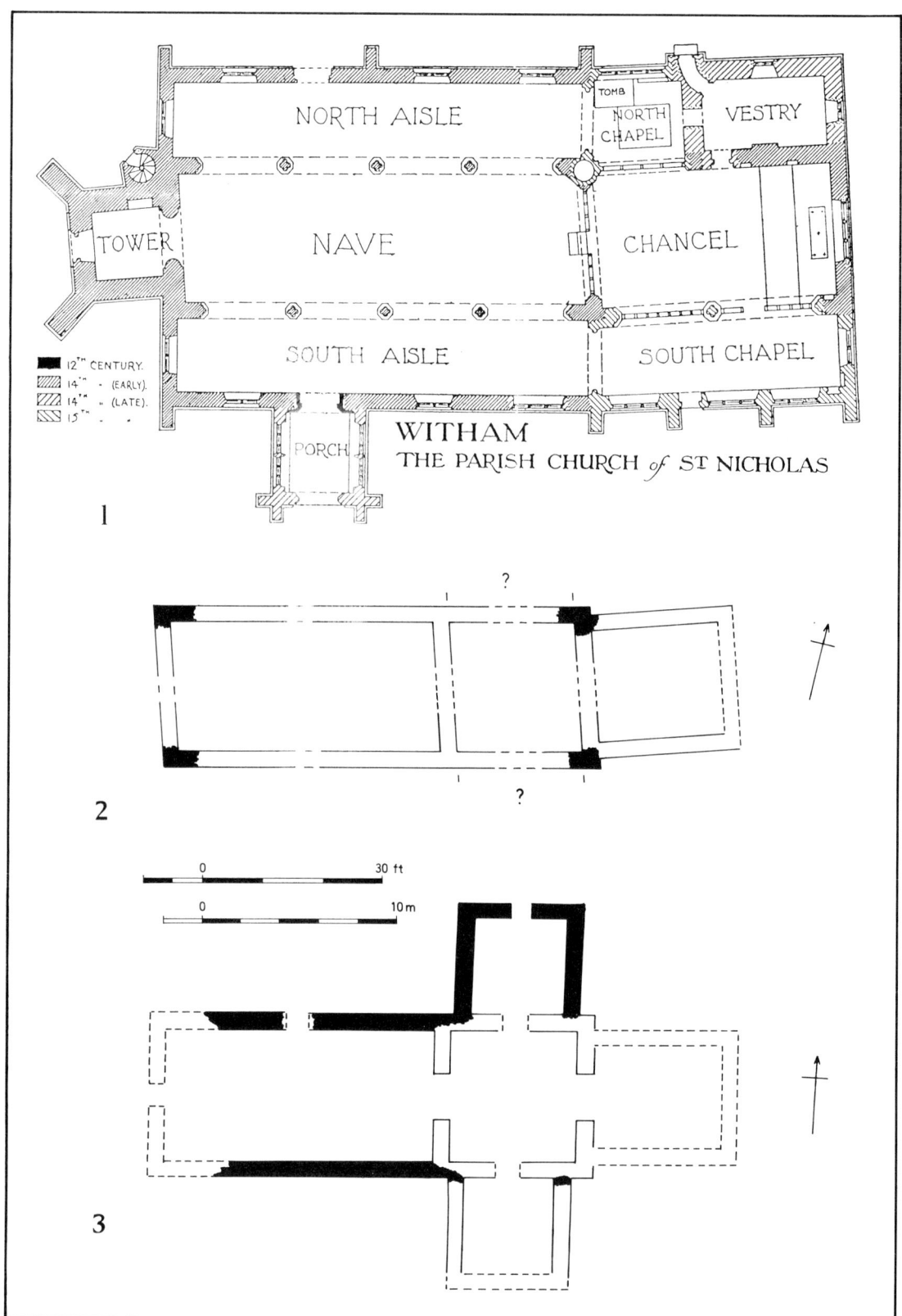

Fig. 41. 1. *Plan of Witham church, as existing. After RCHM 1921, 263.* **2.** *Extrapolated plan of the Anglo-Saxon nave and central space (?crossing), and conjectured outline of the chancel.* **3.** *Plan of the primary phase of Hadstock church, to the same scale. After Rodwell 1976d, fig. 3, revised.*

either side. The nave, however, retains its complete pre-conquest outline, with sides in the ratio of 3:1. This is a very distinctive plan, not only on account of the attenuated form, but also for its dimensional narrowness.

Numerous Anglo-Saxon naves of proprietary churches in south-east England have a length-to-width ratio of less than 2:1: Rivenhall is typical of a very large group of tenth and eleventh-century churches, discussed elsewhere, and dubbed the 'Rivenhall group' (Rodwell and Rodwell 1985, 133–8, fig. 95). Early Norman churches, following in the pre-Conquest tradition, were often similarly proportioned: Faulkbourne is a good example of the mid-to-late eleventh century.[100] Further, the width of the nave in these small churches may be as much as 8.5 m (28 ft), but the long nave at Witham is only 7.0 m (23 ft) wide, measured to wall centres.[101]

Such measurements convey little in themselves, but if they are converted to 'Northern feet' (or their fifteenfold multiple, the Northern rod), these dimensions assume fresh meaning. It has been established that the 15 foot rod (5.03 m) was a common unit of building measurement in Anglo-Saxon England, and that its sub-division was normally into fractions of thirds and sixths (Huggins *et al.* 1982). The size of the nave at Witham is sufficiently close to 60 x 20 N ft (or 11/3 x 4 N rods) to leave little doubt that it was planned with these dimensions in mind.[102] The north and south doorways to the nave, although now located in the medieval aisles, are centred at approximately 20 N ft from the west end, or one-third of the distance along the nave. These doorways are unlikely to have been repositioned laterally when the aisles were added: access points into the church would have been constrained by paths, graves, internal monuments, etc. Moreover, it is clear from the asymmetrical planning of the aisles' fenestration that door positions were pre-determined.

The length of the nave at Witham is such as to prompt enquiry into whether it really represents not one, but two, Anglo-Saxon elements. Explicitly, was there formerly a central space — a quire, crossing or tower — that was united with an originally shorter nave during the medieval rebuilding process? A square central space, defined by a now-lost cross-wall, would of course have left the nave proper with a length-to-width ratio of 2:1, the doorways then being at the centres of the north and south walls. The removal of redundant cross-walls in multi-cellular Anglo-Saxon and Norman churches, in order to create larger congregational spaces, was not uncommon: in unaisled churches scars often remain, providing physical evidence. But in churches with medieval aisles, the plan alone may have to supply the vital clue, until confirmation by excavation is possible.

At Great Easton, near Dunmow, there is a small late Saxon or early Norman church bearing the scars of a lost central space and tower (RCHM 1916, 125–6). The proportions, however, are those of a proprietary church and do not compare favourably with Witham. For more direct comparison it is necessary to look to the minster-type churches of the tenth and eleventh centuries, and in particular to Hadstock, in north-west Essex. Here, the unaisled, transeptal church of St Botolph has been subjected to detailed archaeological study, and its long nave shown to incorporate the site of a former crossing (Rodwell 1976d). Not only does Hadstock provide an analogue for the sequence posited at Witham, but the dimensions and proportions of the nave and central space are identical (Figs. 41.2 and 41.3).

The form of the chancel at both churches is conjectural. Hadstock, however, was cruciform, being provided with north and south *porticus*, and the possibility that Witham was similarly aggrandised deserves serious consideration. There is now no express evidence in the plan or structure for former *porticus*, but it may be no coincidence that if the full Hadstock plan is superimposed on Witham church, it can be seen that the medieval aisle walls would have been erected immediately inside the extremities of the *porticus*. In practical building terms this is a logical progression.

In summary, there can be little doubt that the core of St Nicholas's stands upon the foundations, and echoes the plan, of an Anglo-Saxon minster church of tenth or eleventh-century date. This building bears comparison with other long-naved, cruciform minster churches, such as Tackley, Oxon. (Blair and McKay 1985), Breamore, Hants. (Rodwell and Rouse 1984) and St Mary-in-Castro, Dover (Taylor and Taylor 1965, 214–7).

CHURCHYARD ORIGINS *(Figs. 23 and 42)*

It remains finally to consider the topography of Witham churchyard. Rectilinear graveyard enclosures, marked by banks and ditches and containing between one and two acres, are commonplace in Essex, but the date of formalisation of their boundaries is usually unknown. The establishment of a defined rectilinear graveyard of 1.5 acres (0.6 ha) around Rivenhall Church has been dated archaeologically to the early eleventh century (Rodwell and Rodwell 1985, 122–4), and the much smaller, neatly rectangular graveyard of 0.7 acres (0.28 ha) at Faulkbourne is probably contemporary with the centrally-placed, late eleventh-century church.

Victorian antiquaries repeatedly claimed that certain churchyards were surrounded by ancient 'camps', usually attributed to the Romans or the Vikings; these claims were unsubstantiated. Indeed, very little tangible evidence has hitherto been advanced for Essex churchyard boundaries incorporating pre-medieval earthworks, but the probability that such did happen increases with the widespread recognition of relict ancient landscapes in post-medieval village morphology. The case of Witham is particularly interesting. The basic development seems clear. The later Anglo-Saxon and

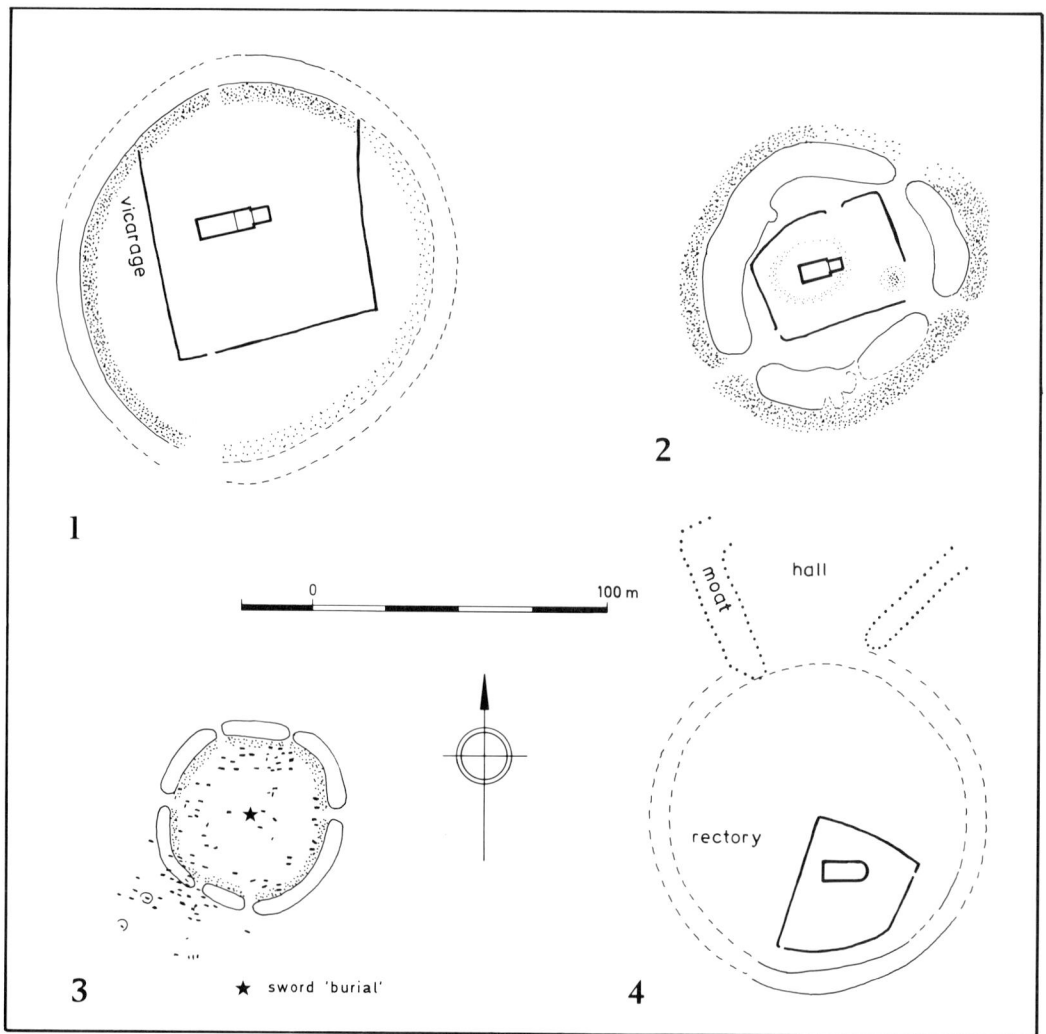

Fig. 42. *Comparative plans of Anglo-Saxon and Norman ecclesiastical sites inside probable prehistoric circular enclosures. Medieval churchyard boundaries are outlined. 1. Witham, Essex: St Nicholas's Church. 2. Church Henge, Knowlton, Dorset. (After RCHM 1975, 115). 3. Springfield, Essex: Bronze Age enclosure and Anglo-Saxon inhumation cemetery, showing excavated graves. (After Buckley and Hedges 1987, fig. 11). 4. Little Braxted, Essex: St Nicholas's Church.*

medieval church stands just north of the centre of a circular or sub-circular enclosure of unknown date (Fig. 23A). The primary religious focus — perhaps a standing cross, or an early timber church — may have been erected at the centre, later to be replaced by a new structure alongside.[103] The date of establishment of a parsonage house within the enclosure, west of St Nicholas's church, is unknown but is unlikely to be later than the mid-twelfth century, when King Stephen granted the advowson of Witham to the canons of St Martin-le-Grand in London (Morant 1768, 411). It has already been noted that Witham vicarage enjoyed manorial status in its own right, and this may have been conferred at the same time.

The formal delineation of the boundaries of the medieval churchyard of 1.3 acres (0.53 ha), on the west, south and east, is easiest explained as a stage in the development of the 'old' town of Chipping Witham in

the eleventh or, more likely, early twelfth century (p. 37). The west boundary separated the graveyard from the vicarage, the south from an open space or green, and the east from Church Street and the planned settlement that was laid out alongside it (Figs. 23A and 25). Hence St Nicholas's Church assumed the appearance of being set more or less centrally within a rectilinear graveyard: such was the early medieval fashion. It was only on the north side that boundary straightening did not take place, and here the churchyard was contiguous with the glebe land.

Churchyards of circular or amorphously curvilinear plan are widespread in western Britain and, like holy wells, were a particular predeliction of the British (or Celtic) Church. Not unnaturally, these features are rarely encountered in the Anglo-Saxon kingdoms, but nevertheless are known: the best example in Essex is at Fryerning, south-west of Chelmsford. The squaring-up process seen at Witham is widely replicated in the West and is well seen, for example, at Knowlton, Dorset (Fig. 42.2). We must return again to the question of the date of the Witham churchyard enclosure. It has already been shown that in terms of size, location and landscape context it is entirely reasonable to posit the reuse of a prehistoric enclosure (p. 57). Indeed, not far away, at Springfield, a Bronze Age henge-like earthwork was adopted in the early Anglo-Saxon period for funerary and religious activity; and by the late Saxon period a settlement had sprung up immediately outside. The settlement failed, however, and the entire site was abandoned in the eleventh century, making it available for investigation in its arrested stage of development (Buckley and Hedges 1987).

Although the recent excavations at Springfield are not yet fully published, the fundamental importance of this site to the study of the origins of the English churchyard is already fully apparent. A circular building lay at the centre of the Bronze Age enclosure, whose site continued to be marked — perhaps by a mound[104] — long after the abandonment of the primary settlement. An isolated pit containing a Late La Tène sword, dug into the centre of the site, is the sole evidence for Iron Age activity. and was most likely connected with a ritual deposit. The pit may, for example, have underlain a burial in a mound that has been removed by ploughing.

Next came a small cluster of early Anglo-Saxon cremations, which were restricted to the area of the posited mound, as though they were satellite burials; meanwhile, a large cremation cemetery developed outside the circular enclosure. Cremation gave way to inhumation; and furnished graves were succeeded by unfurnished ones. Within the northern part of the earthwork lay an orderly group of burials, orientated east-west, and lacking grave-goods. The evidence from Springfield is entirely consistent with the transition from pagan to Christian burial rites in the Middle Saxon period.

The centre of the site, which was largely free of burials, must still have been specially reserved (Fig. 42.3). It might be argued that graves here were inserted into a mound, and have thus been lost by ploughing, but this is not wholly convincing. Burials in and around a mound, or a curvilinear feature, seldom share a common orientation, but tend towards tangential alignments; a similar effect is seen in graves dug close to the apse of a church (cf. Rodwell and Rodwell 1986, fig. 65; Bailey *et al.* 1988, fig. 23). The consistent alignment of most of the graves within the Springfield enclosure points strongly to the presence of a centrally sited east-west feature of paramount liturgical importance. Indeed, a central rectangle measuring *c.* 30 m by 15 m is ghosted by the grave pattern. This is surely the site of a mid or late Saxon timber church? Comparison with

Nazeingbury may be relevant, where the sites of two early timber churches were partly defined by the burial pattern (Huggins 1978). Winwick, Cheshire, supplies another analogue: here the excavation of a Bronze Age barrow disclosed a hitherto unknown early Christian cemetery, and the site of its associated but long since destroyed church was ghosted by the distribution of graves.[105] At present, it can only be said that Springfield and similar sites provide a tantalising model for a long drawn-out sequence that could have obtained at Witham.

Scrutiny might be directed at other early churches with curvilinear graveyard boundaries, lying in river valleys amidst areas of cropmarks of likely prehistoric date. In this connection, mention should be made of an interesting site close to Witham: 1.5 km east of Chipping Hill, at Little Braxted, lies a compact settlement, comprising a hall, church and mill (Figs. 2 and 32). The manor and mill were both recorded in the Domesday Survey, and the tiny church is also eleventh century. The whole complex, including a medieval homestead moat, is contained within a series of boundaries that appear to define a horseshoe-shaped enclosure of *c.* 2.5 ha (6.2 acres), attached to the east bank of the river Blackwater. No archaeological excavation has taken place, but the site has yielded prehistoric and Romano-British artifacts, together with early Anglo-Saxon weaponry, apparently associated with graves.[106]

St Nicholas's Church, Little Braxted, lies awkwardly towards the northern corner of its triangular graveyard. The south side is curved and edged by a road which forms part of the boundary of the horseshoe-shaped enclosure mentioned above, while the north-east and north-west sides of the triangle are straight. The curved section of road is itself flanked on the south — directly opposite the churchyard — by a length of curving, water-filled ditch. The plan, as recorded by the Ordnance Survey in 1874, shows that the churchyard, together with the adjoining road and ditch, all form a quadrant of a circle. The north angle of the churchyard is at the centre-point of that circle (Fig. 42.4).[107] The curious plan of the medieval moat surrounding the former site of Little Braxted Hall assumes meaning when seen as an 'annexe' to a pre-existing circular enclosure.

A possible interpretation of the sequence at Little Braxted is as follows. The church was built a little south of the centre of a circular or sub-circular earthwork with an internal diameter of *c.* 85 m; the hall, rectory and mill lay between this and the river. The settlement was later united by establishing a pair of tangential boundaries from the circular churchyard to the river, thus creating a horseshoe-shaped enclosure. The hall was subsequently dignified with the provision of its own small moat, within which the medieval timber-framed and detached kitchen still stands. The topography of the site was drastically altered in the late sixteenth century, when the moated enclosure was abandoned, the former rectory became the new hall, and a walled garden was built on what had hitherto been part of the circular earthwork (RCHM 1922, 163). The reduction of the area of the churchyard to a quadrant may not have taken place until this time; the two straight boundaries certainly have the appearance of being post-medieval.[108]

It is legitimate to enquire whether there was a particular reason for the choice of circular enclosures for early churchyards. The most obvious explanation must be continuing interest in, and veneration of, an ancient *locus sanctus*, as suggested for Springfield (p. 75), and as also established archaeologically at Winwick.[109] Less easy to demonstrate is the possibility that there is, in certain parts of eastern England, a stratum of early British Christianity beneath that of the more familiar Roman form introduced during and after the seventh century.

Curvilinear churchyards and holy wells are usually held to be a peculiarly Celtic-British phenomenon — although this is now being challenged (Blair, 1992) — and their sparing occurrence in certain areas of traditionally early Anglo-Saxon settlement in eastern England may have deep-rooted significance. The fine example of an intact circular churchyard at Fryerning has already been mentioned, and Hadstock provides another likely instance of this phenomenon in Essex, complete with a holy well dedicated to St Botolph on the boundary. Small numbers of curvilinear churchyards associated with known or suspected early church sites are found all the way up the east coast of England. Examples in Yorkshire include Stanwick, Coxwold, Gilling, Bramham and Kellington (cf. Morris 1989, 455).[110]

Several wisps of evidence relating to early Christianity in the Witham area form a tantalisingly incomplete picture from which it would be dangerous to draw firm conclusions at present. Six further potentially relevant facts are worth recalling. First, that Witham possessed an undoubted British Christian complex in the fourth and fifth centuries at Ivy Chimneys. Second, late Roman objects with Christian associations have been found at Kelvedon (Rodwell, K., 1988, 136) and Rivenhall End (Hawkes 1973). Third, a remarkable find, although not specifically attesting Christianity, has been excavated at Kelvedon: it is a central European ring-brooch of probable fifth-century date, to which an insular British or Irish replacement pin had subsequently been fitted (Welch 1989). No such item has previously been found in Essex, or even in south-east England, and it would be more at home in the early Christian west.

Fourth, Faulkbourne parish church, whose intimate connection with Witham has already been noted (p. 46), bears a rare dedication to St German, the early fifth-century missionary bishop of Auxerre, whose visits to Britain were a landmark in the pre-Saxon era of insular Christianity. There are only two other church dedications to Germanus recorded in the south-east: the first relates to a former chapel site within the abandoned Roman city of *Verulamium*, a place personally visited by the bishop when following in the footsteps of Alban; the second is at Bobbingworth, in west Essex (Arnold-Forster 1899, I, 453–64).

Fifth, it has already been observed that holy wells in and around churchyards were not characteristic of later Anglo-Saxon and medieval Christianity, and it therefore occasions no surprise to find that only a handful are recorded in Essex. But one of those is situated close to Faulkbourne Church and, moreover, bears its own dedication to St German. Sixth, there have periodically been tentative suggestions by place-name scholars of an unexplained British element in a few names in the Witham area: Kelvedon may be one, and other possible candidates include field names at Rivenhall. Even if these are discounted on the grounds of uncertainty, there is an undoubted Celtic element, *pant*, which attaches to the Blackwater: the original name of this river was the Pant (Reaney 1935, 9). Today, the name is reserved to the upper reaches, beyond Braintree.

Stukeley (1723, 80) first proposed the derivation of the name 'Witham' from *Guith-avon*, the 'separating river' (although he was actually referring here to the river Witham in Lincolnshire). Topograpically, the 'separating river' would be an excellent description for the Essex Witham (Fig. 38), but Reaney dismissed it out of hand.[111] The local name Guithavon is well known today, but the first recorded mention seems to be in the nineteenth century (Anon 1845). Its ancestry is unknown, and may be wholly spurious.

Further research into the survival of Celtic placenames in Essex is urgently needed. There has long been a presumption — albeit archaeologically unfounded — that Celtic placenames ought not to occur in Essex, and that Anglo-Saxon forms should have eclipsed them. Scholars have therefore tended to embrace almost any etymological derivation, other than Celtic, for names of uncertain origin.

The Location of Witham Burh

THE HISTORICAL CONTEXT

Witham played a significant role in Edward the Elder's reconquest of eastern England from the Vikings. In 910–11 he recovered London and moved into Hertford and there established the northern *burh* (Hill 1981, figs. 85–86). Edward then set eyes on the Viking stronghold at Colchester, preparing to move towards it. The next logical step was to secure central Essex, and in particular to block the Roman road from London to Colchester, at a point as close to the latter as was tactically possible, without running the risk of being out-manoeuvred on the flanks. From its London base, Edward's army could move rapidly north-eastwards along the Colchester road, until a critical point was reached at Kelvedon. Here, the road crossed the river Blackwater.

Prior to the creation of a chain of mills throughout the Blackwater valley — and these were in place by the mid-eleventh century — the river would have been navigable certainly as far as Witham, and probably up to Kelvedon bridge. There was thus ready access to central Essex from the North Sea. Moreover, the Blackwater debouches into the sea alongside the mouth of the Colne, the river that feeds Colchester. Had Edward's army advanced beyond Witham, even as far as Kelvedon, it would have run the serious risk of being cut off by a detachment of Vikings from Colchester, sailing out of the Colne, into the Blackwater, and appearing from the rear. Witham was therefore the obvious choice for a fortress. It not only provided a central base in Essex, but also prevented the Vikings from moving again towards London. Servicing Witham from the sea, and protecting it from surprise attack via the Blackwater, required a base nearer to the estuary. The prime strategic site for this was Maldon, where the broad marshy estuary suddenly closed in to a defensible — and bridgeable — neck.[112]

Against this topographical and strategic basis there is no difficulty in understanding precisely what was meant by the contemporary chroniclers. The 'A' and 'D' texts of the *Anglo-Saxon Chronicle* record that in 912 King Edward the Elder 'went with some of his forces into Essex to Maldon, and camped there while the borough (*burh*) was being made and constructed (*getimbrede*) at Witham, and a good number of people who had been under the rule of the Danish men submitted to him. And some of his forces made the borough at Hertford, on the south side of the Lea' (*A.S. Chron.*, sub anno 913: for revised dating, see Whitelock 1961, 62). This constitutes the sole documentary evidence for an Edwardian fortification[113] at Witham.

POSSIBLE SITES FOR THE *BURH*

The patriotic desire on the part of antiquaries to establish the true site of Witham *burh*, coupled with the once-obviously impressive nature of the earthworks at Chipping Hill, led, not unnaturally, to an equation being made between the two. It is unnecessary to restate the archaeological evidence in full (pp. 29–33), but it must be emphasised that there is currently nothing to indicate a late Saxon phase of fortification at Chipping Hill, and thus no compelling archaeological grounds for advancing this as the site of the Edwardian *burh*.

Moreover, Chipping Hill Camp was simply in the wrong place from a defensive point of view: it could neither control the road to London, nor inhibit access to central Essex via the Blackwater. While Anglo-Saxon occupation between the inner camp and the river is certainly attested, this is readily explicable as part of an undefended (or minimally defended) settlement associated with the manor of Witham. There can be no denying that, were it not for the reference in the *Anglo-Saxon Chronicle* to a *burh* at Witham, historians and archaeologists would not have advanced the theory that there was one, based on other documentary or field evidence.

Alternative sites in the Witham area must be considered as potential candidates for the *burh* (Fig. 43). First, it is worth noting that there is no necessity for the site to have lain within the modern parish of Witham. In the early tenth century the royal estate bearing the same name undoubtedly included the later parishes of Cressing and probably Faulkbourne, and perhaps Rivenhall too (p. 46). This greatly increases the potential field of search.

After Chipping Hill, the first and most obvious place to consider is the enclosure under the medieval town, the 27 ha *Wulvesford* site. Topographically and strategically, there can be little doubt that this earthwork defence was built to control the ford and the passage of traffic along the main (Roman and later) road, in a way that Chipping Hill never could (Fig. 28). In terms of its plan, and the lack of diagnostic finds, the *Wulvesford* earthwork is unlikely to be of Roman or earlier date. Equally, the plan is not convincingly reminiscent of an Edwardian *burh*, at least not in the planned urban sense of the term. Consideration might also be given to the possibility of a Viking origin, since D-shaped and curvilinear enclosures occupying bends in rivers have long been identified as a characteristic of Scandinavian fortification (Dyer 1972). Superficially, this view might be complemented and supported by the widespread recognition in the last twenty years of a class of regularly planned, rectilinear burghal layouts of the ninth century (Biddle and Hill 1971).

An interesting comparison may be made between the regular plan and the curvilinear plan in *burh* construction at Stamford, one of the Five Boroughs of the Danelaw: here, a Saxon *burh* and a Danish *burh* faced one another across the river Welland. The extent of the Danish settlement, on the north bank, is uncertain, and may have been somewhat greater than previously supposed (RCHM 1977, fig. 4): property boundaries hint at the possibility of a large, U-shaped enclosure attached to the river bank (Fig. 44). This stands in marked contrast to the southern *burh*, constructed by Edward the Elder in 918. The latter, although ill-known in detail, took the form of a gridded rectangle.

Cambridge might be considered as providing an analogue. Here in the southern part of the town, a gently

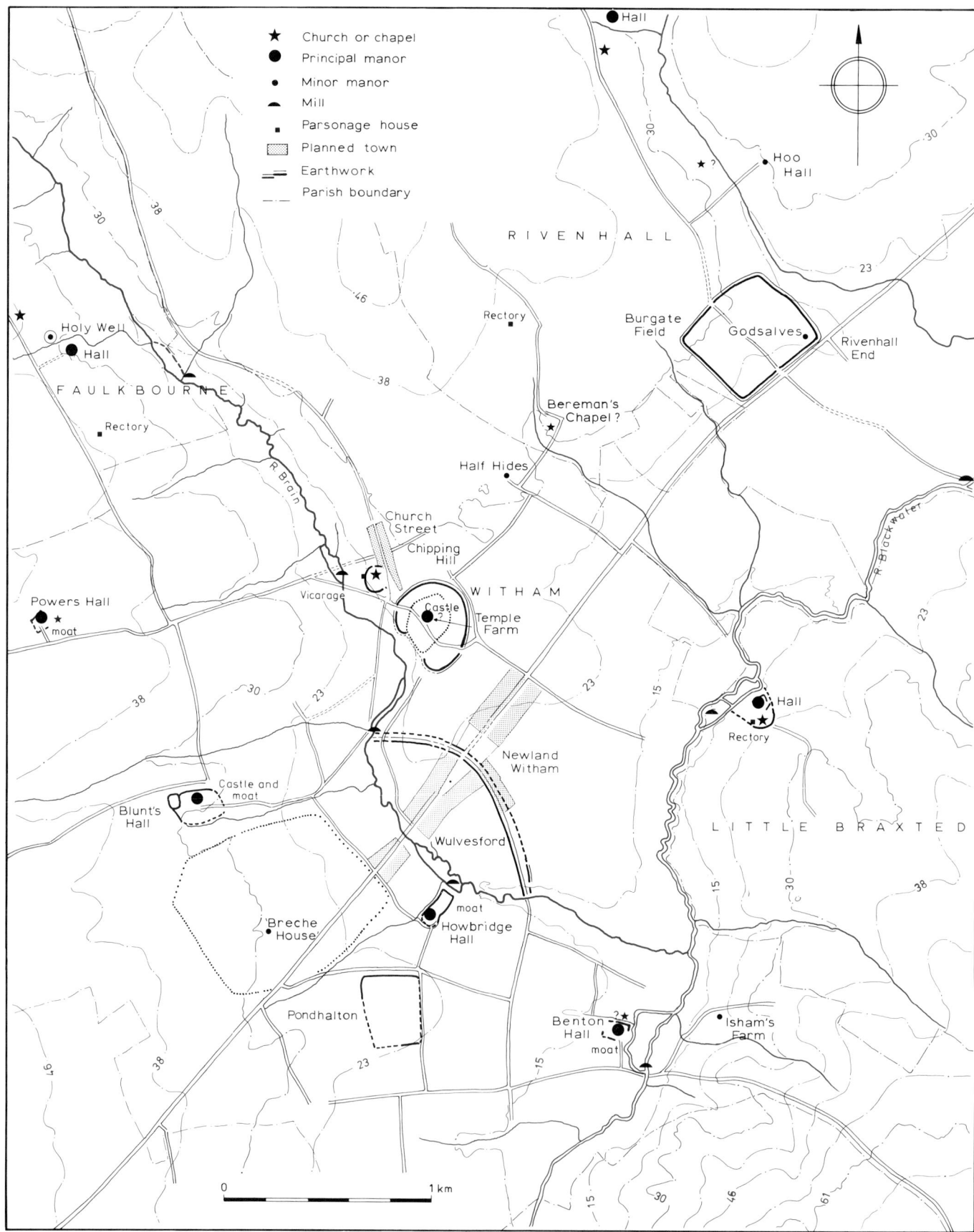

Fig. 43. *The principal elements of the Anglo-Saxon (black) and early medieval (brown) topography of the Witham area. Contours in metres above O.D.*

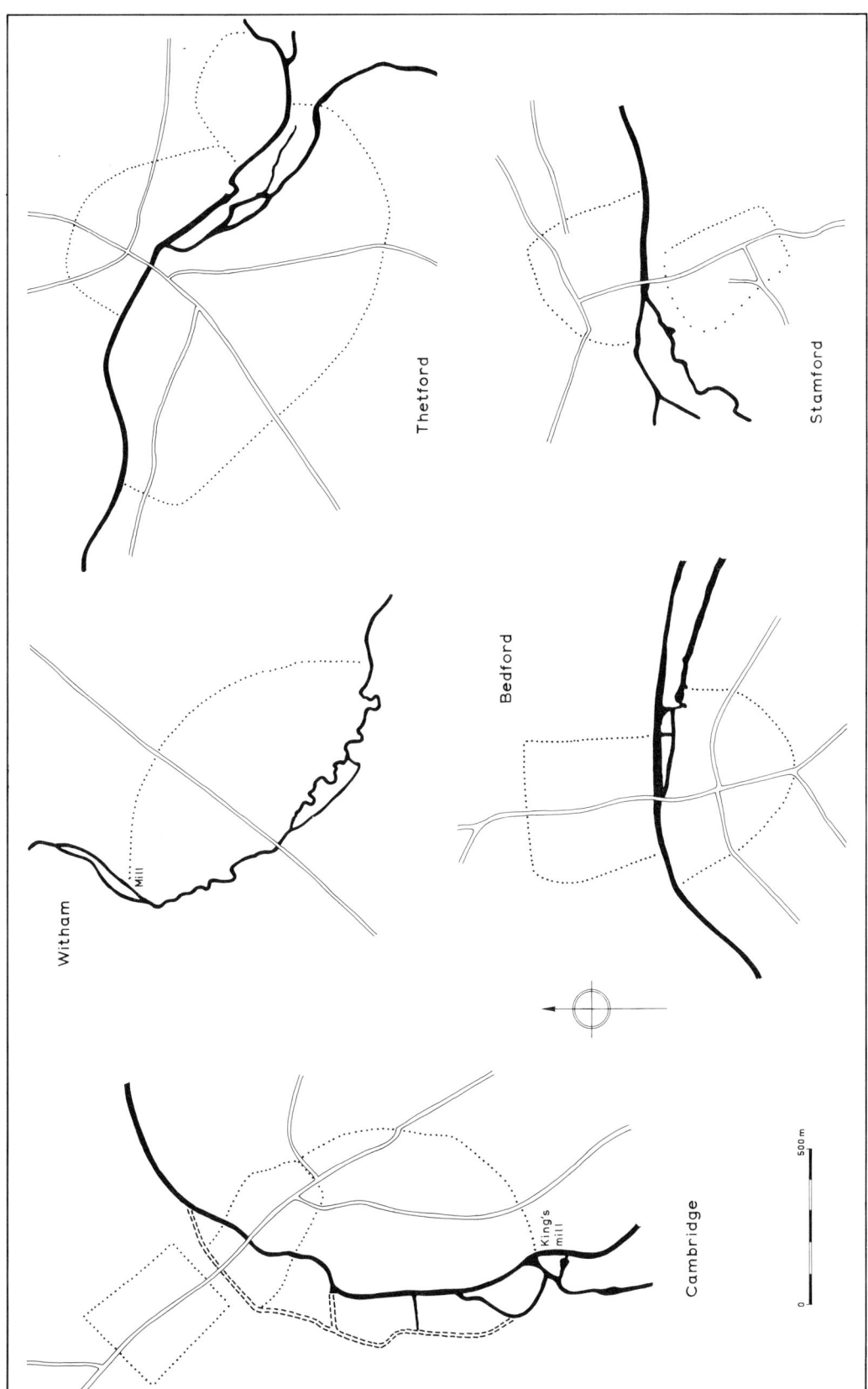

***Fig. 44.** Comparative outlines of burghal earthworks at riverside locations at Cambridge, Witham, Thetford, Bedford and Stamford.*

curving earthwork (the King's Ditch) cut off a bend in the river Cam, severing the line of the Roman through-road, encompassing the bridgehead, and enclosing an area of 36 ha (89 acres). This, it has been argued, was the Danish camp, which was distinct from the Edwardian *burh* that lay directly across the river and occupied the defences of the former Roman town. Another view has seen the King's Ditch, and the associated St John's Ditch, as components of both the English and Danish *burhs* (Lobel 1975, 5; map 2). These lines of reasoning have, however, been fundamentally upset by Jeremy Haslam, who has produced compelling arguments for a temporally more extended and topographically more complex history of urban planning, both at Cambridge, Bedford and elsewhere (Haslam 1983b). He has proposed that the first phase of planned development in the east Midlands and East Anglia was the work of Offa, and that the Vikings, to a large extent, only colonised and adapted existing enclosures.

Certainly, the *Anglo-Saxon Chronicle* leaves no room for doubt that it was Edward's policy to create double *burhs* at strategic river crossings, with a bridge clasped between the two, as an integral part of the defensive apparatus. Bedford sheds light on the problems of attempting to identify an Edwardian 'plan'. The *Anglo-Saxon Chronicle* expressly states that Edward built the southern *burh* at Bedford in 913 (Whitelock 1961, 64). Here, as at Cambridge, the King's Ditch defined a sweeping U-shaped enclosure, based upon the river Ouse. A modest attempt at laying out a street grid is apparent, but it is very incomplete. The northern *burh*, by contrast, exhibits a rectilinear plan and street grid (Baker *et al.* 1979, fig. 182; Haslam 1983a). There is no concurrence between the historically-supported topographical plans from Stamford and from Bedford: the evidence is in collision.

The problem of trying to identify characteristic English and Viking plan-types is compounded at Hertford, where Edward the Elder is recorded as having built both *burhs*, one after the other, in 912. Neither is archaeologically well known, but the northern defence was probably irregular in plan, while the southern was certainly rectilinear (Petchey 1977, fig. 5). In view of the importance of both Hertford and Bedford in earlier Mercian history, there can be little doubt that Edward found one of the defensive circuits at each place already in existence, and either adapted it or built within it. Finally, mention might be made of Thetford, where both bughal defences were curvilinear in plan, and enclosed *c.* 60 ha and *c.* 15 ha respectively (Fig. 44; Rogerson and Dallas 1984, 197; fig. 2). More archaeological evidence is clearly needed before the dating and potential cultural affiliations of *burh* plan-types can usefully be pursued.

The upshot of this enquiry into the plans of *burhs* built or rebuilt in the reign of Edward the Elder is that

no single type can be identified or a clear morphological distinction drawn between English and contemporary Viking constructions. It may be more helpful to enquire into the differences between offensive and defensive fortifications of the period. That there were two planned stages in the establishment of an Edwardian *burh* is evident from the number of instances where there was a recorded lapse of time between the first and second building campaigns. Equally evocative is the fact that in no instance was a bridgehead clasped between two similarly planned enclosures.

Returning to Witham, a case might be argued for the *Wulvesford* enclosure being either a Viking fortification or the Saxon *burh*. On topographical and morphological grounds, the former seems unlikely, if only on the basis that it faced in the wrong direction to be effective as a Viking defensive work. Lying on the east side of the Brain, the *Wulvesford* enclosure only makes sense as an English offensive work. The possibility that there had been a fortified Viking base at Witham, prior to the arrival of Edward must be borne in mind. Other earthworks in the area should not be excluded from consideration.

South-west of the Brain, the only site that could merit consideration in the context of Witham *burh* is the 8 ha rectangular enclosure at Pondhalton Farm (p. 53; Fig. 34). Since, however, this is undated, lacks an internal bank, and appears to be non-defensive, it can probably be dismissed in this context.

The final candidate that demands serious consideration as the potential site of Witham *burh* is the Burgate Field enclosure at Rivenhall End. The name is evocative, but it should be remembered that by the twelfth century the term *burhgeat* (or *burgiet*) had come to denote a legal right as much as an actual structure: Henry of Anjou granted Berkeley (Glos.) to Robert Fitzharding in 1153 *cum tol et them, et soch, et sache et Belle, et Burgiet, et infrangenethef.* On this basis the name Burgate Field might reflect no more than a twelfth or thirteenth-century recognition that the field contained, or had contained, a manor possessing the right of 'burhgeat'.[114] This, however, begs the question, since the topographical study of Rivenhall End has clearly revealed the former existence of a sub-rectangular enclosure of 18 ha (Fig. 31). It is most unlikely to be the work of a private thegn, if only on grounds of size; and no convincing explanation can be offered for it as a contemporary component of a tiny Domesday manor with only 30 acres. The Burgate Field enclosure must be more ancient, a decommissioned earthwork that was simply assigned a new use.

The strategic function of the Burgate Field enclosure was evidently to control the passage of traffic along the Colchester road, without introducing a total obstruction. One possibility for the site's origin might be a late Roman *burgus*, that not only controlled a vital line of communication, but also offered protection for the local populace in times of barbarian intrusion. In this connection, it is worth noting that a particularly interesting strap-end, of a type worn by late Roman officials, was found at Rivenhall End (Hawkes 1972), not however on the site in question but at Durward's Hall, east of the Cressing Brook. Such a *burgus*, much

ruined but still forming a recognisable enclosure, could perhaps have been granted by a late Saxon king to the Domesday free man, Ulsi, or one of his predecessors.

It is difficult to see how the Burgate Field enclosure could be of Roman origin. First, there are no finds of the period from it, whereas there is an attested late Roman site within 0.5 km, across the Cressing Brook,

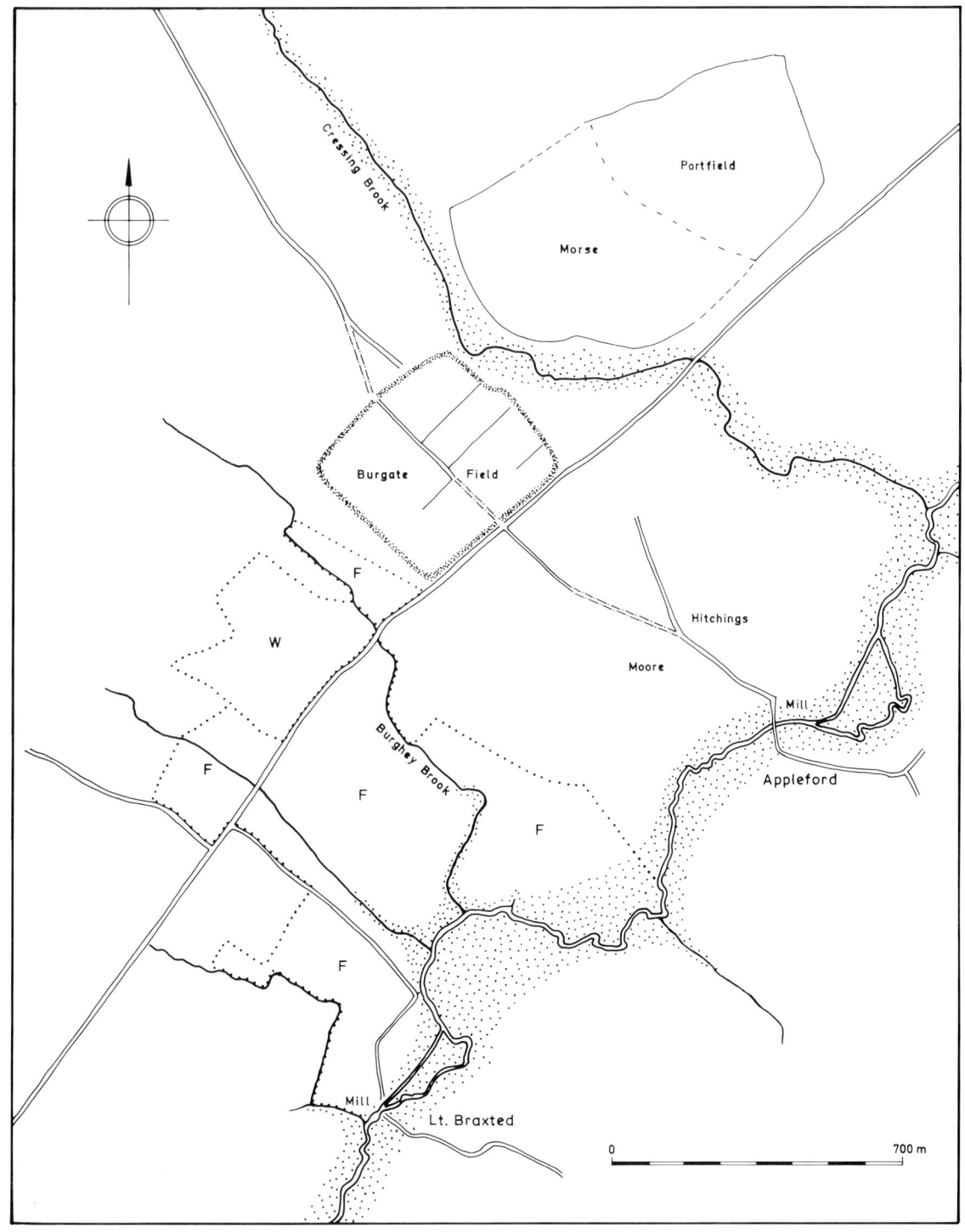

Fig. 45. *Map of the environs of the Burgate Field enclosure, Rivenhall End, showing potentially related features. Detached parcels of Faulkbourne land (F) and Witham land (W) are indicated.*

at Durward's Hall (Hull 1963, 150). Moreover, a *burgus* at Rivenhall End would not accord with the known pattern of Roman settlement and defensive works in the area. Such a site would be easier to understand at Ivy Chimneys, or at Kelvedon where a 5 ha earthwork defence of late second-century origin is already known (Rodwell, K., 1988, 135). A post-Roman origin for Burgate Field is certainly more likely. This being so, the formal rectilinear plan points either to the later Saxon period,[115] or to the medieval era of 'new town' foundation.

The lack of late Saxon artifacts (or artifacts of any period) from Burgate Field is of no more significance than it is for the *Wulvesford* enclosure. The siting of the Burgate Field earthwork was certainly such that it could control the Colchester road, in which task it was helped by the natural protection afforded to its flanks by the Cressing and Burgy brooks. Its position was not perhaps quite as strong as that at *Wulvesford*, which had the particular advantage of being directly accessible from the Blackwater, via a short stretch of the Brain.

Comparisons with other Edwardian *burhs* may help to shed light on the Burgate Field problem. With an enclosed area of 18 ha, it is somewhat larger than the rectilinear southern *burh* at Hertford (13 ha; 32 acres). Stamford was smaller still, but is of interest since it supplies a different analogue for Burgate Field. There, the Anglo-Saxon *burh* occupied a rectangular plot with an area of not less than 6.1 ha (15 acres). There is a suggestion that it was built directly alongside, and parallel to, an existing road leading to the crossing of the Welland. The fortification therefore controlled access along the road, without blocking it completely. It was only later that the road was diverted to run axially through the *burh*, and a street grid was laid out (RCHM 1977, xxxix, fig. 4).

The situation at Maldon is of comparative interest too, being only 10 km (6 miles) from Witham (Figs. 1 and 38). Although not explicitly recorded, Edward's first camp must have been built in 912, when he made Maldon the coastal base for his Essex campaign. But in 916 the *Anglo-Saxon Chronicle* (*sub anno* 920) records that he built and garrisoned a *burh* at Maldon. It is not clear precisely how events over this four-year period should be interpreted. While it could be argued that the initial fortification was simply enlarged and strengthened, Edward's record of *burh* construction elsewhere is likely to point to a different sequence of events. One possibility is that Maldon was another twin-unit, but the need for a double *burh* here could not be the same as at Hertford, Bedford or Buckingham, where the defence of a river bridge was of paramount importance. Maldon lay on high ground forming the southern flank to the estuary of the Blackwater: there is no evidence that the *burh* spanned the river, or was associated with twin bridgeheads. As far as can be judged, the two phases of Edwardian defence were both on the same side of the river.

If this is the case, it considerably eases our problem of understanding the complexity of earthworks now being archaeologically revealed at Maldon (Drury and Wickenden 1982, fig. 1c; Wickenden 1986; Brown 1986). Moreover, it is clear that there were three distinct components to late Saxon Maldon. First, there was the historically important church of St Mary, a potential candidate for an early minster, forming the nucleus of a riverside settlement on the south bank of the Blackwater. Secondly, at a road junction on the hill to the west, was the town with its triangular market place and two churches of St Peter and All Saints. Thirdly, adjoining the town on the west lay the more-or-less sub-rectangular earthwork that is generally held to be Edward's *burh*. The area enclosed was *c.* 8 ha. (19.5 ac).

It is important to note that medieval Maldon lay wholly outside this earthwork, and was probably contained within an enclosure of its own (Eddy and Petchey 1983, fig. 27.1). This supplies critical evidence for the bipartite nature of Maldon: it is suggested that the unoccupied earthwork was a primarily military enclosure of 912, and that the town (a Domesday borough) was an appendage to it in 916. By chance, the medieval and later expansion of the town was entirely in an eastward direction — ultimately linking up with St Mary's and the quay — so that the Edwardian earthwork stood empty until modern times. Like Witham, it was described and illustrated by Strutt (1774, 24; pl.II.3, 4). It is interesting that both Maldon and Witham should have preserved sub-rectangular earthwork enclosures without medieval occupation inside them.

DISCUSSION

Witham is in the anomalous position of having two serious contenders for the site of the *burh*: both the *Wulvesford* and Burgate Field enclosures are topographically and militarily superior candidates to Chipping Hill, which may now be set aside. Chipping Hill Camp could never have played more than a marginal role in the defence of the London-Colchester road, and although there was clearly an Anglo-Saxon royal estate centred here, it seems unlikely that this had any direct association with the *burh*, which was primarily a military installation with an offensive function. All archaeological and topographical evidence relating to the Chipping Hill area may be readily explained in other contexts. If there was any refortification of the camp during the period under consideration, it is more likely to have resulted from temporary Viking use.

The *Wulvesford* site is centrally and strategically located, and fits best the king's perceived needs in 912.

Unlike virtually all Edward's recorded *burhs* — and others which may be attributed to him (Haslam 1988) — there was no urban foundation established at *Wulvesford* as a permanent replacement for the military presence. By analogy with the King's Ditch enclosure at Cambridge, for example, we might have expected to find at least some hints of a regular street layout, one or more churches, a market either within or immediately outside the *burh*, the provision of town fields, and perhaps evidence for the canalisation of the river in order to create efficient wharves along its banks (cf. Haslam 1983b). No trace of any such works or provisions can be found in central Witham, and there can be little doubt that had they ever existed some evidence would have remained in the topographical, parochial or tenurial record. The sole point of comparative interest, apart from the earthwork itself, is the fact that the principal manorial mill at Witham lay at the upstream junction of the *Wulvesford* earthwork with the river Brain. The same location was occupied by the King's Mill at Cambridge (Fig. 44).

If, for the sake of argument, we accept *Wulvesford* as a short-lived, offensive *burh* that was not transmuted into an urban foundation, that still leaves Burgate Field wholly unexplained. Its strategic location, appreciable size, rectilinear plan, evocative placename and singular history throughout the Middle Ages all combine to herald it as a unit of early importance. If it was not the *burh* of 912, it could still have been an urban foundation of slightly later date which, for some unknown reason, failed to prosper, and demised before the Norman conquest. Such an idea is far from being fanciful, since there is now a growing body of evidence to suggest that, from 917 onward, Edward the Elder followed up his reconquest of the Danelaw in eastern England with the systematic foundation of *burhs*, far in excess of the number that happen to have received mention in the *Anglo-Saxon Chronicle*. Jeremy Haslam has briefly introduced and discussed this phenomenon in the context of his proposed identification of the lost *burh* of *Wigingamere* with Newport, Essex (Haslam 1988).

Not all of Edward's foundations survived as double units into the Middle Ages, and some lost their urban characteristics. In a few instances the two components of a double *burh* were not immediately adjacent, as in the case of Nottingham and its counterpart, West Bridgeford. It is not, therefore, inconceivable that the offensive base was at *Wulvesford*, while a site for the intended permanent *burh* at Witham should have been allocated on the edge of the royal estate, rather than at its core. For a new town to succeed it was a *sine qua non* that it had to be provided with a market, mill, town lands, and other support mechanisms. It has been shown above that, with the possible exception of a mill, none of these provisions existed in relation to the *Wulvesford*

site. A different situation obtains, however, in respect of Burgate Field.

First, it is worth observing that the rectilinear boundaries, together with the footpath that crosses the centre of the enclosure from north to south, could be relict from an erstwhile street grid with a central market place (Fig. 31), but no great weight should be placed on circumstantial evidence of this nature. Of far greater significance is the occurrence of the name 'Portfield' a little to the east of the Burgate Field enclosure, in Rivenhall parish (Fig. 45). First mentioned in 1692, Portfield comprised fifty acres, but by the time it was mapped in 1716 it had been reduced to 44 acres, and by 1839 it had been subdivided into three fields.[116] Next to it lay another field of roughly similar size which morphologically has the appearance of being the 'other half' of a unitary layout. This latter field was recorded as 'Morse' in 1385, and by 1692 was divided into three parcels, including Great and Little Moore.[117] The combined area of all these fields was *c*. 120 acres: the intended unit size may therefore have been one hide.

The name Portfield is characteristically found in association with 'town fields' that were provided for the support of an urban community (cf. Haslam 1983b, 23–6; 1988, 29). The name Moore (or Moors) was commonly applied in the Middle Ages to land that had fallen out of cultivation, and become waste or scrub. The field name evidence is therefore of seminal importance to the interpretation of the Burgate Field enclosure.

No less evocative of interest is the curiously irregular block of land adjoining Burgate Field on the west, which spans the Colchester road and stretches south as far as the Blackwater at Little Braxted mill. It has already been noted that the land in question is a portion of Faulkbourne parish, so remotely detached that it remains without satisfactory explanation (p. 46).[118] The fields, comprising some 230 acres, were associated in post-medieval times with Coleman's Farm, a holding of no known historical or tenurial importance. The configuration of the boundaries suggests that the area was anciently cut out of Witham parish (Figs. 39 and 45). Given also the recorded uncertainty as to which parish Burgate Field was in (p. 46), it seems not unreasonable to forge a union between these separate observations, and adumbrate a former tenurial connection between the Burgate enclosure and the 'floating' block of Faulkbourne land. It may be no coincidence that the extent of the land was about two hides.

This assignation, coupled with the abutment of the Faulkbourne land on the Blackwater at Little Braxted mill, may provide the solution to another topographical conundrum. Mills were an extremely frequent occurrence on the rivers of central Essex, and it has been demonstrated that not only were they comprehensively recorded by the Domesday surveyors, but also that the sites of most of these eleventh-century mills are readily identifiable (p. 94; also Rodwell and Rodwell 1985, 175). To a large extent, the establishment of chains of mills probably pre-dated the formalisation of parish boundaries, which may explain why in some instances boundaries that essentially followed riverine courses deviated briefly to take in mill-leats. The general rule seems to have been that the entire mill complex was annexed to the parish to which it belonged; in other words, if a mill-stream lay on the far side of a river from the parent parish, then the boundary was pushed out accordingly to embrace the river, island and mill-stream.

Little Braxted mill enjoys the unusual distinction of having three leats: the present stream, and its predecessor, follow a course to the south of the river, while to the north is another leat without any apparent purpose. Moreover the parish boundary between Little Braxted and Faulkbourne followed that leat (Fig. 32.3). The most logical interpretation of the evidence is that the mill has translocated, and that it originally lay on the leat to the north of the Blackwater (Fig. 33.6). Cropmark evidence for a small enclosure adjacent to the leat, at the point where it rejoins the river, may denote the original mill site (Fig. 2, no. 3). This being so, a case can be advanced for Little Braxted mill having once been attached to the 'floating' Faulkbourne parcel. Was this the burghal mill, which was later taken over by Little Braxted manor?[119]

In summary, the Burgate Field enclosure is surrounded by topographical and tenurial anomalies, each of which could be explained by the presence of a late Saxon *burh* at Rivenhall End. None of this evidence provides a close date for either the foundation or the demise of the posited *burh*, and the assumption that it was the work of Edward the Elder can be no more than that. On balance, it would seem unlikely that the *burh* would have been of late tenth-century foundation: that would have given little time for its building, population, demise and disposal by the king well before 1066. There is no hint of the *burh's* former existence in the Domesday Survey.

The link between Portfield (one hide) and the *burh* must be regarded as strong, and the case for similarly associating the two-hide block of Faulkbourne land has been argued. These would not have been sufficient as town lands for the *burh*, and if we are to seek additional land provision, there are two further blocks, each of

about one hide in extent, which may be offered as likely candidates. They lie between the Colchester road and the Blackwater, opposite Burgate Field and Portfield, respectively. It is extremely difficult to trace the medieval and post-medieval history of these lands. They were fragmentary, variously held, and the field names indicate a good deal of abandoned land. There are several additional parcels with 'Moor' names, and one has the remarkable appellation 'Hitchings'.[120] This name is usually taken as an explicit reference to strip-field cultivation. Since, however, no medieval open-field system of agriculture is known to have been practised in this part of Essex, the occurrence of such a name is striking. Unless some other explanation for Hitchings is forthcoming, we may have here a chink of evidence for an agricultural system that was once in operation at Rivenhall End, but had passed out of currency by the early Middle Ages. Altogether, the several anomalous holdings and groups of fields described at Rivenhall End form a contiguous land block of some five hides around Burgate Field.

The conclusion must surely be that Witham was developed as a tenth-century *burh*, for which a strategically significant site was chosen on the eastern edge of the royal estate. An ambitious earthwork enclosure was built, and lands were assigned for the support of the intended population. But the enterprise was short-lived, and in due course failed altogether, probably before the end of the century. A similar fate befell other late Saxon towns in Essex: Horndon-on-the-Hill is an analagous case (Eddy and Petchey 1983, 63). As a foundation, Horndon is without documentation: the remains of the earthwork enclosure attest its existence, and late tenth-century coinage minted there establishes a *terminus ante quem* for its functioning.

In the case of Witham, the foundation was so unsuccessful or short-lived that it did not manage to acquire the coveted right of minting, and in the context of the tenth century nothing could constitute a more revealing admission of urban failure. Negative evidence though it is, this is an undoubtedly powerful argument. All of Edward's permanently settled *burhs* acquired mints by the second or third quarter of the tenth century: Hertford and Maldon, for example, were both minting under his successor, Athelstan (Blunt *et al.* 1989). That Witham never acquired a mint, Anglo-Saxon or medieval, is confirmation of its non-urban status prior to the arrival of the Templars.[121]

11

The Emergence of Medieval Witham

The 'Old' Town at Chipping Hill

Wherever the *burh* lay, it did not give rise to a late Saxon town of a type that is now widely recognised (Biddle and Hill 1971). Saxon Witham was not formally planned, but if there was any nucleated settlement — and that is at best uncertain — it would have been clustered around an existing road junction, between the minster church and the manorial complex inside the old plateau fort. Possibly, there was a market place too.

CHIPPING HILL MARKET AND 'CASTLE' *(Figs. 23 and 46)*

The antiquity of the triangular 'green' in front of the church, which served as a market place in the Middle Ages, is uncertain. A pre-conquest origin for the market might be inferred by the appellation 'Chipping' (OE *cieping*), but a post-conquest foundation could equally be implied: such was the case at Chipping Sodbury, Glos., where the town was founded in c. 1179 and a market granted in c. 1218 (Leech 1975, 9). Although there is no mention of a market at Witham in the Domesday Survey, this does not necessarily constitute evidence against its existence and, given the prosperous nature of the community implied by the entry, the presence of a market would not be particularly surprising. Markets were entirely ignored by the Domesday surveyors in Essex, even in the boroughs. The first recorded mention of Witham market is in 1153, with reference back to conditions at the time of Henry I (Lees 1935, 152; Britnell 1968, 14). If there was an early market at Chipping Hill — pre-twelfth century — it would probably have occupied the southern part of the circular enclosure containing the church (Fig. 23B). It is less likely that a market would have been held inside the former plateau fort.

Whatever earlier arrangements obtained, the Norman settlement and its church lay outside the north-west gate of the redundant Iron Age camp, in precisely the same way that the town and church of Pevensey (Sussex) lay without the east gate of the ruined Roman fort

(Aldsworth and Freke 1976, 46–7). In cases such as Pevensey, the interior of the ancient *enceinte* was often not abandoned, but housed a manorial complex, the local seat of power and authority. The case for the manorial seat at Witham has been argued (p. 65).

It was not uncommon for parts of these long-defunct earthwork or masonry defences to be refurbished in the twelfth century, turning the manor houses they enveloped into castles. That happened at Pevensey and, it seems likely, on a more humble scale, at Witham too. The filling of the second-phase ditch noted in the 1969 section of the outer defences at Chipping Hill (trench X) can confidently be dated to the early thirteenth century, and its construction can hardly have been a great deal earlier: it would not be unreasonable to assign it to the twelfth century (Fig. 16). Thus a new, and undeniably medieval, act of fortification was introduced. The scale of the work must surely imply a minor castle, and since there is no record of a new fortification being constructed by the king at Witham, it is reasonable to posit the private upgrading of a manor house. The same happened at Blunt's Hall (Trump 1961). Who could have been responsible for a castle at Chipping Hill?

The hundred and manor of Witham, held by the Crown at the time of the Domesday Survey, passed into the hands of Eustace III, Count of Boulogne sometime in the 1120s. Eustace's daughter, Matilda, married Stephen of Blois, who became king in 1135, thus effectively restoring Witham to the Crown. In 1137 Matilda endowed the Order of Knights Templar with their first important rural estate in England. This was at Cressing, and comprised the entire manor, the church and its appurtenances (Lees 1935, xxxix, 145). Cressing is not individually identifiable in the Domesday Survey, since it was then evidently part of Witham. Tenurial separation seems to have occurred in the late eleventh or early twelfth century (before 1125); parochial separation came much later. In 1147, however, Stephen gave also the manor of Witham to the Knights Templar, who thenceforth held a consolidated unit: *In Witham et in Kirsing ... habentur v. hide.* This may be equated with the five-hide manor of Domesday, which must have been split after the conquest and then re-amalgamated. Indeed, Witham-Cressing was still being referred to as though it were a single unit into the thirteenth century (Lees 1935, lxxii-lxxiii; Britnell 1968, 14). By 1185 the Templars had been granted no less than fourteen other holdings in Essex, not including lands in Rivenhall (Lees 1935, lxxiv).

The Templars appear to have met with some difficulty in reaping all the benefits of their new acquisition, since in 1153–54 Stephen had to instruct his sheriff to support the authority of Master Osto and the brethren in holding their market (*mercatum suum*) at

Witham, as it had been held — presumably by Eustace — in the time of King Henry I (Lees 1935, 152). This is the first direct evidence of a market at Witham, and it is not clear how we should interpret the reference to an earlier market: if the Templars were having difficulty in asserting their authority, an appeal to established custom (real or imaginary) might secure royal support. However, subsequent charters of Richard I in 1189 and John in 1199, confirmed the Templars in their manor and market of Witham *sicut ibidem esse solebat tempore Regis Henrici, avi patris nostri* (Lees 1935, 141). None of this, of course, dates the foundation of the market, and the phraseology employed is not overtly

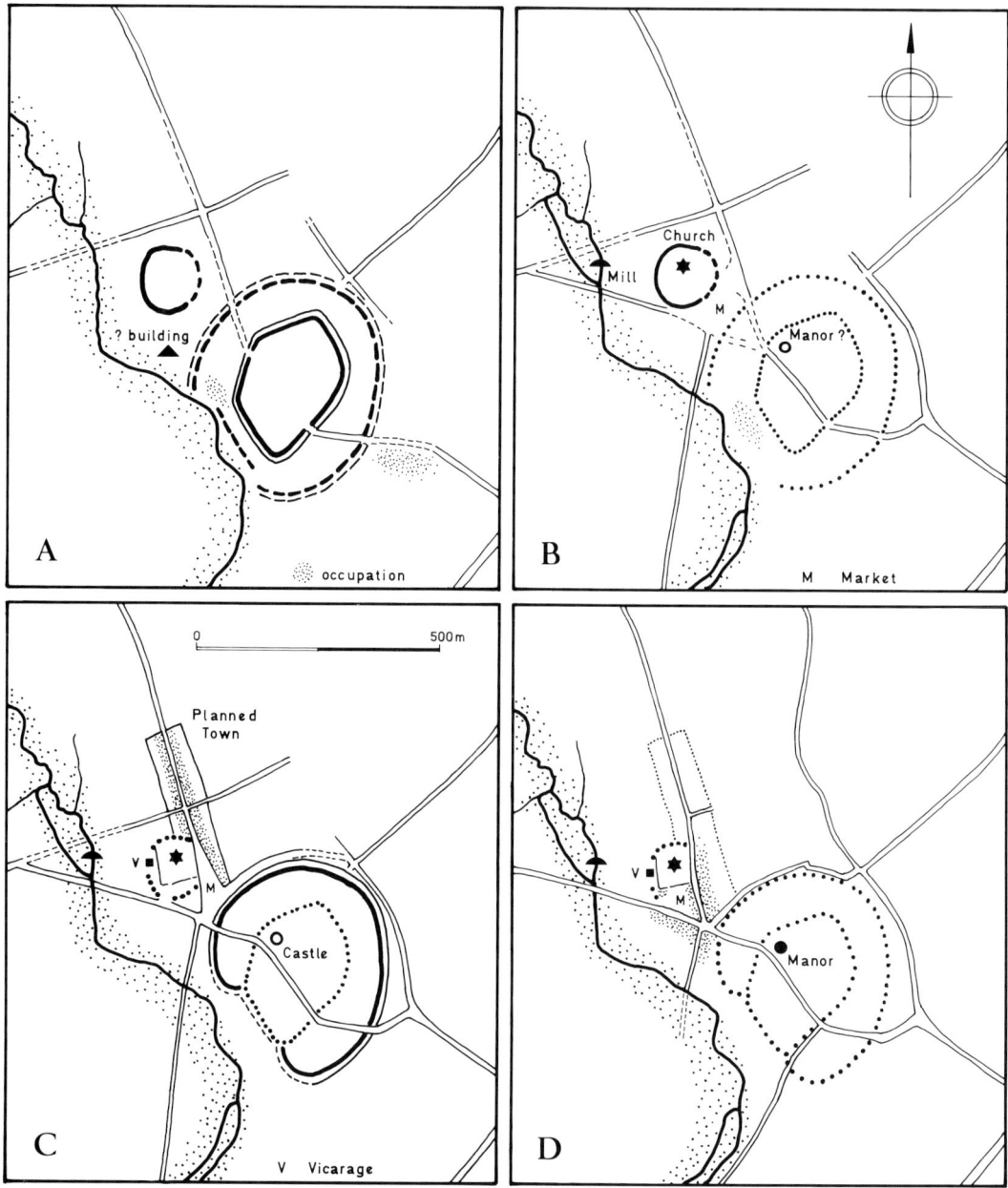

Fig. 46. Suggested development of settlement at Chipping Hill.
A. *Prehistoric earthworks and Roman occupation.* **B.** *Late Anglo-Saxon church and manorial complex.* **C.** *Mid-twelfth century proto-town and castle.* **D.** *Later medieval 'green' village.*

suggestive of an origin in the reign of Henry I. An ol
der foundation is inherently more likely. The allusion to
Henry was merely a convenient means of drawing
attention to the market's lapse during some part of the
reign of Stephen.

The cause of the Templars' problems over holding a
market is not known, but an inspired guess would
connect it with the canons of St Martin-le-Grand in
London, to whom Matilda had previously granted
Witham church.[122] In Henry I's reign the church, the
manor and the market were all in the same hands, but
now they were divided, and circumstances for friction
between the holding parties had been created.

THE FIRST PLANNED TOWN

It was perhaps shortly before the middle of the twelfth
century that the small planned settlement north-east of
St Nicholas's Church was created (p. 34; Fig. 25). This
was undoubtedly conceived as an adjunct to the market.
Several circumstances could be invoked for the creation
of this small 'new town'. First, it is tempting to see it
as having been speculatively planted by the Templars
around the period 1148–53, as a means of augmenting
the revenue obtained from their newly acquired manor.
This is, however, very unlikely because the topography
of the settlement is strongly suggestive of a parcel
having been cut out of the Witham glebe and
churchyard (Fig. 40). That in turn points towards the
second possibility: entrepreneurial activity on the part of
the canons of St Martin's, in the years between 1136
and 1146.

The third option is that the new town was laid out in,
or before, the reign of Henry I, when the manor, market
and church were all royal property. Certainly, the
planning of the small town and the triangular market
place appear to be cohesive; and since the market lay
outside the north-west entrance to the manorial *enceinte*,
a· direct relationship seems to be implied (Fig. 46C).
That would favour a Henrician foundation, rather than
later. Whichever explanation is preferred, it is not
difficult to appreciate that the subsequent separation of
such closely connected properties and institutions into
separate ownerships could have sown the seeds for local
friction.

As Britnell has observed, Chipping Hill market was
essentially a rural affair, 'a local market for local
producers, centrally placed at the hundred meeting
place, but accessible only by lanes', and that 'the
founder, whoever he was, had no expectation of
benefitting from any regular long-distance traffic'
(Britnell 1968, 14). A significant change was not to
come about until the early thirteenth century.

It is clear that throughout the twelfth century the
manor of Witham (with or without its market) and,
separately, Witham church, were held by lords of

considerable wealth and status. It was presumably the
Templars who were responsible for the refortification of
Chipping Hill, for the better defence of their recently
acquired manor. The Templars were certainly minded to
surround themselves by impressive earthworks, and their
preceptory at Cressing was enclosed by one of the
largest moats in central Essex, for which an early to mid
thirteenth-century date has been argued (Rodwell and
Rodwell 1985, 77, n. 59; fig. 129).[123] Cressing Temple
moat is therefore contemporary with the final phase of
earthwork construction identified at Chipping Hill (p.
32).

In passing, it may be noted that Strutt, when
describing the Chipping Hill earthworks in 1774,
referred to the inner work as 'the keep or castle'.
Without pinning too much on this, it is possible that
Strutt's choice of words reflected a local tradition of a
castle or fortified manor here. It may also be no
coincidence that a sixteenth-century farmhouse abutting
the north-west corner of the outer ditch is known as
Moat Farm (Fig. 4B): in 1370 it was *la mote* and in
1415 *the moote* (Reaney 1935, 302). While a medieval
fortification is not necessarily implied by references to
a 'moat', usage in this connection is more common than
in relation to a prehistoric work.

A possible layout for the Norman castle can now be
envisaged: the smaller prehistoric earthwork would have
formed the inner bailey, while an eccentric outer bailey
was created by recutting the larger earthwork. The two
curving banks (archaeologically undated) which link the
inner and outer defensive circuits are most plausibly
interpreted as part of the medieval castle, their purpose
being to conjoin the two baileys and to give them a
common west side (Fig. 4B and 46C). The resultant
earthwork was in the mode of Bourn Castle, Lincs.
(Armitage 1912, fig. 10). Somewhere within the inner
bailey there was presumably a tower, perhaps rising
from an earthen motte. The latter would, if it survived
into the post-medieval period, have been levelled as part
of the seventeenth and eighteenth-century agricultural
improvements that did so much damage to the south and
west sides of Chipping Hill camp (p. 8).

It has already been mentioned that the twelfth century
saw the erection of another fortification at Witham, in
the shape of a small motte-and-bailey castle on the site
of the Saxon manor at Blunt's Hall (p. 49; Fig. 32.1).
Also lacking informative documentation, this castle has
been assigned by its excavator to the years of political
unrest in the middle of the twelfth century (Trump
1961). The absence of glazed wares amongst the pottery
assemblage from the site confirms that the earthwork is
no later in origin.

The date and status of the elongated, rectangular
earthwork around Howbridge Hall are less certain.
Although the nucleus of another Domesday manor,
equal in size to Blunt's Hall, the rectangular plan of this

largely obliterated enclosure has more the appearance of
a thirteenth-century homestead moat than any pretence
at a more major construction (Fig. 32.2). As such, the
Howbridge Hall moat finds ready analogues in the
locality, for example Porter's Farm, Kelvedon, or
Lanham Farm, Rivenhall (Rodwell and Rodwell 1985,
fig. 129). If, however, Howbridge was a two-period
construction — comprising a ringwork and adjoining
rectangular moat — another manor with early medieval
defences is implied.

The New Town at Wulvesford, *alias Newland (Figs. 26 and 47)*

The old town and market at Chipping Witham were
incapable of successful commercial exploitation, and the
only way that the Knights Templar could capitalise on
their chartered asset was physically to move the town to
a more favourable location. The Templars were
exceptionally fortunate in that the London-Colchester
road actually passed through Witham manor: the ideal
opportunity presented itself for the establishment of a
new main-road market town. Furthermore, there was
ample precedent. The bishop of London had
successfully founded two new market towns in Essex in
1199–1200 (Beresford 1967): one was at Chelmsford
(on the opposite side of the river from the Roman
town), the other at an important road junction at
Braintree (on the site of the Roman town). It may have
been the imagined threat posed by these new
foundations that prompted the Templars to seek, and
obtain, confirmation of their Witham market charter
from King John in 1199.

The present town of Witham appears to have come
into existence in, or shortly before, 1212, when the
Knights Templar received from King John a charter
granting them a Thursday market and a yearly fair at
their 'new town' at *Wuluesford: unum mercatum apud
novam villam suam de Wulvesford in parochia de
Wiham.*[124] In another charter, of 1213, John granted the
Templars *terram de Newland.* This supplies the first
reference to what was soon to become known as
'Newland Witham', in contradistinction to 'Chipping
Witham'. The town's main thoroughfare has always
borne the name Newland Street, until modern times
when part was designated as High Street.

If the Templars had been in possession of Witham
manor since 1147, why was it necessary more than sixty
years afterwards for the king to make a special grant of
the *terram de Newland,* which was already part of the
manor? The implication must surely be that the king,
when granting Witham, had retained a component of the
manor that was now required for the development of the
new town. That component was evidently the place
known as *Wulvesford* which, it is argued, may be
identified with the defunct earthwork that enclosed an

arc of land on the east bank of the Brain (p. 41). The
reason for the retention is not difficult to appreciate:
major fortifications in the early Middle Ages were
almost invariably held under direct royal control, and it
is most unlikely that the king would readily have
relinquished a site of such strategic potential as
Wulvesford, and certainly not in the restless years of the
mid-twelfth century. But by 1212 political circumstances
had changed, and the old earthwork would probably no
longer have been of serious military interest, and could
be released for redevelopment.

The new town, flourishing on its main road site,
never adopted its charter name of *Wulvesford,* but was
almost invariably referred to as Newland Witham. The
local name was not however lost, and a tithe list of *c.*
1320 refers to 'the bridge called *Woluesford*'[125] The old
town, Chipping Witham, continued with its physically
separate existence. Although the new Thursday market
was only 0.9 km distant from the Chipping Hill Sunday
market, the Templars, surprisingly, did not abandon the
latter, but appear to have operated the two in tandem.
The 'old' market, as it became known, continued to
function for a considerable time. At least a partial
manorial separation seems also to have been effected
within Witham, since there were separate manor courts
for Chipping and Newland, although they were held in
the same place, and at the same time (Morant 1768,
107).

The parish, however, remained united: considering
the physical separation of the two settlement
components, it is surprising that a substantial market-
place church or chapel-of-ease did not emerge at
Newland. The towns at both Chelmsford and Braintree
had been provided with substantial parochial churches.
In fact, it would appear that Newland did at some stage
have a chapel, although its site is unknown, and there is
only one oblique reference to it: in an Inquisition of
1309 it was reported that the manor of Witham had a
chapel and chaplain, separate from those at the
preceptory at Cressing (Fowler 1907, 177). The
reference cannot be associated with Witham parish
church, and it is unlikely that there would have been
any need for a chaplain at the old manorial focus inside
Chipping Hill Camp. Logically, the chapel in question
would have been in or adjacent to the market place at
Newland.

The chapel may have disappeared with the
suppression of the Hospitallers, and the inhabitants of
Newland Witham had to wait until 1842 for the erection
of a second parish church, All Saints. This, in turn, was
declared redundant in the 1970s, and the ancient parish
reunited.

Following the establishment of Newland Witham, the
nature of settlement at Chipping Hill changed. No
longer did it have pretensions to a quasi-urban status,
becoming instead a prosperous village set around a

green. In essence, it is still that today. We have no means of telling whether all the twelfth-century plots laid out along Church Street were taken up, but once the town had moved to its new main-road location, and begun rapidly to prosper — as it clearly did — commercial holders of tenements at Chipping Hill would have been so seriously disadvantaged that a move was inevitable if they were to remain in business. We may suspect that the Church Street tenements were abandoned by the middle of the thirteenth century, and the market which had been held there in tandem will have dwindled. It seems to have ceased functioning in 1379.

The site of the former market, at the south end of Church Street, became infilled with late medieval houses, and similar properties began to border the previously open space to the south of the parish church. They formed a village around a green (Fig. 46D). These were not tenements, with long narrow plots, but spacious timber-framed houses with halls and crosswings, dating from the fifteenth and early sixteenth centuries; some may have had even earlier origins. At least seven can be counted today, and others have disappeared. The 1608 survey of the manor makes it clear that there were very few tenements at Chipping Hill, but a number of larger properties. The Tithe map indicates their generous layout (Fig. 24), and the same is seen on early photographs (eg. Gifford 1984, pl. 44).

By the time of the Tithe survey the Church Street plots were once again being built up, within the confines of the medieval layout. There were still some vacant plots. Until recently, Church Street was lined with modest tenements, built piecemeal in the seventeenth, eighteenth and nineteenth centuries. Some have been replaced with modern housing, and there has been infilling.

PLANNING AND GROWTH OF NEWLAND

Witham, as a town, was basically uprooted and moved to a new site, where its commercial success is attested by its rapid expansion. The remaining problems to be resolved are, how new was the 'new' town of 1212, what was its size, and how did it grow? *Wulvesford* was evidently something more than an abandoned fortification: settlement is indicated by a reference in 1185 to Henry de Wluesford, who was one of the Templars' tenants (Lees 1935, 3), although we do not know precisely where he was living. The size of *la Neweland*, as initially conceived and laid out, is unknown, and the first topographical information has to be gleaned from a survey of *c*. 1258, in which sixty-one plots were enumerated, together with the tenants of the *novum forum*.[126]

The listing of the plots is topographically very revealing: thirty-nine of them were half an acre (0.2 ha)

in extent, and acquired the colloquial appellation *les Halfacres* (Britnell 1968, 15). The list is worth reproducing and analysing. It is in two parts: plots which had been built upon by *c*. 1258, and those which remained vacant.

Developed Plots

Number of plots	Area as given	Acreage
4	1 rood	1/4 acre
35	1/2 acre	1/2 acre
2	3 roods	3/4 acre
6	1 acre	1 acre
1	1 acre, 1 rood	1 1/4 acres
3	2 acres	2 acres
1	2 acres, 3 roods	2 3/4 acres
1	3 acres	3 acres

Totals 53 plots   39 acres

Undeveloped Plots

Number of plots	Area as given	Acreage
4	1/2 acre	1/2 acre
1	3 acres	3 acres
1 piece	1/6 acre	1/6 acre
1 messuage	1/6 acre	1/6 acre
1 curtilage	1/6 acre	1/6 acre

Totals 8 plots   5 1/2 acres

It is immediately striking from these figures that, not only is a moderate sized town with a range of plot sizes implied, but also that two fundamentally different systems of planning have been at work. One system relates to the subdivision of the acre into quarters (roods), the other into sixths. This alone provides a good indication that Witham in the mid-thirteenth century was not a single-period planned town. Topographical analysis firmly reinforces this point. It has been shown that five distinctly separate groups of burgage plots are identifiable from cartographic evidence (p. 39).

The block in Bridge Street, group A, was distinguished by three characteristics. First, it was isolated on the west side of the Brain. Second, the individual plots were small, being one-third and one-sixth of an acre in extent. Third, the boundaries tended to be irregular, and there was a generous margin of flexibility in the plot sizes (Fig. 26). The original plan probably allowed for eighteen plots, each of one-third of an acre. On average, plots seem to have measured 12 rods, or poles (60 m) in depth, and had a frontage of 4 rods (20 m). Thus the development comprised six acres in all. The close similarity between the Bridge Street development and that in Church Street, Chipping Hill, is too obvious to require further elaboration (p. 34). Since it has already been argued that Church Street dates from the middle of the twelfth century, if not earlier, it logically follows that Bridge Street represents the first stage in the development of Witham new town.[127] It is therefore suggested that the small block of burgages in group A represented an initial planned development on a modest scale, by the Templars, sometime during the second half of the twelfth century

(Fig. 47A). This settlement was presumably known as *Wulvesford*, and was likely the place of residence of Henry de Wluesford in 1185 (p. 39).

The new town could not expand south-westwards along the main road, on account of the land here belonging to other manors (Blunt's Hall and Howbridge Hall); in any case, this would have involved moving yet further away from the historic core of Witham. Logically, growth needed to take place in the opposite direction, and that is what occurred. The first requirement would have been to gain possession from the king of the old *Wulvesford* earthwork, which was achieved in 1213. Thus *la Neweland* was created. The

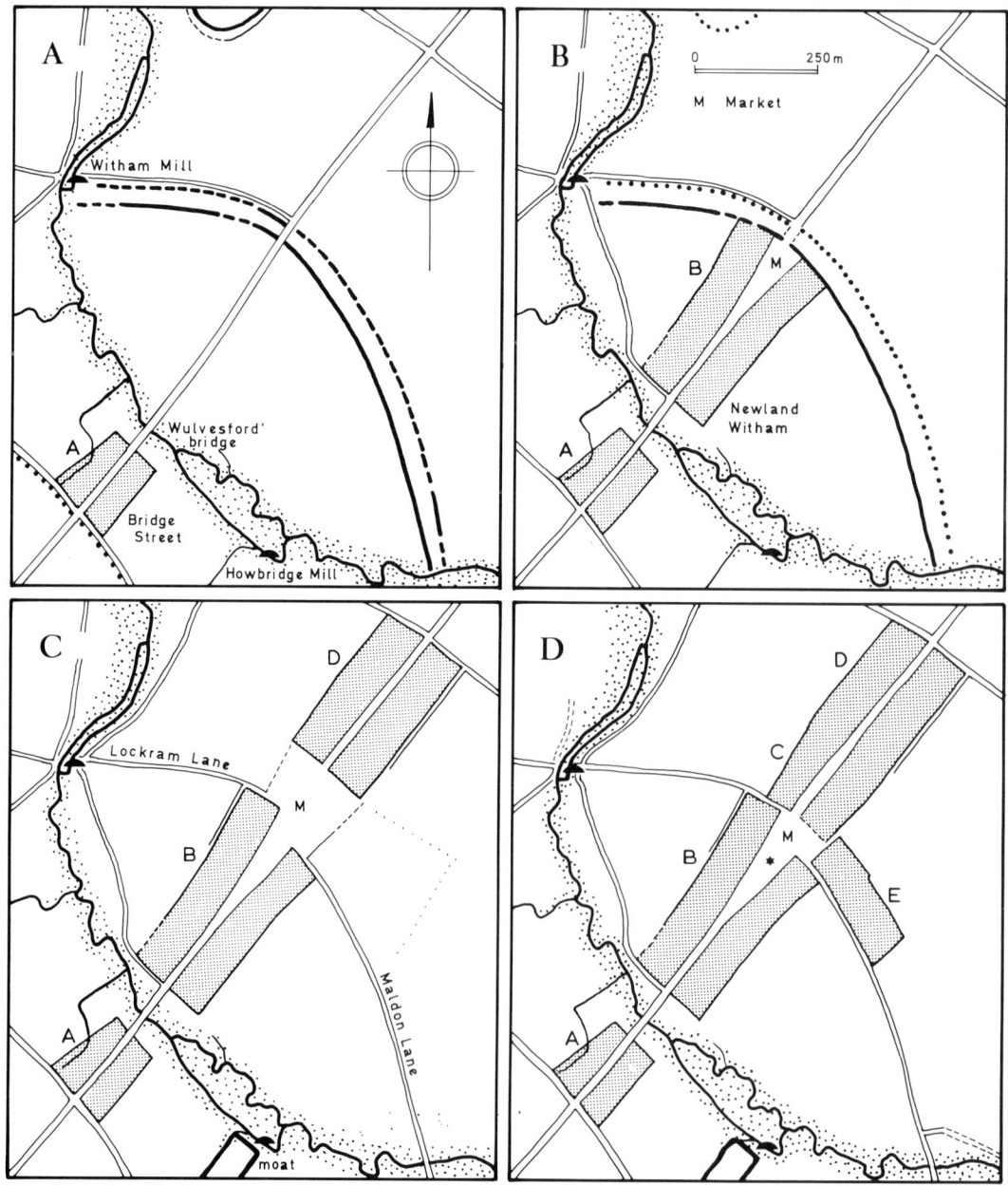

Fig. 47. Plans showing the suggested progression of urban development (stippled blocks A to E) at Newland Street, Witham, between the mid or late twelfth century and the mid-thirteenth century.
A. Later twelfth century. B. c. 1213. C. Second quarter of the thirteenth century. D. Mid-thirteenth century.

second and principal block of burgages, group B, was then laid out. These were of markedly regular form, and filled the frontages of the Colchester road between the river and the earthwork, where it intercepted the road. This was a convenient point to site the north-east entrance to the town, which was perhaps marked by a gate at the end of the newly created triangular market place (Fig. 47B).

The town still comprised a single street — Newland Street — with a frontage stretching between the river and the *Wulvesford* earthwork, a distance of around 400 m (c. 1300 ft). This would have comfortably accommodated thirty (or perhaps thirty-two) half-acre tenement plots, fifteen (or sixteen) aside. Arguably, that was the intended capacity of the new town in 1212. The depth of all the plots here was 16 rods (80.5 m), and the standard frontage must therefore have been 5 rods (25.2 m). The medieval layout is plainly shown on the Tithe map (Fig. 27) and first edition Ordnance Survey map (1874), which confirms that in the town centre the rear boundaries of the tenement plots lay c. 80 m from the street frontage, but there has been so much subdivision and amalgamation of plots over the intervening centuries that it is not easy to determine precisely how many original burgages there were per side.

Newland Street (now High Street) was moderately broad and parallel-sided for two-thirds of its length, but the easternmost section opened out rapidly to form a triangular market place. It was probably at the change of direction where the cross was sited, '*que stat in medio vico qui ducit de la Newelond versus Colecestr*'.[128] The cross was taken down shortly before 1790, and there seems to have been a common well close by it (Smith 1970, 3). The rear boundaries of the burgages on both sides of the road were outwardly angled in sympathy with the plan of the market place, thus maintaining a constant plot depth. The frontage line of the thirteenth-century market place is still preserved on the north-west side, with the remains of an intrusive central 'row' in front of it. Late medieval and post-medieval encroachment on to the market place from the south-east has masked the frontage line here, but hints of it can still be detected in boundary and building alignments.

It has already been argued that the *Wulvesford* earthwork, which crossed Newland Street at what is now the Maldon Road junction, is most unlikely to be of medieval origin (p. 39), but its existence could hardly have been ignored when the Templars were laying out their new town. Indeed, an early fourteenth-century source appears to make reference to the earthwork as *la Hollediche*, 'the ditch in the hollow';[129] while a survey of 1608 mentioned 'a certain hollow called Lyon Mead' (1½ acres), lying behind properties at the junction of Newland Street and Maldon Road.[130] The earthwork would have formed a very effective and ready-made

town enclosure, albeit that the area contained was four times larger than required. However, with the earthwork at one end of the town, and the river crossing at the other, Newland Witham was in a position to exercise total control over the passage of traffic along this section of the London-Colchester road, to its obvious commercial and financial advantage. The evasion of tolls and market dues would have been extremely difficult.

What lay at *Wulvesford*, east of the river, before 1212 is unknown. It would be surprising if there had been no roadside settlement close to the river crossing, within the royal enclosure, either of a straggling nature or, more likely, huddled around the ford (or bridge) across the Brain.[131] The Tithe map of 1839 provides a hint of jumbled property boundaries in the northern angle between Newland Street and Mill Lane (which runs alongside the river), but whether these are relict from a pre-urban phase, or merely the result of a later breaking down of the formal plan, cannot be superficially determined.

There was no possibility of cramming the sixty-one plots listed in c. 1258 within the defined space, unless a grid of streets was created, and that plainly did not happen. Thus the allusion to so many holdings indicates rapid growth beyond the earthwork limits, and this is reflected in the town's morphology. There are in fact three further blocks of properties to consider.

The name Newland Street formerly encompassed a stretch of the Colchester road extending as far beyond the *Wulvesford* earthwork as within it. Half of that north-eastward extension — which in plan resembles an extra-mural suburb — was still lined by regularly spaced tenements in the mid-nineteenth century. The rear boundaries of these plots were not contiguous throughout the length of this 'suburb', and thus two distinct blocks of additional planned town may be inferred (groups C and D; Fig. 26). The farthest block, group D, may be considered first.

Prior to its demolition in 1932, this section of Newland Street was fronted on the south by a large seventeenth and eighteenth-century house, known as The Grove, and on the north by its private park. The manner in which both these components were fitted into the landscape, and particularly the boundaries around The Grove, provides circumstantial evidence for the continuation of the medieval planned town as far as the very end of Newland Street (where it was apparently crossed by a medieval lane). The local topography strongly supports the hypothesis that The Grove was built upon a part of the town that had either been abandoned, or where the tenement plots had never been fully taken up. Moreover, it can be no coincidence that the first field beyond the medieval cross-lane was known as Town End Field.[132]

Thus the full linear extent of the planned medieval

town, in its third phase, would have been in the order of 1150 m, of which block D occupied 325 m. There is clear evidence for a back lane on the south-east side of Newland Street, and slight circumstantial evidence for one on the opposite side (Fig. 47C). One of these lanes was called 'le Backside' in 1608.[133] The depth of the burgages appears to have been 85 m, or 17 rods, and the few surviving lateral divisions suggest that the plots may have been very much larger here than in block B. While there are some frontages of 25 m to 30 m, the major divisions on the south-east side of the street fall at 85 m intervals. Three generously measured plots of two acres each are indicated. If no subdivisions have been lost on the north-west side of Newland Street, another two-acre plot, and a three-acre one may be discerned. It is interesting to note that in the survey of *c.* 1258 three plots of two acres, and two of three acres, are mentioned (p. 89); this is the only part of the town in which such large plots occur.

The original market place would have been central to the extended town, east of the river. The enlargement represented by block D must be dated to before *c.* 1258. Since only one of the large plots was still undeveloped at that time of the survey, we may deduce that enlargement had probably taken place some years previous.

Block C lies between B and D. It was separated from B by the then entirely redundant earthwork (represented by *la Hollediche* and Lockram Lane to the north, and Maldon Road to the south of Newland Street); and it joined uneasily with block D. There can be little doubt that C was an infill-block. The rectangular site that it occupied, immediately outside the former town entrance, suggests that this may have been a suburban market.

Finally, this leaves block E on the east side of Maldon Road. Here, we find the major lateral boundaries defining three or four plots of fairly large size: slight differences occur in the depth, between 75 m and 80 m (15–16 rods). There is no hint of planned development on the west side of Maldon Road. Block E has more in common with block B, than D: chronologically, it may have fallen between the two, though the fact that it was somewhat out on a limb may point to a terminal stage of development (Fig. 47D).

Although it is impossible to calculate the number of individual plots in the town at any given moment[134] — since the processes of amalgamation and subdivision would have been continuously operative — gross areas are however calculable. Block A occupied six acres, block B fifteen or sixteen acres, block D 131/2 acres, block E 43/4 acres, and block C between three and five acres (depending on how much of this central area was still encumbered by earthworks). Thus the outside limits for the size of the medieval planned town, as a gross unit, are between 421/4 and 451/4 acres. This provides a remarkable degree of correspondence with the 441/2 acres of plots recorded in the survey of *c.* 1258 (p. 89).

From these calculations there can be no doubting that all blocks, A to E, had been laid out before the middle of the thirteenth century. Thus, in a period of about half a century Witham developed rapidly through five physical stages. Its zenith had been reached, and no further additions were made.

Witham in its earlier stages was an archetypal linear town, with no hint of a street grid, back lanes or backland development. Its plan bears favourable comparison with those of Henley-in-Arden and Chard. The latter exhibits the additional similarity of having a distinctly separate and earlier village focus centred on the parish church. Brackley is another example in this category (Aston and Bond 1976, fig. 19). The closest parallel in Essex for Witham is Brentwood, which is situated on the same road, but much nearer to London. Here, in 1221, permission was obtained to erect a chapel-of-ease for the use of the town dwellers, appendant to the parish of South Weald (Eddy and Petchey 1983, 27–8).

The medieval street frontage at Witham seems only to have been pierced at three points: the most significant was Maldon Road (Maldon Lane in 1608). This followed the line of the *Wulvesford* earthwork, entering the market place from the south. Not quite opposite, on the north, was Lockram Lane, about which little is known (it was sometimes referred to as Queen's Street, or Church Street). Evidently medieval in origin and associated with the weaving industry, it seems to have skirted the outer lip of *la Hollediche*, and led from the market place to Witham mill. The third breach in the street frontage was close to the bridge, where Mill Lane took a riverside course, not only to Witham mill, but continued on to Chipping Hill (the latter part of this line was called Guithavon Valley in the nineteenth century).

That the physical extent of Witham remained virtually unchanged between the thirteenth and the seventeenth centuries is demonstrated by a remarkably detailed survey of the manor in 1608.[135] No fewer than thirty-nine entries refer to tenements, cottages and other holdings in Newland Street, often specifying whether on the north or south side. Moreover, the areas of all but two are given: these total almost 411/2 acres. A further three properties, covering just over 11/2 acres, were recorded in Maldon Lane. The extent of Newland Witham was thus somewhat in excess of 43 acres in 1608. This figure corresponds remarkably closely with the 441/2 acres recorded in the survey of *c.* 1258, and the *c.* 42–45 acres calculated from cartographic evidence of the nineteenth century (above).

The continuing process of subdivision and amalgamation of the medieval plots may be glimpsed in 1608 from entries such as 'one tenement divided into two, and two other tenements newly built'. The complete plot size was only half an acre, presumably one of the original medieval 'halfacres', but it now supported four tenements. Another entry — mentioning 'greens and le backside' — evidently referred to some of the larger, and then unihabited, plots at the north-east end of the town. The area given, 6½ acres, was probably an allusion to two three-acre plots, and a 'halfacre'. This must either have been the site upon which The Grove was built later in the seventeenth

century, or, more likely, the last three plots on the opposite (north-west) side of Newland Street.

MILLS *(Fig. 48)*

Medieval Witham was well endowed with mills, but there are considerable difficulties in disentangling both

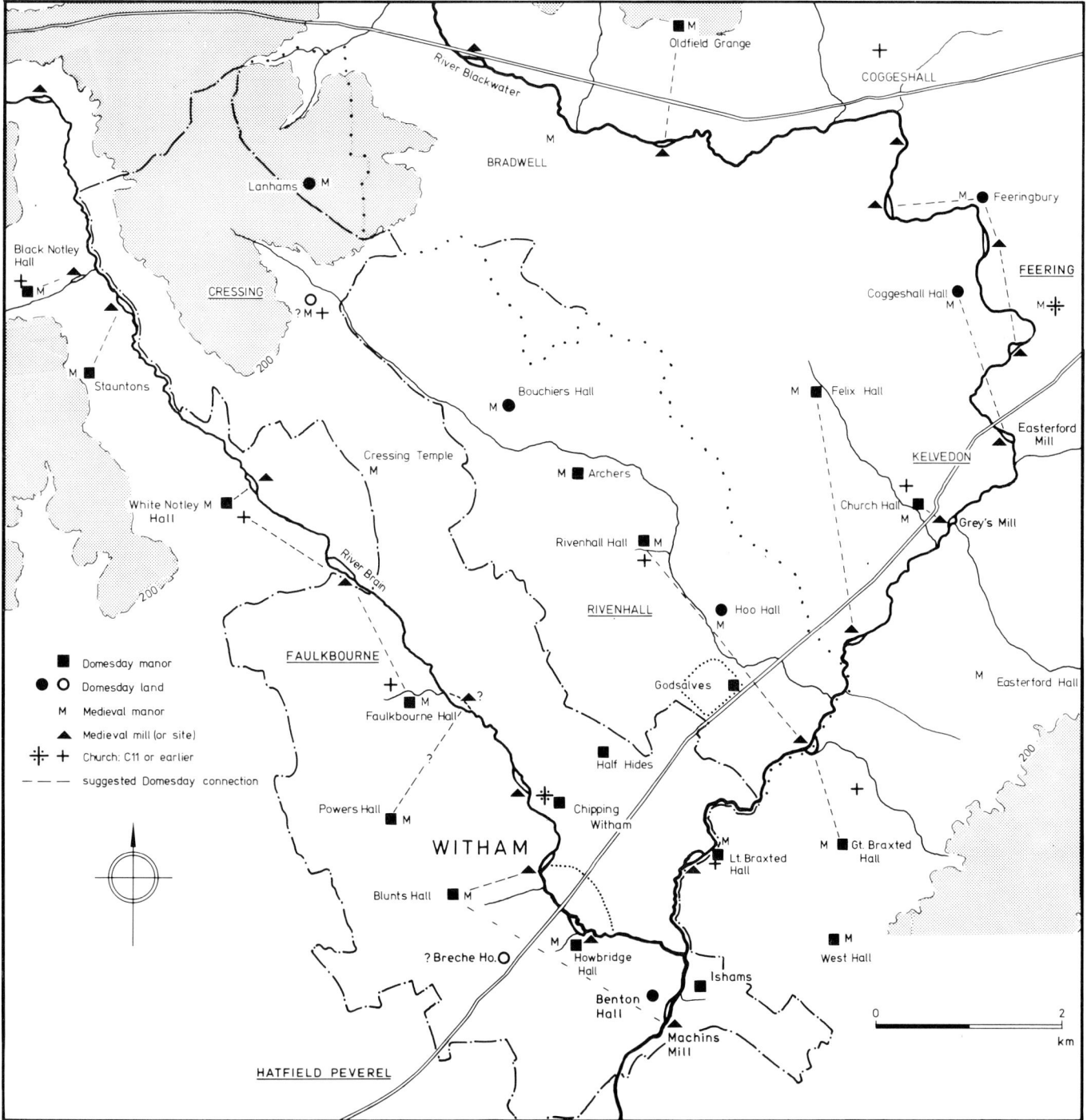

Fig. 48. *Map showing the locations of Domesday manors and other land holdings in the Witham area. The connection between these holdings and mills on the rivers Blackwater and Brain are indicated. The full extent of the combined parishes of Witham, Faulkbourne and Cressing is marked with a chain line, and the parish of Rivenhall with a dotted line.*

the identities and histories of the individual sites. While the Essex Domesday surveyors showed no interest in markets, and little in churches, they assiduously recorded mills: a prodigious number lay in the valleys of the Blackwater and Brain. Since most of these are also known from medieval references, and their leats have survived as topographical features into modern times, a near-complete picture of the eleventh-century exploitation of the two rivers can be assembled (Rodwell and Rodwell 1985, fig. 123).

No fewer than five mills recorded in Domesday lay within the medieval parish of Witham, and one in Faulkbourne (Fig. 43). Witham (alias Newland) mill was at the centre, inside the *Wulvesford* earthwork. Upstream, and just west of the church, lay Chipping Hill mill. Further upstream, just south-east of Faulkbourne Hall, the pattern of boundaries suggests the site of another mill, long since disappeared. This could have been Witham Parva (Powers Hall) mill.[136]

Downstream from Witham, and the last on the Brain, was Howbridge Hall mill.[137] Then, on the Blackwater, adjacent to Bennington (Benton) Hall lay another mill, known more recently as Blue mills or Machin's mill. Logically, this should be equated with the Domesday mill of Bennington, which the survey tells us was acquired, or built, between 1066 and 1086. Another problem arises, however, in that the larger of the two manors of Blunt's Hall also possessed a mill, and a charter of 1425 explicitly equates this with Machin's mill.[138] It is very unlikely that the streamlet which rises near Blunt's Hall and flows eastward into the Brain could ever have supported a mill, and nor is there any field evidence for one. Since there was meadow in the Blackwater valley (adjoining Machin's Mill) belonging to Blunt's Hall in late medieval and more recent times, it is entirely reasonable to seek the manorial mill thereabouts.

If Machin's mill had always been the property of Blunt's Hall manor, it would leave Bennington without a mill. There are several possible solutions to the dilemma. First, one of the sites may have included a double mill, or a shared mill that was incorrectly recorded in Domesday. The configuration of leats at Chipping Hill could possibly be interpreted as having supported two mills, but the efficacy of such a system is questionable. On the suggestion of a shared mill, it is worth recalling the arrangement at Rivenhall reported in Domesday: between 1066 and 1086 it lost half a mill to Great Braxted (Round 1903, 379). A further contemporary example would appear to be the loss of Faulkbourne mill to White Notley. Yet another explanation is that Blunt's Hall mill was not on or adjacent to the manorial lands, but at some distance, and not on a site that has supported a mill in recent times. The area around the confluence of the Brain and Blackwater might bear closer inspection.

There is, however, a further potential solution to the problem which commends itself in the particular circumstances obtaining at Witham in the twelfth and thirteenth centuries, namely that further (undocumented) transfers of mill ownership took place. The manor of Chipping Witham possessed only one mill in the eleventh century: that was presumably Chipping Hill mill. This would have had to provide the full milling capacity for the Knights Templar both at Witham and at Cressing (where there were no mills). As the Templars expanded their holdings, and particularly in consequence of the foundation of the town of Newland Witham, the need for further mills would have become overwhelming. This would have provided the context for the construction or, more likely, acquisition of Newland mill.

The location of Newland mill, close to Blunt's Hall and adjoining its manorial lands, makes it the obvious candidate for the Domesday mill under that name. But selling its mill to the Templars would have left Blunt's Hall without a manorial mill, and that in turn provides an explanation for the acquisition of Machin's mill on the Blackwater, as a substitute. Benton Hall, beside which the mill stood, was a modest holding in the eleventh century, which had not aspired to manorial status, and which evidently fell into decline (p. 52). Thus Machin's mill and a large tract of meadow (re-named Blunt's Mead) was acquired, by Blunt's Hall manor. This solution fits all the recorded facts and does not require the loss of hypothetical mills for which there is no field evidence.

Some Post-Medieval Developments

It is not proposed here to explore the post-medieval history of Witham, beyond mentioning those developments that impinged upon the principal areas of earlier archaeological importance. Whatever the motivation to defend the ancient centre at Chipping Hill in the twelfth and thirteenth centuries, the need receded. The site, and with it the manor of Witham, passed from the Knights Templar to the Knights Hospitaller, and upon the suppression of the latter reverted to the Crown in 1540. In the reign of Charles I the joint manor of Witham and Newland was sold to Henry Smith (alias Neville), the new lay owner of Cressing Temple. The ancient site of Witham manor house, at the centre of Chipping Hill Camp, was marked by Temple Farm until 1882, when it was lotted and sold for building development. The house alone remains, now called The Grange.

The Grove and The Avenue (Figs. 26 and 49)

Meanwhile, in the late seventeenth century, The Grove was built in Newland Street by Robert Barwell, a wealthy industrialist who manufactured baize. With the house, he laid out a park that straddled Newland Street. North-west of the road, and directly opposite the front of the house, a stately avenue of limes was planted, leading towards Chipping Hill and the parish church. Where the avenue crossed the outer defences of the camp a landscaping operation was carried out, and that was the phase of earthwork destruction to which Morant (1768, 106) alluded (Fig. 4B). It is interesting that the avenue, although well established by 1839, and possibly perpetuating a much more ancient land boundary, was entirely omitted from the Tithe map.[139] It was, however, depicted in 1777 on Chapman and André's map of

Fig. 49. Postcard view (pre-1914) along The Avenue, from Chipping Hill towards The Grove. (Reproduced by courtesy of the Essex Record Office).

Essex; and was still a sufficiently notable feature of Witham in the early years of the present century to merit publication as a postcard view (Fig. 49). The limes that appear in the photographic record were certainly not seventeenth century, and it may be deduced that the avenue was replanted in the early nineteenth century. The present road called The Avenue is now unrecognisable as a historic feature, being suburban housing of the 1930s; the limes were felled about thirty years ago.

Witham Lodge and Ivy Chimneys

Another, very modest, park was created towards the middle of the nineteenth century around White Gate Farm, which was later pretentiously renamed — in keeping with its new-found status — Witham Lodge. The farm was almost certainly an eighteenth-century creation (before 1777), and was rebuilt as the Lodge about 1812, or very soon after.[140] The new sinuous drive to Witham Lodge was laid, doubtless intentionally, to follow the local contour created by the west corner of the Iron Age earthwork (Fig. 29). Cartographic evidence indciates a date for the drive between 1799 and 1812. Farming activities were removed before 1839 to a new site, Lodge Farm, on the edge of the park. The act of emparkment resulted in further levelling of the Iron Age earthworks, although they were already substantially degraded by the early nineteenth century.

Finally, there are hints on the Witham Tithe map that a more-or-less equally spaced series of long and narrow plots had been laid out on the north-west side of Hatfield Road, sometime before emparkment took place around Witham Lodge. Although the area had been divorced from Blunt's Hall by this time, there are marginal indications on the estate map of 1812 that the plot system was already in existence. The plots were individually defined by banks and ditches, two of which were sectioned during the 1971 excavation. They were assigned on archaeological grounds to the eighteenth or early nineteenth century. Further evidence for the detailed layout is reflected in the arrangement of boundaries shown on the 1874 Ordnance Survey map. Other, ordered field and plot layouts can be seen in the vicity of Blunt's Hall and Cupper's Farm (Fig. 50).

The grouping of plots along Hatfield Road with similar dimensions demonstrates that this was not a haphazard act of enclosure for agricultural purposes, but was another planned phase of Witham's suburban extension, beginning at Duck End (Bridge Street) and ending at White Gate Farm. The plots averaged 4 acres (1.6 ha) in size, and had a frontage of 250 feet (76 m). A common rear boundary appears to have been envisaged, but this has been partly lost through plot extensions. Although undocumented, this was almost certainly a late eighteenth-century speculation by a landowner who hoped to sell off individual plots for the erection of spacious Georgian houses on the western fringe of the town. In the event, none was built.

Several plots at the north-east end of the layout were subsequently occupied by the Union Workhouse (later Hospital), built in 1839. The only property that superficially appears to occupy one of these plots is Ivy Chimneys, but the present house dates from the sixteenth century. The plot system was evidently laid out with respect to it, and indeed perhaps by its then owner. The house and its gardens are shown in similar form on maps of 1777, 1799 and 1839, and the origins of the property have been discussed on p. 63. The sale particulars of 1803 do not refer to potential building plots, and the loss of the accompanying map precludes direct comparison with the Tithe map.[141]

The surviving post-medieval buildings of Witham have been generally discussed by Wadhams (1972), and described in various local publications.

Witham: An Archaeological Perspective

In conclusion, it may reasonably be claimed that the development of Witham is a substantially more complex subject than it appeared to antiquaries in the eighteenth and nineteenth centuries, to Wheeler and Cottrill in the 1930s, and even to scholars in the 1960s. Effectively, only a single question was being asked of the archaeology of Witham: was Chipping Hill Camp the site of Edward the Elder's *burh*? To try to answer an explicit historical question with a minute amount of archaeological evidence from a single site is at best a dangerous pursuit. Moreover, twenty or so years ago, when Chipping Hill was thought to be the *only* site of importance in the area, such an approach did not seem unreasonable. Now, however, as a result of excavation, historical research, topographical study and landscape analysis in Witham and the adjoining parishes, an entirely new perspective has been gained.

No longer can the construction of a *burh* in 912 be considered as the principal event in Witham's formative history: set against a background of three millennia of intensive and diverse activity, it was but a small episode. When Cottrill began excavations a little over half a century ago, there was no indication of a Late Bronze Age and Middle Iron Age plateau fort at Chipping Hill, or of the settlement and Late Iron Age earthworks at Witham Lodge, let alone of an extensive and orderly system of prehistoric tracks and fields; there was no suggestion of a Roman villa on the river terrace, and the Roman pagan and early Christian cult-centre at Ivy Chimneys was unsuspected; the geography of the royal vill and minster church centred on Witham had not been explored; the Burgate Field enclosure lay undetected, along with the major earthwork at *Wulvesford*; the records of the Knights Templar were

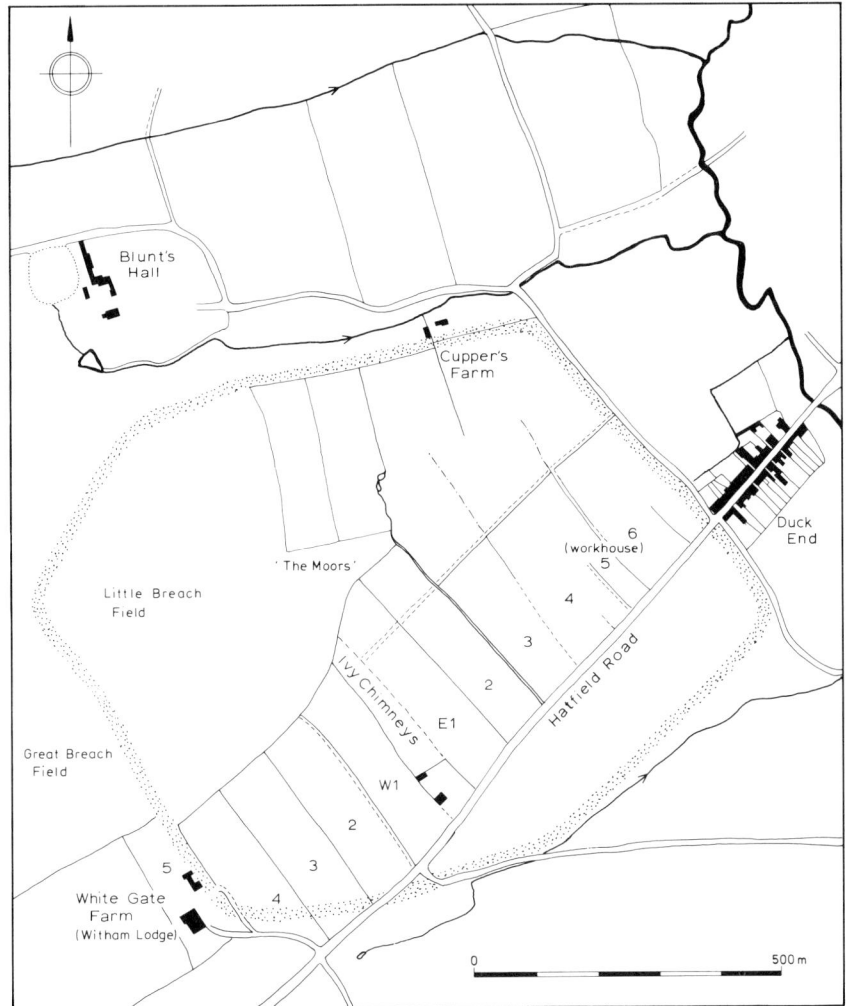

Fig. 50. *Plan showing a regular series of undeveloped post-medieval plots laid out between Witham Lodge and Bridge Street (Duck End), and based upon Ivy Chimneys. Other early modern land divisions related to Blunt's Hall and Cupper's Farm are indicated. The probable outline of the Witham Lodge Iron Age earthwork is indicated by stippling.*

then unpublished, and the inter-related processes concerning their tenure of Witham manor, and the foundation of their new town and market, were scarcely matters of contemporary concern to archaeologists; and no idea was entertained that undocumented medieval fortifications might be found at Chipping Hill and Blunt's Hall. The history of Witham must now be viewed as an amalgam of all these, and perhaps more.

13

Appendix: Specialist Reports and Excavated Finds from Chipping Hill Camp

Finds from the Railway Cutting, 1844

LA TÈNE IRON POKERS *(Fig. 51)*

The only surviving finds from the construction of the railway are three iron objects, now identified as fire pokers of the La Tène II-III period (p. 10). They are in the Chelmsford and Essex Museum (Accn. no. N.22208).

The Witham pokers have been described in detail elsewhere, and discussed in the context of the class of objects to which they belong (Rodwell 1976c). A brief description will suffice here.

Poker 1. This is the most complete and best preserved poker, and has an overall length of 1.024 m. It is wrought from a single bar and comprises a shaft of circular section, *c.* 16 mm in diameter; one end has been flattened and expanded to form a shoulder and blade 24.5 cm in length. The blade has a maximum width of 4.5 cm at the shoulder, from which the sides taper slightly, terminating in a well rounded tip. The blade is rectangular in cross-section, and the longitudinal section shows the two faces to be parallel for most of their length, but tapering to a wedge shaped tip. The rectangular neck joins to the blade with slightly concave shoulders.

There is a hint that the end of the shaft was drawn out to a square, tapering point, for the attachment of a pommel. Close to the point are the remains of a circular iron ferrule, and there is another mid-way along the shaft. There can be little doubt that these ferrules were intended to secure a binding of organic material which provided both a grip and insulation against conducted heat.

Pokers 2 and 3. These are both in a poor state of preservation, but it is clear that they were virtually identical to no. 1, the only discernible difference being the slightly shorter blade in relation to the length of the shaft. There can be little doubt that the three pokers were the product of a single workshop, and were buried as a 'set', or hoard.

Finds from the Excavations of 1933–35

The primary purpose of the Chipping Hill excavations was to obtain a selection of artifacts from a supposedly well-dated later Anglo-Saxon site, and when hand-made pottery with grass-marked surfaces came to light it was believed to be relevant to that quest (Cottrill 1934). At the time, virtually nothing was known about Anglo-Saxon pottery in Essex, a few pieces from the pagan period excepted. Equally, knowledge of the pre-Belgic Iron Age in the area was very scant. While pottery of the Early Pre-Roman Iron Age was recognisable, the successive ceramic phase had not as yet been identified. It was material of this period — the Middle Iron Age — that constituted the bulk of the pottery from Witham. Had the assemblage been fully published at the time it would have made a valuable contribution to Iron Age studies: instead, it has remained in obscurity.

The recognition of Middle Iron Age pottery as a locally distinctive type came only with the excavations at Ardleigh (Erith and Holbert 1970), although dating was still a matter for guesswork. The situation changed dramatically with the discovery and excavation of the Middle Iron Age village at Little Waltham in 1970–71, and pottery of this period was finally set into a wider chronological framework (Drury 1978). Similarities between the pottery from Witham and that from Little Waltham are so close that comparisons with the latter are cited wherever possible.

The original catalogue of finds and most of the material itself have been lost (p. 12): listing of the pottery in 1933 alone reached at least 292 sherds. Only thirty items in all are now extant. About half of the pottery drawings included in this report were prepared in the 1930s by Cottrill (and two drawings are by G.C. Dunning): they now constitute the sole record of some of the more complete vessels.

The small finds, which included coins, bronze, iron and bone objects, are all lost. Two of the restored Iron Age pots have been located in the collections of the Institute of Archaeology, London, where they were used

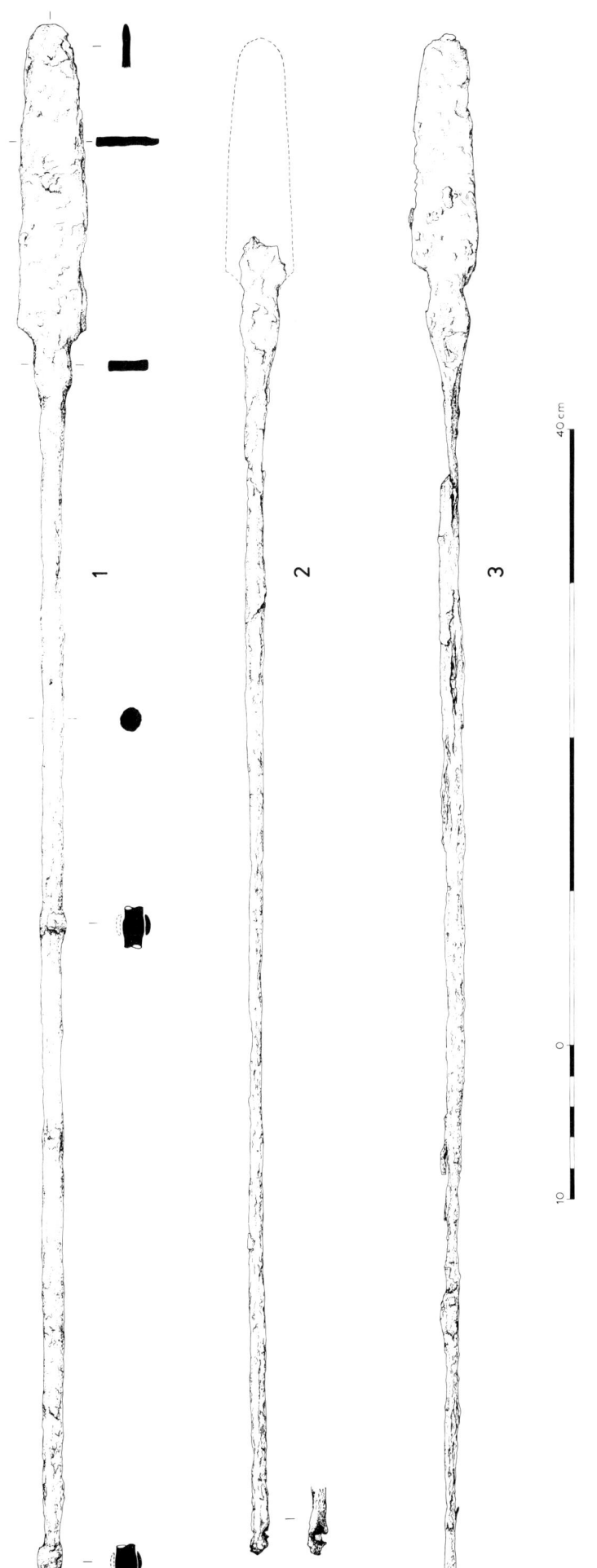

Fig. 51. La Tène II-III iron fire pokers from the railway cutting at Chipping Hill, 1844. Scale 1:4.

as teaching exhibits by Wheeler. Otherwise, the surviving material is in the Colchester and Essex Museum; this mainly comprises small pieces of Iron Age pottery that were, until 1973, in the custody of the late Professor C.F.C. Hawkes at the Institute of Archaeology, Oxford.

IRON AGE POTTERY *(Figs. 52 and 53)*
(All, except nos. 2 and 3, drawn by F. Cottrill)

Fine Wares

1. Pear-shaped jar with upright rim and beaded base; a contemporary note adds, 'a cross scored

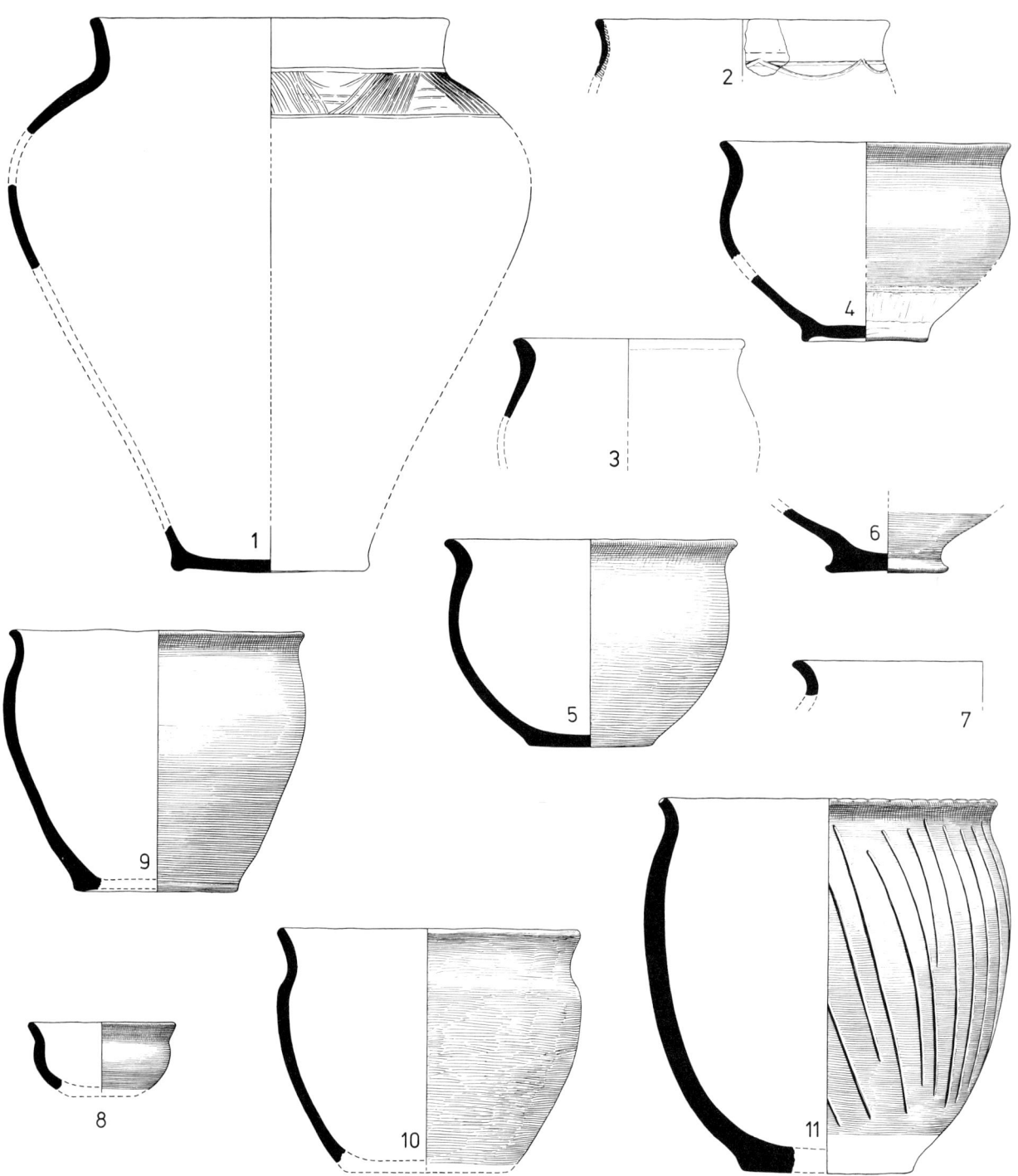

Fig. 52. Pottery from the 1933 excavations at Chipping Hill: Iron Age. Scale 1:4.

on the base: cf. pottery from The Caburn, Sussex'. Presumably this vessel was a grey or black fine ware with a highly burnished exterior, having a reserved zone on the shoulder bearing the burnished or lightly scored band of linear decoration. This comprises obliquely set groups of parallel lines with plain triangles between; in one triangle there appear to be traces of a simple swag. No local parallel can be cited for this unusual vessel. The form occurs amongst the curvilinear-decorated pottery from Canewdon (Pollitt 1953, pl. XX.2); and a large basal cross is a common feature of Thames-side footring bowls (cf. Drury and Rodwell 1973, fig. 14.34). The upright rim, high shoulder and decoration are, however, most closely paralleled on vessels from Sussex (eg. Cunliffe 1978, fig. A:32.3, 5). A particularly close comparison for the upper part exists in a vessel from Allen's Pit, Oxon., although this has the addition of lug-handles; the suggested date is fifth to third century B.C. (Cunliffe 1978, fig. A:9.10). Trench H, not extant.

2. Flared rim of a bowl or jar, with badly flaked internal surface. Very fine, medium brown fabric containing occasional lumps of calcined flint (Little Waltham fabric C); burnished, dense black exterior. The shoulder is decorated with a horizontal line and other fragmentary features, perhaps shallow swags, as reconstructed. These were scored with a blunt instrument, after burnishing. Too little survives to reconstruct either the vessel form or the decorative scheme, but there can be little doubt that this is a further example in the diverse series of curvilinear styles found in Essex (cf. Elsdon 1975, fig. 3). For shallow swags cf. Hunsbury, Northants.: Cunliffe 1978, fig. A:21.5, 6). Trench H: Cottrill cat. 149.

3. Flaring rim of a bowl in fine, dark grey ware tempered with a little fine white sand; surfaces heavily abraded and (now) light grey in colour. The rim form is distinctive and is normally associated with burnished footring-bowls of Little Waltham form 13 (cf. Drury and Rodwell 1973, fig. 14.38), and with pear-shaped jars such as that from Canvey Island, decorated with curvilinear ornament (*ibid.* fig 14.45). The fabric is probably a good copy of Little Waltham fabric A. Trench H.

4. Footring bowl with flared rim: Little Waltham form 13. The feint vertical markings on the lower part of the body are typically found on the best vessels in this fine ware series, which are invariably in a black, well burnished fabric (Little Waltham fabric A). Trench H, not extant.

5. Wide-mouthed bowl, almost complete but in fragments; restored. Dense, soft black fabric containing some fine sand, and a few larger grains up to 2 mm across; small surface lacunae, possibly resulting from dissolved out, finely crushed shell tempering. Surfaces brown to grey, with slight traces of burnishing on the exterior; heavily burnt. This vessel, although possibly only a semi-fine ware, belongs to the same bowl series as nos. 3 and 4, and is representative of the type which lacks a footring (cf. Drury 1978, fig. 48.203). Trench H. (Coll. Institute of Archaeology, London)

6. Base of a bowl with an unusually flared foot. Presumably this is a fine-ware vessel related to no. 4, and may be an exaggerated form of a Little Waltham type (Drury 1978, fig. 48.203). Trench H. Not extant.

7. Everted rim of a large bowl. Grey-brown fabric containing much fine white sand; surfaces burnt red, but presumably once black; the exterior was well burnished. Form uncertain (cf. Little Waltham forms 11 and 13); the fabric is a good copy of Little Waltham fabric A. Trench H. Cottrill cat. 148.

8. Small cup, similar in profile to a vessel from Little Waltham (there in fabric C: Drury 1978, fig. 51.261). See also no. 2. Trench H. Not extant.

Semi-Fine Wares

9. Jar, similar to Little Waltham form 3. Presumably a semi-fine ware with black burnished exterior. Trench H, not extant.

10. Wide-mouthed bowl related to Little Waltham form 9. Probably a semi-fine ware, as no. 9. Another sherd (Cottrill cat. 127, not illustrated) from the shoulder of a vessel of similar form is in a fine textured, dense black fabric with a crudely burnished exterior. Trench H, not extant.

11. Thick walled, barrel-shaped jar with an out-turned rim and well defined base; more than half complete, and now fully restored. Medium grey fabric with black core, and reddish-brown to grey surfaces, badly burnt; tempered with fine sand and occasional lumps of flint, and possibly also some finely crushed shell, as evidenced by small surface lacunae. No indications of burnishing. The body of the vessel is decorated with deeply scored lines, and there are very small finger-tip impressions on the rim. The vessel is a hybrid between semi-fine and coarse wares, and is clearly related to a common coarse-ware series from eastern England and the Midlands (Cunliffe 1978, figs. A:13 and A:22; Matthews 1976, fig.

99, nos. 55–60; Drury 1978, fig. 42.17). Trench
H. (Coll. Institute of Archaeology, London)

12, 13   Wide-mouthed bowls with flaring rims.
          Probably of similar form and fabric to no. 10.
          Unlocated, not extant.

14.   Sherds of a simple bowl (rim now lost). Dense
          black fabric with sparse sand grains (Little
          Waltham fabric G); surfaces brown to black,
          evidently burnished both internally and
          externally. Cf. Drury 1978, figs 45.80, 47.168,
          9, etc. Trench H: Cottrill cat. 200.

Coarse Wares

15.   Rim and basal sherd of a wide-mouthed jar,
          crudely made, in grey-brown fabric tempered
          with much crushed flint. This is not closely
          datable, and may be Early or Middle Iron Age
          (cf. Drury 1978, fig. 45.80). Unlocated: Cottrill
          cat. 265–6.

16.   Rim of a jar decorated with finger-nail
          impressions: cf. no. 18. Unlocated, not extant.

17.   Rim of a bowl or jar decorated with finger-nail
          impressions: cf. no. 19. Unlocated, not extant.

18.   Several sherds of a small globular bowl with a
          mildly everted rim. Soft, dense black fabric
          containing sparse sand grains and lacunae
          resulting from vegetable tempering (Little
          Waltham fabric G); black and brown surfaces,
          rough textured. There are finger-nail
          impressions on top of the rim, and were it not
          for the distinctive decoration this vessel would
          pass for early Anglo-Saxon 'grass-tempered'
          ware. The type is exactly paralleled at Little
          Waltham: form 3 (Drury 1978, fig. 45.103).
          Trench H: Cottrill cat. 13.

19.   Many sherds of a small globular bowl with a
          flat-topped rim and exceptionally heavy base.
          Soft, black fabric containing some fine sand
          (Little Waltham fabric H); reddish-brown
          surfaces. The surfaces have been lightly
          smoothed, if not truly burnished. Simple finger-
          nail marking on the rim; cf. Drury 1978, fig.
          49.223. Trench H: Cottrill cat. 181–3 and 218.

20.   Basal sherds of a thick-walled jar (cf. no. 19);
          soft, black fabric with a little vegetable
          tempering (Little Waltham fabric G). Unlocated:
          Cottrill cat. 146 and 150.

21.   Basal sherd in Little Waltham fabric H; black
          exterior, well burnished; burnt. Unlocated:
          Cottrill cat. 197.

22.   Basal sherd in Little Waltham fabric H.
          Unlocated: Cottrill cat. 185.

23.   Rim sherds of a simple jar with slightly out-
          turned lip. Soft, black fabric tempered with a
          little fine sand (Little Waltham fabric H).
          Although now abraded, there are traces of

horizontal striations, possibly crude combing.
Unlocated: Cottrill cat. 19.

24.   Simple bowl: cf. no. 23. Unlocated, not extant.

25.   Clubbed rim of a large, thick-walled storage jar,
          described as being tempered with 'large flint
          grains'. It stands out from the remainder of the
          collection in both size and evident coarseness.
          Date uncertain, but likely to be of the Late
          Bronze Age or Early Iron Age. Unlocated, not
          extant.

ROMANO-BRITISH POTTERY *(Fig. 53)*

28.   Simple outcurving rim of a jar, in hard, grey
          fabric, sightly sandy; medium grey surfaces.
          Probably first century A.D. Unlocated: Cottrill
          cat. 267.

LATE ANGLO-SAXON POTTERY *(Fig. 54)*

(Nos. 29 and 30 drawn and described by G.C. Dunning)

29.   'Upper part of a large pitcher of Thetford-type
          ware, complete with three strap-handles and a
          parallel sided bridge-spout. The rim is everted,
          angular and bevelled on the inside, and there
          are two girth-grooves on the shoulder. Fine,
          sandy grey fabric with a smooth surface.' For a
          closely similar vessel cf. Rogerson and Dallas,
          1984, fig. 162.206. Despite much recent work,
          the dating of Thetford ware is still very
          imprecise: the finer wares appear to be later,
          and this vessel is unlikely to be earlier than the
          eleventh century. Trench G, upper filling of
          'hearth' pit: Fig. 12.4, F21.

30.   'Rim of a flanged bowl in dark brown to black
          shelly fabric of St Neot's ware type.' Tenth or
          eleventh century. Trench G, topsoil.

Other sherds of St Neot's type were allegedly found
in trench H, along with ninth-century coins, according
to a note by J.G. Hurst (1955, 65). However, the coins
are now known to be Celtic (see below), and since
trench H was in an area where Roman occupation is
known, the date of the pottery must be doubtful. Hurst
did not examine the material personally, and it is likely
that it belonged to a class of late Roman shell-tempered
pottery, with a superficial resemblance to St Neot's
ware, which has subsequently been identified in central
Essex (Going 1987, 10).

31.   Complete section of a small flat-based bowl,
          with a thin, flat, slightly drooping rim. No
          fabric description survives, but this vessel
          clearly belongs to the early medieval tradition.
          Possibly twelfth century. Unlocated, but
          presumably from trench G.

OBJECTS OF FIRED CLAY *(Fig. 53)*

26. Part of a clay weight — usually regarded as a loomweight — of triangular form, pierced through the corners. These weights are common in local contexts of Middle and Late Iron Age date. Trench C, pit; not extant. See also p. 111.

27. Simple ovoid lump of fired clay, rough in texture, but with no evidence for any added tempering material. It has been labelled as a sling-shot, and is comparable to the manufactured clay sling-shots from the pre-Belgic phase at Maiden Castle, Dorset (Wheeler 1943, 49; pl. XXXII B). Similar items have turned up at other hillforts, such as The Caburn,

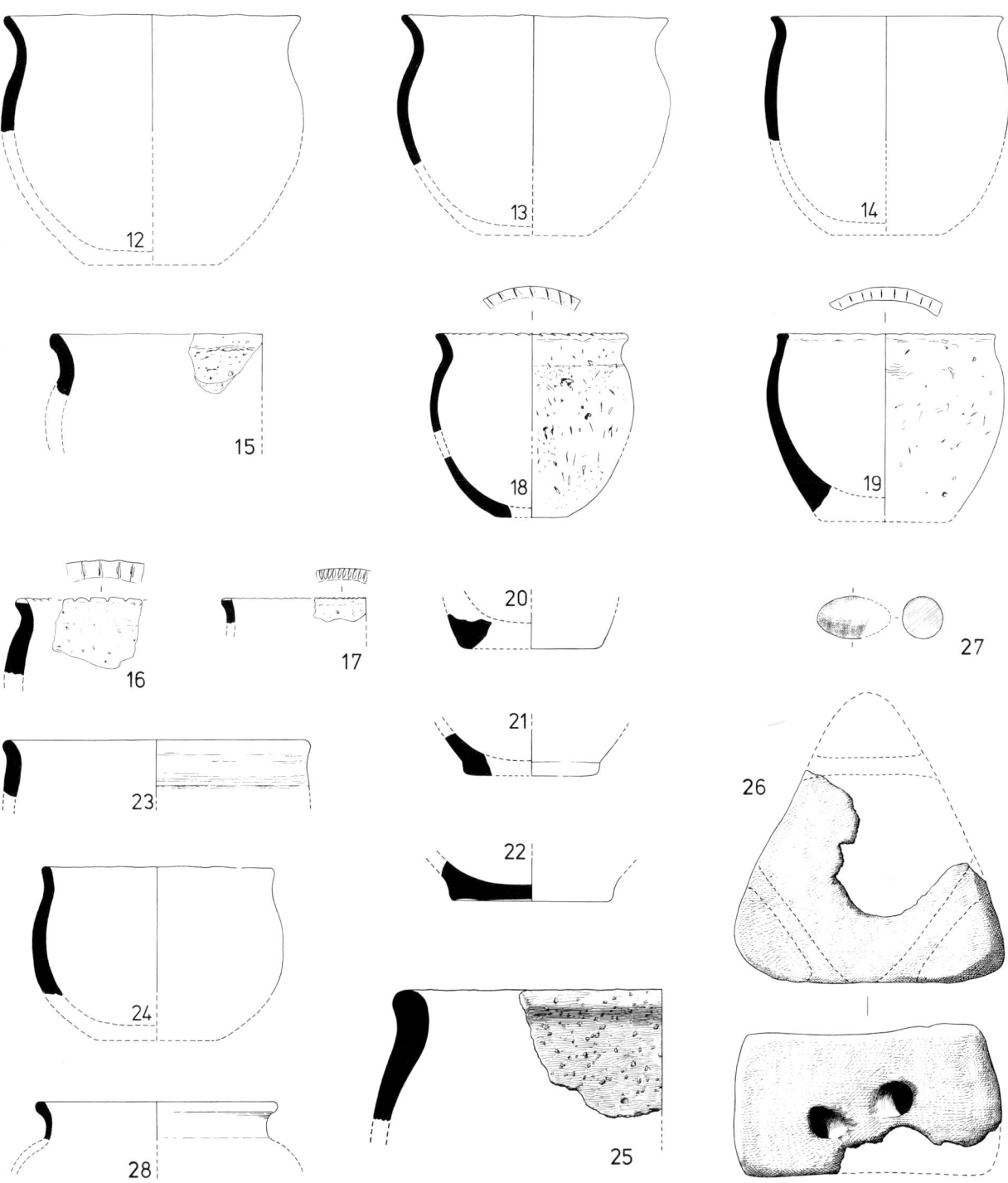

Fig. 53. *Pottery and fired clay from the 1933–35 excavations at Chipping Hill: 1–25. Iron Age pottery; 26. Fired clay loomweight; 27. Fired clay sling-shot; 28. Romano-British pottery. Scale 1:4.*

Sussex (Curwen 1929, pl. XI.46), and a good series has been published from Danebury, Hants. (Poole, in Cunliffe 1984, 398–9; fig. 7.44). Trench H, hollow.

The Witham object is of very light weight, and could hardly have been as effective a sling-shot as a rounded river pebble. It is difficult to suggest any other viable interpretation for these objects; and Wheeler noted that clay shots were rare at Maiden Castle, when compared to the number of sling-stones. Clay sling-shots have not been reported from any other Iron Age site in Essex, and it is perhaps noteworthy that they have not been found at *oppida* such as *Camulodunum* and *Verulamium*.

It would seem that manufactured shots of this type are a phenomenon of the pre-Belgic, or non-Belgic, Iron Age. At Danebury, they are firmly assignable to the first half of the first century B.C. An example found in a late Roman context at Old Winteringham, Lincs., must be regarded as residual from a much earlier, but unexplored, phase of occupation on the site (Stead 1976, fig. 123.212).

A second clay sling-shot was reported as being found at Witham, but is no longer extant.

ROMAN GLASS *(Fig. 55)*

The vessel was exhibited at the Institute of Archaeology, London, in 1938, and described as

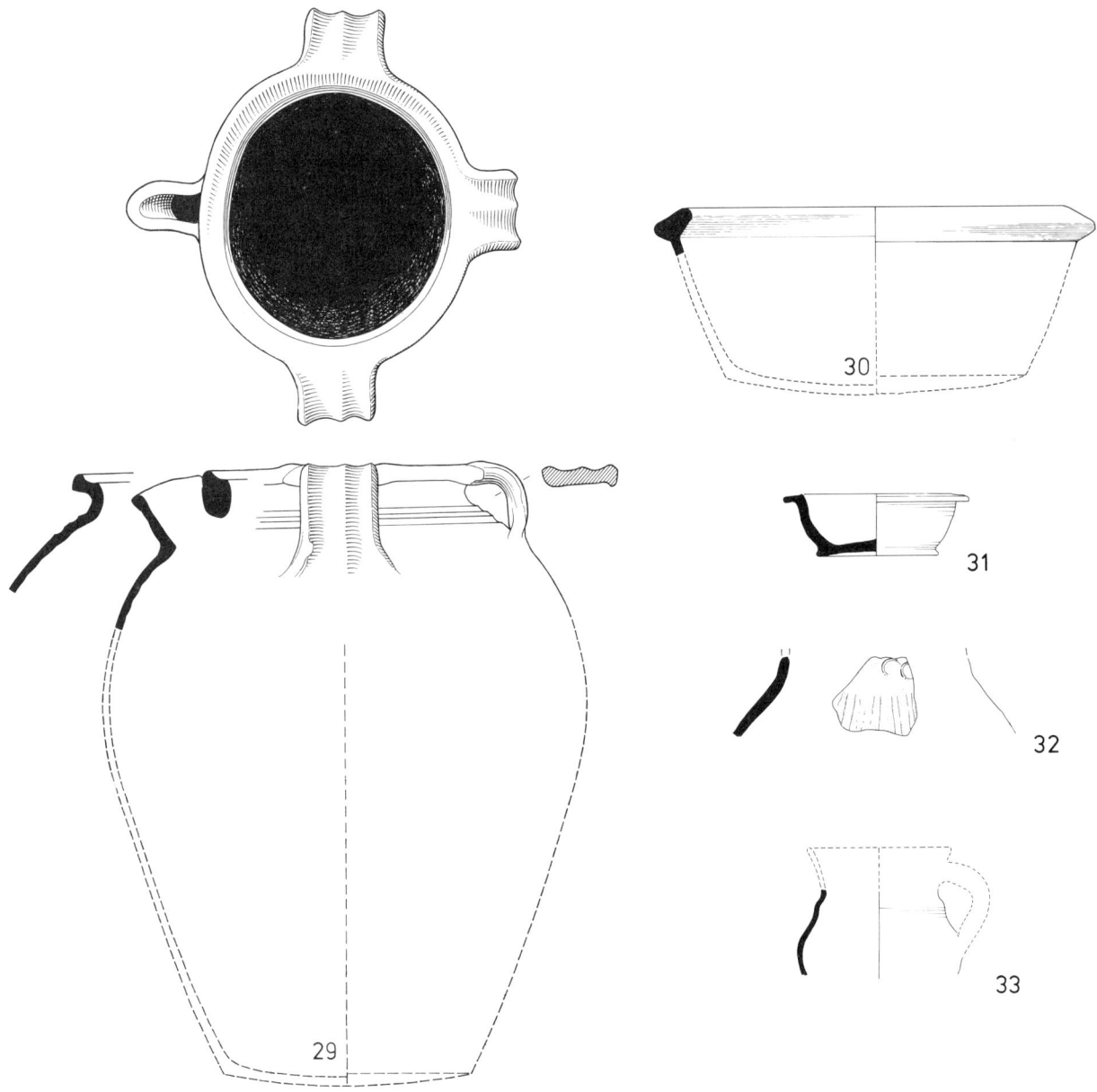

Fig. 54. Pottery from the 1933–35, 1969 and 1971 excavations at Chipping Hill:
29–31, late Saxon; 32, medieval; 33, post-medieval. Scale 1:4.

'Anglo-Saxon' in the *Catalogue of an Exhibition of Recent Archaeological Discoveries, 1933–38* (1938), p. 27. It was said to have been found 'with' the St Edmund penny. The vessel was seen in 1938, and again in 1954, by Dr D.B. Harden, who corrected the mis-identification, *in litt.* (Colchester Museum files). From trench G 'at south-west corner in yellow soil, 3 ft down'. Deposited in Colchester Museum in 1974, but could not be traced in 1990.

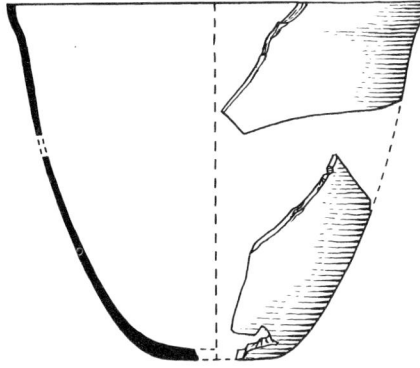

Fig. 55. Late Roman glass bowl from Chipping Hill, 1934. Scale 1:2.

There were thirteen fragments of glass in all, including the rim, side and base, of a bowl. The vessel was described in manuscript (1954) by Harden.

> Dull greenish glass: some surface frosting and dulling, no irridescence; very bubbly and many blowing spirals visible. Rim knocked off and ground, with slight constriction below; sides taper gently and curve to flattened base. No decoration.
> This bowl is of a typical fourth-century Roman shape; the thickness of the glass, the ground rim with constriction below, and the sides tapering to a flattened base, all indicate this (cf. Haberey 1942, 256, no. 4, fig. 2a, etc.). Many more references could be given, but this, which cites examples from a cemetery of the last third of the fourth century, will amply prove the point.

The vessel belongs to Isings's general category of plain hemispherical bowl, form 96, dated to the second half of the fourth century and first half of the fifth (Isings 1957, 113–14).

IRON OBJECTS *(Fig. 56)*

Various iron objects, all now lost, were found in Iron Age and later levels. The more significant items were illustrated, and although the original sheet of drawings was also lost, a photographic copy was in the hands of M.R. Petchey in *c.* 1980, but cannot now be traced (one item, no. 4 below, had been copied and redrawn by the present writer). The objects included:

1. A series of conjoined rings. It has been suggested that this object was an Iron Age tankard handle. From trench H.

2. The curving tip of a single-edged blade was described at the time of its discovery as a *scramasax*: it was evidently part of a large Iron Age knife. From trench H.

3. The looped end of an Iron Age bucket handle.

4. An equal-armed cruciform object (incomplete) which would appear to have been a mount for leather (perhaps a book cover), as evidenced by the projecting studs, or rivets, on the back face. The complete object would have measured 40 mm overall. It is likely that this is only the core, over which was once wrapped a thin covering of precious metal. There can be little doubt that the cross was Anglo-Saxon, and a contemporary note by Dunning suggested that it was 'Carolingian'. The object finds ready analogues amongst later Anglo-Saxon mounts incorporating cruciform designs, usually from sites with ecclesiastical associations. There are, for instance, both plain and ornate examples from Whitby, Yorks. One of these, a small, plain bronze cross mounted with a thin silver covering, is generally similar to the Witham find (Wilson 1964, 194, no. 113; pl. XXXIX).

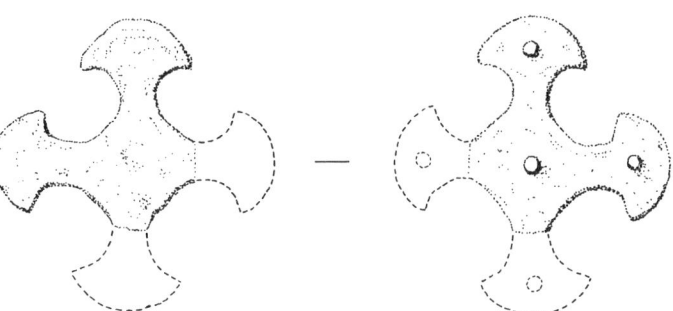

Fig. 56. Iron core of a late Saxon cruciform mount from Chipping Hill, 1934. Scale 1:1.

From trench G, in the uppermost filling of the pit (F21) that yielded the Saxo-Norman pitcher (Fig. 54.29).

BONE OBJECT

A bone comb with ring-and-dot ornament, now lost, is reported as having been found in an Iron Age pit in trench C. This was presumably a weaving comb of the usual single-ended type.

CELTIC COINS

Reports mention, variously, the finding of two, and five, potin coins of class I type in the pit or 'working hollow' in Trench H. The probable explanation here is that two coins were found in 1934, and a further three when the trench was completed in the following year (when one newspaper report mentions that four had been found). The coins are now lost, but were seen and noted by the late D.F. Allen (Allen 1971, 145). The finding of as many as five potin coins (and no other types) in a restricted area suggests that they were either buried as a small hoard, or were dispersals from a larger hoard in the vicinity; cf. the hoard of 51 coins recently recovered from an Iron Age hut gully at Stansted, Essex (Brooks 1989).

ANGLO-SAXON COIN *(Fig. 57)*

Note by Marion M. Archibald

A single silver coin, recognised at the time as a St Edmund Memorial penny, was found in the upper levels of trench G. It was seen by the late S.E. Rigold, who referred to it, *inter alia*, in Rogerson and Dallas 1984, 67. It is believed that Rigold had custody of the coin. Curiously, there is no correspondence about it in Cottrill's files, and the coin's present whereabouts is unknown. Photographs showing both the obverse and reverse, probably taken at the Institute of Archaeology, London, in the 1930s, are in Colchester Museum. The coin was evidently broken into two parts at the time of its discovery. The photographs show that it was otherwise in very good condition, with no obvious signs of wear.

The photographs were submitted to Miss M. M. Archibald, who kindly reports as follows:

'The inscriptions on the coin are:
Obv.:   +SEIMEGR (S on its back; round-backed E)
Rev.:   +AOALBERT (letters A barred)
Diameter: (based on photograph only): 19 mm

Fig. 57. Obverse and reverse of the St Edmund Memorial penny from Chipping Hill, 1934. Scale 1:1. From a photograph in the Colchester and Essex Museum).

The coin belongs to the later phase of the St Edmund Memorial issue, when the king's name has become very blundered. The moneyer's name retains greater literacy here, but shows the first stage in the devolution process in the replacement of the second letter in the moneyer's name, Adalbert, with O. The moneyer's designation has already gone from the reverse, and only the R of REX survives on the obverse.

Adalbert is one of the many Continental names found on the St Edmund coinage. He was a prolific moneyer, and no die-identity has been found in the British Museum, in the other collections published in the *Sylloge* series, or among the writer's other records. The marks on the coin's surface appear to be accidental damage rather than deliberate test-marks.

This coin is not, however, from the very end of the St Edmund coinage, but is comparable to many coins in the Cuerdale, Lancs. (1840) hoard, which was deposited in *c.* 905. Its diameter suggests that it was not even among the most recent coins in that hoard, which are on smaller flans, and are more illiterate. This coin was therefore probably struck *c.* 900. Such coins remained current in quantity until Edward the Elder reimposed Anglo-Saxon control in East Anglia during the second decade of the tenth century. Apart from stray survivors, few are present in hoards deposited after 920. Coins at this period did not however 'circulate' in the full sense, and could easily survive in virtually unworn condition for ten or more years after issue. The date bracket for this coin's deposition is therefore *c.* 900–15, earlier rather than later within the bracket being preferred.'

Another reference to finding 'ninth-century' coins in trench H (Hurst 1955, 65) is apparently erroneous. The potin coins mentioned above were mistaken in the 1930s for primitive Anglo-Saxon coinage, at a time when the former were ill-known as a class.

Finds from the Excavations of 1969 and 1971

In contrast to the prolific finds of 1933–35 in the south and west regions of Chipping Hill Camp, very few artifacts were recovered during the more recent excavations on the northern defences. These finds were limited to about thirty small sherds of pottery, and animal bones. Unfortunately, some of the better pieces of medieval pottery were lost after being loaned for an exhibition in Witham in 1971. A handlist of the remainder of the finds has been deposited with the site archive in Colchester Museum. Pottery identifications by Mr Paul Drury during the compilation of this list are gratefully acknowledged. None of the material is of intrinsic interest, and no more than a brief summary is called for here.

IRON AGE AND ROMANO-BRITISH POTTERY

A handful of small, abraded and undiagnostic fragments of Early to Middle Iron Age pottery was found in ditch fillings. A fragment of a fine-ware carinated bowl was recovered from near the bottom of the inner ditch, but is not securely stratified (trench Y, F13): *c.* fourth century B.C. A single Romano-British sherd came from the middle filling of the secondary outer ditch (trench X, F11).

ANGLO-SAXON POTTERY

A small sherd in reddish-brown, vegetable-tempered fabric with a grey core is of early Anglo-Saxon type. It has the remains of four perforations, each *c.* 4 mm in diameter, and was found in the middle filling of the outer ditch (trench X, F10). Perforated vessels of this kind, known alternatively as colanders and wool-comb warmers, have been found in fifth and sixth-century contexts in Essex.

A wired-base fragment of fine, Thetford-type ware, and another sherd in a shelly black fabric with brown surfaces, related to St Neot's ware, were found in the top of a pit or well-shaft cut into the backfilled inner ditch (trench Y, F17). Late Saxon or early medieval.

MEDIEVAL AND LATER POTTERY *(Fig. 54)*

All the positively identifiable sherds of medieval pottery from the fills of the outer ditches (trench X) date from the later twelfth and thirteenth centuries, and can be matched in the large assemblages from Chelmsford and Rivenhall (Rodwell and Rodwell 1992, forthcoming). The sherds comprised both coarse and fine unglazed wares (including products of the Mile End kilns, Colchester), and glazed jugs from the Hedingham kilns. One is capable of illustration.

32. Three sherds (and others, lost) of a jug in fine reddish-brown fabric; cream slip under green speckled glaze on exterior. Decorated with circular stamps around the neck, and vertical stripes applied *en barbotine* on the body. Hedingham ware, thirteenth century. Trench X, ditch F11, lower fill.

A few post-medieval sherds were recovered from the topsoil and one pit.

33. Body sherd of a cup of hard-fired grey fabric with brown surfaces and brown glaze both internally and externally. Probably sixteenth century. Reconstruction based on an example from Chelmsford. Trench Y, pit F14.

Specialist Reports and Finds from the Excavation of 1988

PREHISTORIC POTTERY by Nigel Brown

A small quantity of prehistoric pottery (348 sherds, weighing 2.605 kg) was recovered from the excavations. The pottery was recorded using a system devised for later prehistoric pottery (details in Archive). Fabrics present are:

Definitions
Size of inclusions   S = less than 1 mm diameter
   M = 1–2 mm diameter
   L = more than 2 mm diameter

Density of inclusions   1 = less than 6 per cm^2
   2 = 6–10 per cm2
   3 = more than 10 per cm^2

Fabrics
A Flint, S 2 well sorted
B Flint, S-M 2
C Flint, S-M 2
D Flint, S-L poorly sorted
E Flint and sand, S-M 2
F Sand, S-M, 2–3, with addition of occasional L flint
G Sand, S 3
H Sand, S 2
I Sand, S-M, 2–3
J Sand, S 2 with veg. voids particularly on surfaces
M Grog, often with some sand or flint and occasional small rounded or subangular voids
O Quartz and flint and some sand S-L poorly sorted
P Sparse very fine sand occasional M-L or sparse irregular voids
R Shell temper M-L 2, soft fabric
Z Unclassifiable

The pottery from the two excavations WH2 and WH3 is discussed together.

The earliest material present is Grooved Ware. This was largely recovered from a small feature (WH3, 107) beneath the old land surface. A few small sherds came from the old land surface itself (WH3, 5). The Grooved Ware includes sherds with grooved and impressed decoration (Fig. 58.1), incised and stabbed decoration (Fig. 58.2), and rims with both internal and external decoration (Fig. 58.3). It occurs in shell, grog and, occasionally, sand-tempered fabrics.

The pottery from the old land surface (WH3) is predominantly flint-tempered (90% by weight), and includes sherds diagnostic of the later Bronze Age. The round-toothed comb impressions on a sherd from WH2, 88 (Fig. 58.4) may be matched in Deverel-Rimbury ceramics from White Colne, Ardleigh (Erith and Longworth 1960), North Shoebury (Brown forthcoming) and Shoebury (Colchester Museum Records). A sherd from WH3, 6, with burnished surfaces seems to be derived from a Late Bronze Age carinated bowl. The upper part of a plain convex-sided jar with internally bevelled rim (Fig. 58.5), from the old land surface, is clearly appropriate to a Late Bronze Age Plain Ware assemblage (Barrett 1980). It can be matched at Broads Green (Brown 1988a) and Springfield Lyons (Brown in prep.). A sherd (Fig. 58.6) from a slot beneath the old surface (WH3, 17) is so similar in rim form, fabric and surface treatment that it seems likely to derive from the same vessel. Most of the pottery from the old land surface is largely unabraded and must have been incorporated in the deposit soon after breakage. A few flint-tempered sherds from the lower ditch fills include a small rim (Fig. 58.7), probably of Late Bronze Age date. It may be that this material derives from the old land surface through which the ditch was cut.

Most of the pottery (60% by weight), was derived from the upper ditch fills, features which cut the upper ditch, and other cut features. This material is of Middle Iron Age character; 91% by weight is sand-tempered, as is typical of such assemblages (Drury 1978; Brown 1991). Diagnostic sherds include rims of round-bodied bowls (Fig. 58.8–11), many of Little Waltham form 13 (Drury 1978, fig. 37) or variations on that form. Bases are either flat or footring. Slack-shouldered coarse jars are also present (Fig. 58.12–13). One jar rim (not illustrated) has slight finger-tip impressions on top, but the assemblage is largely undecorated. One rim sherd (Fig. 58.14) has what may be a furrowed neck, a feature which occurs in the Darmsden-Linton assemblage at Lofts Farm (Brown 1988b).

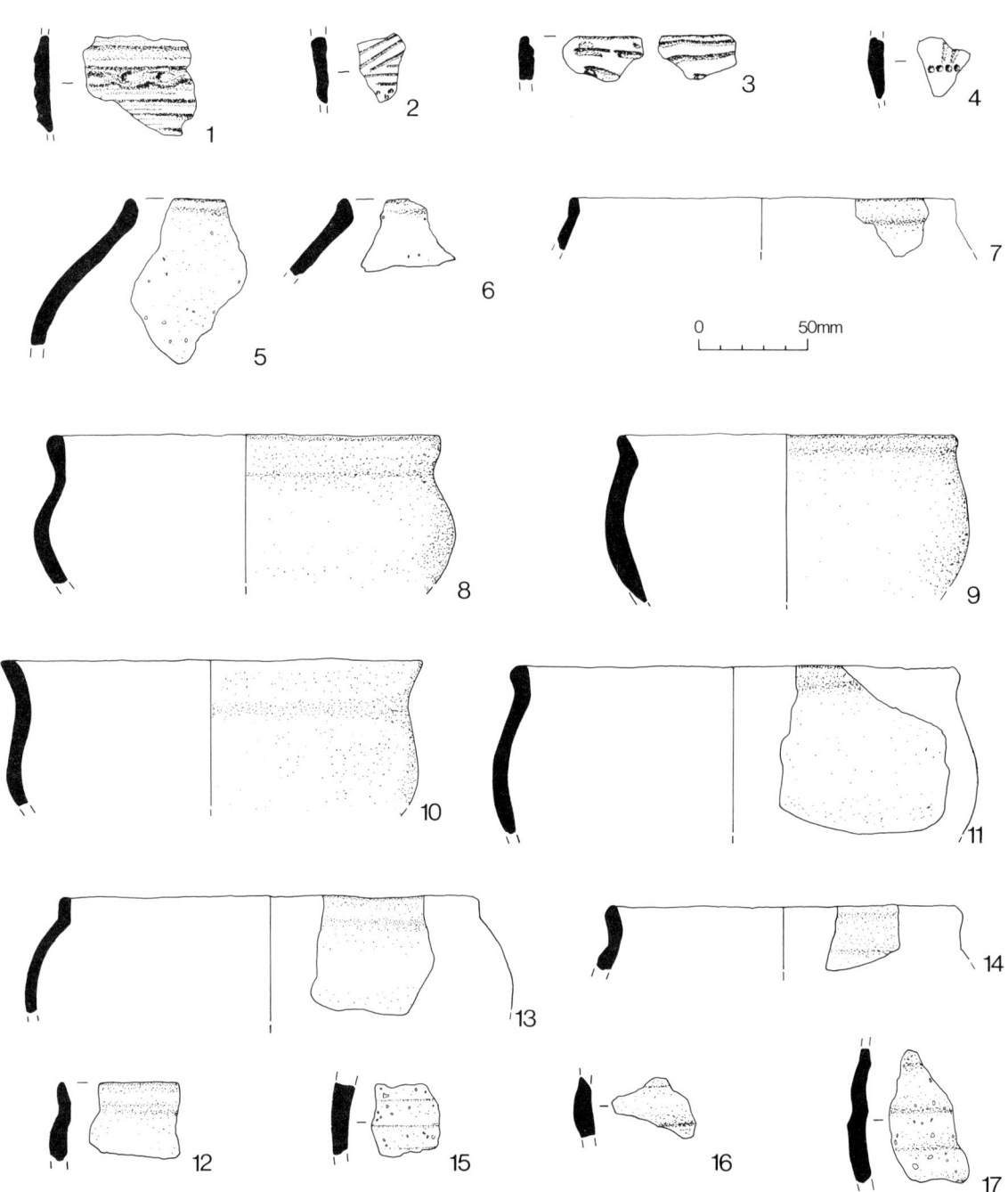

Fig. 58. Prehistoric pottery from the 1988 excavations. Scale 1:3.

Three body sherds have furrowed surfaces and/or shallow grooved lines (Fig. 58.15–17). These sherds may be paralleled in Darmsden-Linton assemblages, although they could equally belong to Middle Iron Age curvilinear decorated vessels (eg. Prittlewell; Brown 1983, and Asheldham Camp; Brown 1991).

Whilst these few decorated sherds may indicate the presence of some Early Iron Age Darmsden-Linton style

Catalogue of Illustrated Sherds

No.	Context	Fabric	Class	Description
1	WH3. 108	M	-	Horizontal grooved lines above and below row of ?fingertip impressions.
2	WH3. 108	I	-	Incised geometric decoration with two stabbed impressions below. Abraded interior.
3	WH3. 108	R	-	Upright rounded rim with internal and external grooved lines.
4	WH2. 80	D	-	Round toothed comb impressions, with part of two shallow grooved lines below.
5	WH3. 60	C	I	Sooty black deposit on neck.
6	WH3. 17	C	I	-
7	WH2. 77	B	IV	Partly abraded surface.
8	WH2. 14, 32 and 150	F	IV	Surfaces originally smoothed but damaged by burning. Little Waltham Form 13.
9	WH2. 97	J	IV	Smoothed surfaces partly abraded. Little Waltham Form 13.
10	WH2. 48			Smoothed surface partly abraded. Little Waltham Form 13.
11	WH2. 134	G	IV	Smoothed surfaces abraded. Little Wlatham Form 13.
12	WH2. 169	J	I	Damaged rim? Little Waltham Form 4.
13	WH2. 21	H	I	Little Waltham Form 4.
14	WH2. 74	H	II	Smoothed/burnished exterior, abraded interior ?furrowed neck.
15	WH2.74	C	-	Smoothed partly abraded. Shallow grooved line on exterior.
16	WH2. 74	D	-	Smoothed surfaces partly abraded. Shallow grooved line on exterior.
17	WH2. 74	D	-	Furrowed exterior.

material, most of the assemblage is typically Middle Iron Age. Although not closely datable, a range of *c*. 300–100 BC may be suggested.

Bowl forms predominate in this small assemblage and the majority of sherds (75% by weight), where such a distinction can be made, are fine wares. This may indicate ceramic refuse derived from food consumption, rather than cooking or storage. Joining sherds of one bowl (Fig. 58.8) were recorded from the upper fill of the ditch (WH2, 150), a posthole (WH2, 32) and a shallow feature (WH2, 15), possibly indicating that the features were backfilled at about the same time. Several sherds of this vessel appear to have been burnt.

IRON AGE COIN *(Fig. 59) by David Rudling*

Cast bronze 'Potin' coin, Class 1. 1.09 g. 16 mm diameter.

Obverse: Celticised head of Apollo right
Reverse: Celticised bull, charging left

0   10mm

Fig. 59. Obverse and reverse of Iron Age potin coin from Chipping Hill, 1988, site WH2. Scale 1:1. (Photo: Essex County Council).

This coin is of the angular bull variety which has recently been dated by Van Arsdell (1989, 87, No. 129–1) to 85–50 BC. The main distribution of such coins (Van Arsdell 1989, 465) indicated that they were issued by the Cantii/Kentish tribes. (From WH2 context 98, an upper fill in the hill fort ditch).

THE FLINT *by Robin Holgate*

The excavations produced 432 humanly-struck flints (Table 1) from both sites (Table 2). The bulk of the assemblage probably dates to the later Neolithic period, although some pieces are Mesolithic and possibly earlier Neolithic in date. On the whole, the flints are in mint condition and a large proportion of those from WH3 were probably *in situ*.

Raw Material. The material used for flaking mostly consisted of dark grey-brown nodular flint with occasional cream cherty patches. In one instance, a dark

grey chert nodule had been used. Cortex was present on just over two-thirds of the pieces in the assemblage, and was often relatively thin and abraded. Much of the flint was of a reasonable quality for flaking, with few flaws and incipient cracks being discernible. It is likely that most of the flint came from local river terrace gravel deposits which, in this area of Essex, are known to contain a high proportion of flint (Bridgland 1988). About 4% of the pieces in the assemblage had also acquired a blue-white patination.

Technology. The assemblage is dominated by unretouched flakes and implements produced on flakes. The majority of these flakes had been detached from cores using hard hammers; their butts were generally more than 2 mm in width; and butt edges were unabraded. One shattered piece had formed part of a hammerstone showing that, in some instances at least, flint nodules had been used as hard hammers. Of the cores, one was a small discoidal core and the other three consisted of large flakes from which some half a dozen small flakes had been detached.

About 10% of pieces had been struck from cores using soft hammers, including five blades, eight bladelets, a cutting blade and a microdenticulate which probably date to the Mesolithic period on account of their flaking characteristics. Three of the remaining soft hammer struck pieces were axe-thinning flakes of either Mesolithic or Neolithic date. The remainder of the assemblage probably post-dates the start of the later Neolithic period, although some pieces would not be out of place in an earlier Neolithic context.

Typology. Of the implements recovered during the excavations, cutting tools predominate. The cutting flakes have use wear damage on one or both lateral edges; the three knives have invasive retouch along one edge, with two of these knives also having bevelled edges on the opposing lateral edge; and the combination tool is a piercer with a lateral edge that has also been used as a cutting flake. After the cutting tools, scrapers are the next most common implement, all but one of which have abrupt retouch; the exception has invasive retouch and was produced on either an axe-thinning flake or a flake struck from a discoidal core using the Levallois technique. Combination tools and invasively retouched scrapers usually occur in later Neolithic and Beaker period assemblages in southern England (Holgate 1988, 60–1), whilst the fragmentary chisel arrowhead can also be dated to the later Neolithic period.

Conclusion. The flints recovered from the excavations show that activity of some description took place on the site during the Mesolithic period and possibly during the earlier Neolithic period as well. Most of the flints probably date to the later Neolithic period and, given the multiplicity of implements present in the assemblages, could represent part of a domestic flint assemblage associated with occupation of the site during the third millennium BC.

Table 1. The flint assemblage.

Flakes	346
Blades	27
Bladelets	9
Cores	4
Shattered pieces	4
Miscellaneous retouched pieces	8
End scrapers	6
Side scrapers	3
Cutting flakes	15
Cutting blades	1
Knives	3
Piercers	2
Microdenticulate	1
Combination tool	1
Ground flint axe flake	1
Chisel arrow head	1
TOTAL	432

Table 2. Summary of contexts producing flints.

WH2
Unstratified contexts	23
Ditch fill	33
Possible old land surface	9
TOTAL	65

WH3
Unstratified contexts	6
Old land surface	328
Features below old land surface	32
Context associated with rampart	1
TOTAL	367

SHALE BOWL *by Hilary Major*

A plain fragment from the body of a shale bowl, or other vessel, 11 mm thick, with a maximum surviving diameter of 135 mm. The surface is well-finished. From context 134, an upper ditch fill, which also contained Middle Iron Age pottery.

The production and trade of Kimmeridge shale vessels was well established by the end of the Iron Age,

although little pre-Roman shale has been found in Essex, and it must have been very much a prestige item in this area. Other shale vessels from Essex include unspecified forms from an Aylesford-type burial at Great Chesterford, excavated in the 1860s (ECC SMR PRN 4981) and, slightly later in date, a tazza from a Belgic burial at Colchester (cited in Wheeler 1943, 318).

BAKED CLAY LOOMWEIGHT *by Hilary Major*

A corner from a triangular loomweight, with a perforation 14 mm in diameter. The loomweight was 64mm thick. The fabric was fairly soft, orange-brown, with a partly reduced core, and with occasional inclusions of small pebbles. This came from context 134, an upper ditch fill, containing Middle Iron Age pottery, the shale bowl fragment (above) and the possibly ritual dump of animal bone (below). The loomweight type is common in Essex (Major 1982) and other examples have been found at Chipping Hill (Fig. 53.26) and in the Witham area. They were in use throughout the Iron Age.

ANIMAL BONE *by Owen Bedwin*

Bone and teeth were recovered only from WH2 (Saxons). In general, the gravel subsoil in the area would not have been expected to have provided suitable conditions for their survival, and the complete absence of such material from WH3 (Button Factory) reflects this.

The presence of fairly well preserved bone and teeth in WH2 indicates a far more favourable micro-environment. Two factors may be responsible; the first being the gravelly silt subsoil, less acid than the gravel in WH3, the second being the domestic debris dumped in the upper part of the ditch, contributing to better conditions for bone survival. Consequently, the fragments from WH2 were mainly in good condition, though some were rather soft, with unabraded breaks and external surfaces.

A total of 127 fragments were identified as to species; of these, 107 were from Middle Iron Age contexts, the remainder being undated but all post-Middle Iron Age. Of the 107 dated fragments, the species represented were:

Ovis (53.3%); *Bos* (20.6%); *Sus* (21.5%); *Canis* (2.8%); *Equus* (1.9%).

There was, in addition, an almost complete, articulated dog skeleton from context 134 (one of the Middle Iron Age ditch fills).

As regards interpretation, the association of the bone with Middle Iron Age pottery, charcoal and some small baked daub fragments suggests that the bone is essentially food debris, dumped in the upper part of the ditch. The assemblage, however, is not large enough to warrant generalisations about Middle Iron Age diet or economy.

The only exception to this interpretation concerns the dog skeleton already mentioned. This lay on its right side, missing only the rear left leg; its age at death was 1–2 years. Against its forelegs rested a horse skull, intact as excavated, but which shattered on lifting. From the evidence of its teeth, the horse was male, aged 4–5 years at death. Fifty centimetres from the dog's tail was the right hand half of a pig skull, split down the centre line; age at death was 1–2 years. This group seems more likely to reflect ritual activity than domestic dumping.

THE CARBONISED PLANT REMAINS
by Val Williams and Peter Murphy

INTRODUCTION

Samples were taken from the two trenches WH2 and WH3. In WH2, the ditch fills, and other discrete features, for example post-holes and distinct layers, were sampled. Contexts dated from the Late Bronze Age to Middle Iron Age. WH3 was a section through the back of the bank which revealed two well-defined buried land surfaces. These, and other discrete features, for example a linear slot, pits and post holes, were sampled. These contexts were dated from the Late Neolithic to Late Bronze Age. Plant remains were extracted from the samples by manual water flotation, collecting the flots in a 500 micron mesh sieve. The dried flots, were sorted under a binocular microscope at low power. The plant remains extracted and identified are listed on Tables 3–6. (Remains from undated contexts are listed in Tables 7 and 8, which form part of the Archive.)

CROP PLANTS

Site WH2
Cereals or chaff were recovered from all but 3 samples (88, 92, 150). *Triticum dicoccum*, (emmer), *Triticum spelta* (spelt), *Hordeum* sp. (barley) and some *Avena* sp (oats) are the main species present.

Wheats. Many grains are in poor condition and heavily distorted, but of the identifiable portion, most are elongate with many having asymmetrical cross-sections. Several are of the 'drop' form typical of emmer. A small number of shorter grains are possibly artefacts of carbonisation although there is one definite grain of a free threshing variety from context 74 (undated at present).

Emmer and spelt chaff (glume bases and spikelet forks) occurs in ten samples and in most cases emmer appears to predominate, for example in contexts 80, 119 and 154. A similar predominance of emmer was noted at the Late Bronze Age enclosure at Lofts Farm, Essex (Murphy 1988).

Barley. Most of the grains are in very poor condition and are distorted by carbonisation but a proportion of asymmetrical (lateral) grains and grains of a hulled variety were noted. Barley chaff occurs in only two samples (48 and 154) and consists of one rachis node and two awn fragments.

Oats. Oat grains, floret bases and awn fragments were only recovered from seven samples. Context 48 has three floret bases of *Avena sativa*, while context 154 has a floret base possibly of *Avena strigosa*. On all other floret bases, the articulation scars have not survived.

Site WH3
Cereals and chaff are only present in seven samples from trench WH3. The only species represented are wheat and barley.

Wheat. Grains were found only in four samples (3 from context 9, the other context 90) all from the buried land surface beneath the bank. All are in very poor condition but appear to be elongate. Chaff is very rare (one rachis internode from context 51, glume bases from context 86 and context 90 and one spikelet base from context 4). In only one case (context 90) was a tentative identification of a *Triticum dicoccum* glume base made.

Barley. Grains were recovered from four samples and no chaff was noted. All grains are in a very poor condition and only two could be identified as asymmetrical (lateral) grains.

THE WEED FLORA

Site WH2
All samples had some remains of carbonised weed seeds although in some cases (contexts 81, 88 and 92) these are only single seeds or fragments. A flora indicative of damp grassland is represented by *Montia fontana*, *Carex* sp. and *Isolepis setacea*. The predominant arable weeds are *Bromus mollis/secalinus* (especially from context 48), indeterminate large and small grasses, *Chenopodium album* and indeterminate Chenopodiaceae. The remaining weed taxa include *Stellaria media*, *Atriplex* sp., *Malva sylvestris*, *Vicia/Lathyrus Polygonum articulare*, *Polygonum persicaria/lapathifolium*, *Polygonum convolvulus*, *Rumex* sp and *Valerianella* sp. A single fragment of *Prunus spinosa* stone and a total of 9 *Corylus avellana* nutshell fragments are possibly

domestic refuse although they occur in cereal and chaff-rich deposits (contexts 13, 48 and 119) unlike samples of a similar date from Springfield Lyons, Essex (Murphy 1990) where grain and nuts and fruit appear to be mutually exclusive.

Site WH3

Although all samples contain some weed seeds, many are so poorly preserved as to only be included in an indeterminate seed category. Of the identifiable species, *Chenopodium album*, cf. *Atriplex* sp. and indeterminate Chenopodiaceae are the most common although it should be stated that all samples from WH3 were heavily contaminated with modern seeds of these species. The remaining weed taxa include *Bromus mollis/secalinus*, indeterminate grasses and grass fragments, *Silene* sp., *Stellaria media*, *Vicia/Lathyrus*, *Polygonum aviculare* and *Rumex acetosella*. *Corylus avellana* shell fragments are present in contexts 24, 51, 55, 87 but again in very small quantities, probably representative of domestic waste.

DISCUSSION

One problem encountered with the material was that eleven samples had no contextual information and are, therefore, undated. Although several of these samples contained quite rich cereal and weed assemblages (Tables 7 and 8, Archive) they will not be considered further.

LATE NEOLITHIC TO LATE BRONZE AGE
(Site WH3; Tables 3 and 4)

The features below the buried land surface in trench WH3 are of probable Late Neolithic to Late Bronze Age date. The samples produced little carbonised material

but did include occasional cereal remains and *Corylus* nutshell fragments. Assemblages of this type would not be out of place in a Late Neolithic context, but such a sparse scatter may easily represent intrusive material of a later date.

The buried land surface dated by the excavator to the Late Bronze Age or earlier, produced a similarly sparse assemblage which is not datable from its composition.

LATE BRONZE AGE AND POST LATE BRONZE AGE
(Site WH2; Table 5)

Late Bronze Age contexts were located at the base and edge of the hill fort ditch. Two samples produced very sparse assemblages and a third (context 151) produced so little as to be inconclusive. But the sample from context 48 produced comparatively abundant cereal remains, largely of wheats including emmer and spelt, but also with some barley and oats, an associated weed flora and *Corylus* nutshell fragments. There is a grain to glume base ratio of 1.6:1. The excess grain may represent a part processed batch of cereal although the possibility of differential preservation of glumes and cereals during combustion should not be dismissed. Similar emmer and spelt assemblages of Late Bronze Age date are known from other Essex sites, at Lofts Farm (Murphy 1988) and Springfield Lyons (Murphy 1990). Context 48 also contained a high proportion of weed grasses including oats, although some of the latter are of a cultivated species.

MIDDLE IRON AGE (Site WH2; Table 6)

Middle Iron Age contexts consisted of the upper ditch fills and the fills of a pit and two post-holes. Samples produced moderately large assemblages of cereals with

Table 3. Features below old land surface (Late Neolithic or Late Bronze Age or earlier) from site WH3, Chipping Hill, Witham, Essex. Carbonised remains of cereals, crop weeds, etc.

Context No.	17	24	51	55	108	121
Cereal indet. (caryopses) (a)	2	-	4 fr	-	-	-
Triticum spp. (rachis internodes)	-	-	1	-	-	-
Hordeum sp. (caryopses) (a)	1	-	-	-	-	-
Rumex acetosella agg.	-	-	-	1	-	-
Polygonaceae indet.	-	-	-	-	-	1
Corylus avellana L.	-	-	1	-	9	-
Indeterminate seeds etc.	-	8	1	1	-	1
Sample weight (kg)	1.80	5.50	4.90	5.70	3.00	2.65
% flot sorted	100	100	100	100	100	100

(a) only embryo ends counted.

wheats being predominant but also including some barley. On the evidence of the chaff fragments, emmer appears to be the main wheat represented, as with two samples (34 and 38) from contexts of this date at Asheldham Camp, Essex (Murphy, unpublished data). A weed flora, with *Corylus* nutshell fragments and a fragment of *Prunus spinosa* fruit stone, is also present although weed grasses do not appear to be so common as they were in the Late Bronze Age samples. The assemblages from contexts 80, 119 and 154 probably represent cereal processing waste with grain to glume base ratios of 1:1.8, 1:4.8 and 1:33.5 respectively, although it is not impossible that material from sources other than cereal processing has become incorporated.

Table 4. Old Land Surface below bank in WH3 (Late Bronze Age or earlier), Chipping Hill, Witham, Essex. Carbonised remains of cereals, crop weeds etc.

Context No.	4	4	9	9	9	10	10	81	81	86	87	87	90
Cereal indet.													
(caryopses) (a)	-	-	2	2	3	-	-	-	-	1	-	-	2
(spikelet fragment)	-	-	1	-	-	-	-	-	-	-	-	-	-
Triticum spp.													
(caryopses) (a)	-	-	4	1	2	-	-	-	-	-	-	-	1
(glume bases)	-	-	-	-	-	-	-	-	-	1	-	-	-
(spikelet bases)	1	-	-	-	-	-	-	-	-	-	-	-	-
Triticum dicoccum Schübl													
(glume bases)	-	-	-	-	-	-	-	-	-	-	-	-	1cf
Hordeum sp.													
(caryopses) (a)	-	-	2	-	1	-	2	-	-	-	-	-	-
Bromus mollis/secalinus													
(caryopses) (a)	-	-	-	1fr	-	-	1fr	-	-	-	-	-	-
Gramineae indet.													
(caryopses)	-	-	-	-	-	1	-	-	-	-	-	-	1cf
(culm nodes)	-	-	-	-	-	-	-	-	-	1	-	-	-
(culm base)	-	-	-	-	-	-	-	-	-	-	1	-	-
Silene sp.	-	-	-	1	-	-	-	-	-	-	-	-	-
Stellaria media (L.)Vill.	-	1	-	-	-	-	1	-	-	-	-	-	-
Chenopodium album L.	-	-	2	1	-	-	-	-	-	-	-	-	-
cf. *Atriplex* sp.	-	-	-	2	2	-	-	-	-	-	-	-	-
Chenopodiaceae indet.	-	-	-	2	3	1	-	-	-	-	-	-	2
Vicia/Lathyrus sp.													
(cotyledons)	-	-	-	-	-	-	1	-	-	-	-	-	1fr
Polygonum aviculare agg.	-	-	-	-	1	-	-	-	-	-	-	-	-
Corylus avellana L.	-	-	-	-	-	-	-	-	-	-	1	1	-
Indeterminate seeds etc.	3	-	5	4	12	4	1	4	-	2	-	-	-
Indeter. roots/rhizomes	1	-	-	-	-	-	-	-	2	-	1	-	-
Sample weight (kg)	3.00	5.30	4.30	1.80	4.70	4.10	4.00	5.00	5.30	5.10	4.40	2.70	4.60
% flot sorted	100	100	100	100	100	100	100	100	100	100	100	100	100

(a) Only embryo ends counted

Table 5. Late Bronze Age and post Late Bronze Age Contexts from site WH2, Chipping Hill, Witham, Essex.
Carbonised remains of cereals, crop weeds, etc.

Context No.		48	81	88	151
Cereal indet.	(caryopses) (a)	31	–	–	3
Triticum spp.	(caryopses) (a)	171	-	-	-
	(rachis internodes)	5	-	-	2
	(glume bases)	13	2	-	7
	(spikelet bases)	37	1	-	1
	(spikelet forks)	5+1(b)	-	-	-
Triticum dicoccum Schübl	(glume bases)	7	-	-	1
	(spikelet forks)	5	-	-	-
Triticum spelta L.	(glume bases)	9	-	-	1
	(spikelet forks)	1	-	-	-
Hordeum sp.	(caryopses) (a)	7	-	-	-
	(rachis node)	1	-	-	-
Avena sp.	(caryopses (a)	14	-	-	-
	(awn fragments)	30	-	-	1
	(floret bases)	6	-	-	-
Avena sativa	(floret bases)	3	-	-	-
Bromus mollis/secalinus	(caryopses) (a)	101	-	1fr	1
Gramineae indet.	(large & small caryopses)	16	-	-	-
Stellaria media (L.) Vill.		1	-	-	-
Caryophyllaceae indet.		1	-	-	-
Montia fontana L.		1	-	-	-
Chenopodium album L.		5	1	-	2
Vicia/Lathyrus sp.	(cotyledons)	2fr	-	-	-
Polygonum convolvulus L.		1+7fr	-	-	-
Polygonaceae indet.		1	-	-	-
Corylus avellana L.		8	-	-	-
Indeterminate seeds etc.		1	-	-	1
Sample weight (kg)		4.30	4.90	3.70	4.40
% flot sorted		25	100	100	50

(a) Only embryo ends counted
(b) Terminal spikelet fork

Table 6. Middle Iron Age and probable Middle Iron Age contexts from site WH2, Chipping Hill, Witham, Essex. Carbonised remains of cereals, crop weeds, etc.

Context No.	8	9	13	21	22	32	80	92	95	119	134	150	154
Cereal indet.													
(caryopses) (a)	1	-	7	1	1	2	13	-	4	6	-	–	4
(awn fragments)	1	-	-	-	-	-	-	-	-	-	-	-	5
(rachis internodes)	-	-	-	-	-	-	-	-	-	1	-	-	-
Triticum spp.													
(caryopses) (a)	4	1	33	2	-	3	9	-	4	7	-	-	-
(awn fragments)	-	-	-	-	-	-	1	-	-	-	-	-	-
(rachis internodes)	-	-	-	-	-	-	4	-	-	1	2	-	20
(glume bases)	4	-	1	-	-	3	15	-	1	24	5	-	88
(spikelet bases)	1	-	1	-	-	1	4	-	-	4	2	-	4
Triticum dicoccum Schübl.													
(glume bases)	1	-	2	-	-	-	9	-	1	19	2	-	24
(spikelet forks)	1	-	3	-	1cf	-	1	-	-	5	-	-	4
Triticum spelta L.													
(glume bases)	-	-	1	-	-	-	2	-	-	1	1	-	4
(spikelet forks)	-	-	1	-	1(c)	-	2	-	-	-	-	-	1
Hordeum sp.													
(caryopses) (a)	-	-	11	1	-	-	5	-	1	2	-	-	1
(awn fragments)	-	-	-	-	-	-	-	-	-	-	-	-	2
Avena sp.													
(caryopses)	-	-	3	-	-	1	4	-	-	2	-	-	-
(awn fragments)	-	-	-	-	-	-	1	-	-	-	-	-	1
(floret bases)	-	-	1	-	-	-	2	-	-	-	-	-	4
cf. *Avena strigosa*													
(floret bases)	-	-	-	-	-	-	-	-	-	-	-	-	1
cf. *Brassica* sp.	-	-	1(b)	-	-	-	-	-	-	-	-	-	-
Bromus mollis/secalinus													
(caryopses) (a)	2fr	-	3	1	-	3fr	3	-	3fr	3	2	1fr	3
Gramineae indet.													
(large & small caryopses)	3	4	5	3	1	3	-	-	2	1	2	5	1
(culm nodes)	1	-	1	-	-	-	-	-	-	-	-	-	-
Stellaria media (L) Vill.	-	-	-	-	-	-	1	-	-	-	-	3	-
Stellaria sp.	-	-	-	-	-	1	-	-	-	-	-	-	-
Montia fontana L.	-	1	1	-	1	-	1	-	-	-	-	-	-
Chenopodium album L.	1	10	62	2	2	8	4	1	17	53	3	4	23
Atriplex sp.	-	-	1	-	-	-	-	-	1	-	-	-	-
Chenopodiaceae indet.	5	3	13	2	2	6	2	-	10	20	-	1	11
Malva sylvestris L.	-	-	1	-	-	-	-	-	-	-	-	-	-
Vicia/Lathyrus sp. (cotyledons)	2	-	-	-	-	1	-	-	-	-	-	-	1
Prunus spinosa L.	-	-	1fr	-	-	-	-	-	-	-	-	-	-
Polygonum aviculare agg.	-	-	1	-	-	-	-	-	-	-	-	-	-
Polygonum persicaria/lapathifolia	-	-	1	-	-	-	-	-	2	-	-	-	-
Polygonum convolvulus L.	-	-	-	-	-	-	-	-	-	1fr	-	-	1+11fr
Rumex sp.	-	-	-	-	-	-	-	-	1	1	-	-	-
Polygonaceae indet.	-	1	1	-	-	1+1fr	1	-	-	1	-	-	-
Corylus avellana L.	-	-	-	-	-	-	-	-	-	1	-	-	-
Valerianella sp.	-	-	-	-	-	-	-	-	-	-	-	-	1
Isolepis setacea (L.)R.Br.	-	-	-	-	-	-	-	-	-	-	-	1	-
Carex sp.	-	-	1	-	-	-	-	-	-	-	-	-	-
Indeterminate seeds etc.	7	2	8	1	3	7	4	1	3	6	-	8	13
Indeterminate buds	-	1	-	-	-	-	-	-	-	-	-	-	-
Indeterminate thorns	-	-	-	1	-	-	-	-	-	-	-	-	-
Sample weight (kg)	5.30	4.50	3.75	3.80	5.00	4.10	1.80	0.74	4.20	3.50	4.00	1.30	4.80
% flot sorted	50	50	25	50	50	50	50	100	100	50	25	50	12.5

(a) only embryo ends counted

(b) testa frag.

(c) spikelet base

MICROMORPHOLOGICAL ANALYSIS OF
THE TWO BURIED SOILS FROM WH3
by C. A. I. French

INTRODUCTION

A thin buried soil (the primary buried soil, context 38) was sampled in two places for soil micromorphology (described as profiles A and B, below). In addition, the secondary buried soil (context 35) was also sampled (described below as profile C).

All three samples were impregnated with crystic resin, and described in thin section after Bullock *et al.* (1985a; 1985b). The results are discussed in two sections, with the detailed soil micromorphological descriptions, and the photographic record included in the Archive, as Appendices 1 and 2 respectively.

THE LATE BRONZE AGE BURIED SOIL

Profile A
The upper *c.* 10 cm of the profile is characterised by an apedal, relatively dense, homogeneous fabric. This fabric is a loam composed of more or less equal proportions of quartz sand, silt and clay. There is little evidence of biological activity or recognisable organic matter, which survives mainly as an amorphous, ferruginised aggregate or organic material within the groundmass, very rare fragments of plant tissues with almost unrecognisable cell structure, and very few small flecks of charcoal in the groundmass.

The most remarkable feature of this soil is the presence of abundant, non-laminated dusty (or impure) clay within the groundmass and of quartz grains, but only rarely within the void space. These intercalations tend to be thin (<25 um) and are commonly ferruginised. The abundant intercalated dusty clay suggests that the soil was subject to the addition and within-soil movement of silt and clay fines and organic matter. This slaking process results from the mechanical breaking up of the soil, which leads to the mobilisation of the fine fraction by rain and soil water, usually as the result of tillage (Jongerius 1970; 1983). The 'dirty' appearance of the fine fraction, caused by the inclusion of very fine comminuted charcoal, organic matter and silt, is also indicative of tillage. Thus this soil horizon is a colluvium, derived locally from erosion associated with cultivation.

The presence of very rare laminated dusty clay as partial infills of voids and channels is indicative of the translocation of impure clay, probably as a result of minor soil disturbance (Courty and Fedoroff 1982; Fedoroff 1968; Macphail 1986; Slager and van de Wetering 1977). The illuviation of fine material in this way could have easily occurred from the disturbance caused by the construction of the overlying rampart.

The amorphous sesquioxide impregnation (with iron and manganese) of up to one-third of the fine fabric, as well as the few rounded sesquioxide nodules within the groundmass are indicative of the alternative wetting and drying of this soil. This hydromorphic process would be coincident with the slaking of fine soil material by soil water, as well as a result of burial by the rampart causing impedence to soil water movement.

At *c.* 10-11 cm down the surviving profile, there is a marked change to a dense, highly ferruginised and organic zone, although the composition of the soil fabric remains similar to the remainder of the profile, both above and below this zone. It is dominated by ferruginised organic matter, both in amorphous form and less commonly with some cell structure still visible, as well as by frequent comminuted flecks of charcoal and a few faunal excrements. This material almost resembles polymorphic organic matter, which is characteristic of the spodic horizon in podzols (de Coninck 1980), and has been similarly subject to biological mixing by earthworm/enchytraeid activity under slightly acidic conditions. Thus this zone is suggestive of a mull/moder horizon (or Ah) (Limbrey 1975, 78) or former turf line.

The remaining *c.* 11-14 cm of the surviving profile has a similar loamy, but slightly less dense, fabric to the overlying colluvium and turf horizon. It contains frequent (but less abundant than in the overlying turf zone), amorphous, ferruginised organic matter, as well as occasional non-laminated dusty (or impure) clay coatings of the quartz grains and groundmass, which is also indicative of the addition of slaked fine material to the pre-rampart soil. These characteristics suggest that this is A2 horizon soil material (Limbrey 1975, 79), with a relatively minor colluvial component. Finally, both the turf and the underlying A2 horizon appear to be slightly broken up or disturbed in appearance, probably as a consequence of the activity associated with the construction of the rampart.

Profile B
The surviving profile exhibits more or less identical soil characteristics with a similar tripartite horizonation to profile A just described: colluvium (*c.* 0-8 cm), turf line (*c.* 8-9 cm) and A2 horizon (*c.* 8-9 cm) and A2 horizon (*c.* 9-11.5 cm).

Profile C (Secondary Buried Soil)
The complete profile, *c.* 7.5 cm thick, which had probably developed on top of the initial rampart, exhibited an apedal, homogeneous loam to clay loam fabric composed of more or less equal proportions of quartz sand, silt and clay. The soil fabric is dense, it contains little organic matter, and this is mainly present as a few amorphous, ferruginised organic aggregates and few very fine flecks of charcoal. There are also very abundant non-laminated dusty clay coatings throughout

the groundmass, in voids and on quartz grains. These intercalations of impure clay are the result of within-soil mass movement. Finally, up to *c.* 75% of the fine fabric is impregnated with amorphous sesquioxides (primarily iron).

These soil characteristics are generally similar to those observed in the upper two-thirds of profiles A and B, although there is a greater predominance of intercalculations of impure clay, especially within the groundmass. There is no doubt that these intercalations derive from the slaking of silt and clay fines as explained above in section 2.1.

The following process may be envisaged to explain the abundant impure clay intercalations within this horizon. The colluvial soil which composes the upper surface of the earlier rampart became an exposed surface which was then subject to considerable trampling, which in turn led to further slaking of the silt and clay fraction. Repeated trampling and re-slaking caused further fragmentation and re-distribution of the slaked fines. This continual sequence of events was probably caused by the construction of the second, overlying rampart.

The origin of the between-rampart colluvial soil may be similar to that of the original pre-rampart soil. The great abundance of intercalated silt and clay throughout the soil fabric suggests that the soil composing the upper surface of the rampart was re-deposited, but well homogenised, former colluvial soil. This soil must therefore have been gathered from the immediate vicinity, from land subject to localised downslope soil erosion and/or the addition of fine material transported in overbank floodwaters of the adjacent River Brain.

Comparative Sites
Although very little micro-pedological work has been done on buried soils associated with earthworks of a broadly similar date, there are at least four relatively well studied examples. The most comparable material comes from Cornwall (1958) and Dimbleby's (1962) micro-pedological and pollen investigations of the heathland site at Keston (Caesar's) Camp, Kent, which showed that the buried humo-ferric podzol had developed under primary woodland. Thus this soil, sealed by the rampart, was already well degraded by the Iron Age period.

At Bury Wood Camp, Wiltshire, a buried Iron Age soil developed on calcareous Jurassic limestone was found to be cultivated (thin section by I. Cornwall) (Grant King 1963). On calcareous gravels, the ditch of the fifth-century BC ringfort of Tattershall Thorpe, Lincolnshire, showed indications of a minor colluvial element in an otherwise naturally infilled ditch, with a fluctuating but high local ground water table (French forthcoming). On the fen edge/Welland valley terrace

gravels northeast of Peterborough, the investigation of the buried soil within the interior of the ringfort known as scheduled monument 222 (dated to 2090+/-80 BP (Har-8512) corrected to 380 Cal BC to Cal AD 80) revealed that the buried soil is an intact former brown earth. This soil had been ploughed, and contained considerable quantities of dumped occupation debris (French 1988). It also had been subject to the addition of minor amounts of alluvial silt and clay, prior to the soil being sealed by a later, major unit of alluvium.

CONCLUSIONS

1 The buried profile beneath the initial rampart is composed of three elements: colluvially re-deposited soil; turf (a mull/mode Ah horizon); and an organic upper A (or A2) horizon.
2 The pre-rampart soil was a slightly acidic, organic loam. The organic matter component displays some features of the upper part of a podsol. In this respect, this profile bears a slight resemblance to the pre-rampart soil at Keston (Caesar's) Camp, Kent.
3 The pre-rampart soil was subject to the addition of small amounts of colluvial fine material and associated ferruginization, as well as to the accumulation of a layer of colluvium above it *c.* 8-10 cm thick.
4 There was some slight soil disturbance of the profile, probably associated with the construction of the overlying rampart.
5 The overlying colluvial soil was also a loam, and was probably derived from the same subsoil from which the buried soil was developed. Downslope erosion and/or overbank flooding could have been responsible for the deposition of colluvium both within and on the pre-rampart soil.
6 The thin 'soil' (*c.* 7.5 cm thick) observed between the two ramparts is probably the trampled, bare upper surface of the earlier rampart.
7 The abundance of slaked silt and clay in the upper 7.5 cm of the first rampart suggests that it was composed of colluvially influenced soil, similar in character to that of the colluvial soil that had accumulated on the pre-rampart buried soil. Therefore, the soil material composing the rampart is most probably derived from the immediate vicinity of the floodplain.

ACKNOWLEDGEMENTS

I would like to thank Dr R. I. Macphail of the Department of Human Environment, Institute of Archaeology, London, and the same department and Fenland Archaeological Trust for the use of their laboratory facilities.

Notes

1. Wm. Holman, 'History of Essex', unpublished manuscript in the Essex Record Office, Chelmsford: ERO T/P 195. The original compilation dates from *c.* 1710–30. The section entitled 'The History of Witham' (T/P 195/10/1) is probably no later than *c.* 1720. Holman echoed contemporary antiquarian opinion on the identification of Chipping Hill: 'This is the place where our modern commentators upon Antoninus's Itinerary have at last agreed to fix that famous terminus, Ad Ansam ...' (fol. 1).

2. Sale particulars, *The Temples Estate* (1882). ERO B5160.

3. In 1933 the excavations were sponsored by the Society of Antiquaries and the Royal Archaeological Institute: a small workforce was employed, which included some notable local characters. In 1934 the Society of Antiquaries, the Essex Archaeological Society and New College, Oxford, were joint sponsors: the workforce comprised students from Oxford. Supervisors were Miss Thalassa Cruso (Mrs Hencken), Miss Norah Jolliffe and the late J.B. Ward-Perkins.

4. Letter dated 23 August 1935. Cottrill's correspondence file is deposited at Colchester Museum.

5. The finds from Witham were taken back to the London Museum (then at Lancaster House). Two Iron Age vessels were restored and used by Wheeler as teaching aids at the London Institute of Archaeology, where they still remain. Some sherds and a sling-shot from the 1933 season, together with the Roman glass, were personally retained by Cottrill. He gave the sherds and sling-shot to Professor C. F. C. Hawkes in 1945, who passed them on to W. J. Rodwell in 1973; they are now in Colchester Museum, as is the glass which Cottrill himself deposited in 1974. The neck of a Thetford-ware pitcher and other sherds were at one time with the late Dr G. C. Dunning, but their present whereabouts has not been traced. Likewise, the fate of the four Celtic coins and a silver St Edmund Memorial penny is unknown. The bulk of the finds undoubtedly perished during the 1939–45 war. In a letter to Hawkes, dated 22 March 1945, Cottrill recalled 'The sad truth about the Witham pottery is that most of it was buried in the ruins of the "old kitchen" at the London Museum by the Luftwaffe.'

6. The Witham Tithe map (1839) and successive editions of the Ordnance Survey 1:2,500 and 1:10,560 maps (1874 onward) chart the destruction of the Chipping Hill earthworks with depressing clarity. Prior to *c.* 1820 Temple Farm was the only building complex inside the earthwork circuit; by 1844 the railway and Witham station had been constructed, and by *c.* 1874 Temple Villas, Millfield Terrace, the Albert Hotel and sundry other properties had been erected. In 1882 Temple Farm was sold for speculating development, and the eastern half of the earthwork was completely infilled with mean, terraced housing. Further development followed, including a glove factory.
   When excavations began in 1933 about half of Temples Field was all that remained in an undeveloped state, but in 1936 Witham Urban District Council granted consent, amidst protest, for infilling this plot with housing. The last twenty years have seen substantial redevelopment: new roads have been cut through the site, some of the older properties demolished (including the glove, later button, factory), and large gardens have been built upon. The whole site is now packed with pretentious 'executive style' commuter housing and dreary blocks of flats.

7. The 'street' referred to is the London-to-Colchester road. This description formed the basis of accounts by Holman (see note 1) and later writers.

8. The coins were of Valens (364–78): obv. *Valens Pius Felix Augustus*, rev. *Securitas Reipublicae*; and Gratian (367–83): obv. *D. N. Gratianus*, rev. *Gloria Novi Saeculi*' (Holman ms., fol. 2; see note 1).

9. Details of Barwell's tomb in Witham parish church were recorded in the Holman ms., fol. 43.

10. The field name 'Temples', and Temple Farm, are both derived from the medieval ownership of the site by the Knights Templar.

11. Eg. Strutt entirely omitted Temple Farm, which lay against the northern side of the inner earthwork (Fig. 4B).

12. ERO D/CT 405. The surveyor for the Tithe Commissioners was James Beadel, a local farmer, who also happened to be the owner of Temple Farm.

13. The earthworks were shown in rudimentary form; an even more debased version of the same plan was

published by the Victoria County History: Gould 1903.

14. The plan and field survey notes are held by the National Monuments Record, London. Under the 'Remarks and Recommendations' section of the survey *pro forma* is the following: 'It is most important that this, one of the few remaining authentic earthworks of the Anglo-Saxon period, should be scheduled for protection.' There is also a note that 'Excavations for gravel have been made for several years past in the ramparts and continue, in spite of protests.' The site never was Scheduled as an Ancient Monument. A renewed attempt to protect the last significant remains of the earthworks was made in 1936, but H.M. Office of Works declined to Schedule the monument (Cottrill correspondence: see note 4).

15. The only site notebook covers the 1933 season, and part of 1934: the contents are scrappy and not completely intelligible. Several sheets of plans and sections were compiled at the time by Miss Cruso, but not labelled. These drawings were deposited by Cottrill in Colchester Museum in 1974, but have subsequently appeared in the Sites and Monuments Record held by the Archaeology Section of Essex County Council. There are eighteen small, snapshot-type photographs in Cottrill's files, together with prints from four half-plate negatives, all unlabelled. The four glass plates, taken in September 1933 by T.C. Gall of Colchester, are in the possession of the Essex Archaeological Society (Colchester Museum). There is also a related series of nineteen contact prints from lost plates held in the Sites and Monuments Record, Essex County Council. Their origin is unknown, but they may be Cottrill's own set (or copies) of his official excavation photographs. Indeed, four of the prints are evidently taken from the surviving Gall plates at Colchester (with retouching, to remove background objects such as buildings and fences). The E.C.C. photographs were probably all by T.C. Gall; and some are potentially misleading on account of the negatives having been reversed when the existing prints were made.

16. On 22 March 1934 and 21 February 1935.

17. Society of Antiquaries: 31 glass lantern slides, cat. nos. 5191–5204 and 6092–6108. Prints were made from these in the late 1970s, at the instigation of M.R. Petchey (then of Essex County Council), who was preparing an account of Cottrill's excavations for publication, a project which was never brought to fruition. When the Society's slide collection was transferred to the National Monuments Record in 1980–81 it was found that the Witham material was missing, and subsequent attempts to trace its whereabouts have failed. The prints made for Petchey have not been traced either. Some of the missing slides were made from Gall's photographs (see note 15), while others were from lost drawings of plans, sections and artifacts.

18. Cuttings from the *Braintree and Witham Times* and *The Observer* in Cottrill's files, Colchester Museum. See also Chelmsford Borough Library: Essex Coll., ZP 025 175.

19. For the mostpart, detailed feature descriptions are not available. A simple numbering system has been introduced here to facilitate reference to the principal features.

20. In the 1882 sale particulars, Temple Field (lot 76) was described as containing 'a very valuable and deep bed of gravel'. The accompanying plan showed a large pit at the north end of the field, in the angle between Chipping Hill and Moat Farm. ERO B5160.

21. Under-excavation is a frequent problem in Essex soils, especially in dry summer conditions; the situation is made worse when the trench sides are stepped, as was the case at Witham. The differences between fills and the naturally mixed and banded clays and gravels can be very difficult to detect even under favourable conditions.

22. The *Braintree and Witham Times*, 16 August 1934, reported that the post-Roman date of the inner rampart had been 'definitely established' by the discovery beneath it of a Roman amphora sherd. While it was still believed that the inner earthwork was late Saxon, this was an unexceptionable find, but when a prehistoric date was subsequently accepted, the amphora was seen as an embarrassment, and had to be explained away. A note by Cottrill in the Colchester Museum files baldly states that the amphora had been 'planted'. Unfortunately, the sherd does not survive, but with hindsight we may suspect that this was of the Dressel 1 variety, and thus a genuine find. The occurrence of Dressel 1 amphorae in pre-Roman strata is now commonplace; other nearby sites, including Kelvedon, have yielded sherds (Rodwell 1976b, 318–21; fig. 18).

23. A section drawing of trench E exists, but is generally uninformative and has not been reproduced.

24. There are difficulties here with conflicting evidence. Cottrill plotted the trench on a copy of the 1:2,500 Ordnance Survey map, in such a position that it fell within the line of the outer bank, as mapped by Montgomerie. Cottrill's 1934 lecture notes make it clear that the outer ditch was under investigation at this point; moreover, the *Braintree and Witham Times*, 30 August 1934, reported the discovery as 'the lip of yet another ditch'. Either the trench was incorrectly plotted, or this was not the outer ditch at all but the edge of an otherwise unrecorded feature.

25. Letter with accompanying sketch in Colchester Museum, dated 16 August 1934.

26. *Braintree and Witham Times*, 30 August 1934.

27. Cottrill's lecture notes, 1933, p. 13.

28. The tip of a single-edged iron blade was described as a *scramasax*, but was probably only a large knife.

29. A spikelet from an ear of wheat was identified as an impression in burnt daub: letter from J. Percival to Cottrill, 19 September 1935.

30. Now occupied by the modern properties 'Kelsale' and 'Serenus'.

31. A simplified feature numbering system is used here for ease of cross-reference between text and figures.

32. The pottery comprised four sherds, from two different vessels. These are sagging-base cooking pots of twelfth-thirteenth-century date in a medium brown

fabric, tempered with fine sand and grog: cf. fabric group 12 at Rivenhall, for which see Drury *et al.*, in Rodwell and Rodwell 1992 forthcoming.

33. The pottery comprised 30 sherds from about ten vessels, which included some large pieces of glazed jugs of Hedingham ware.

34. One sherd is a wire-marked base of Thetford-type ware; the other is a body sherd of coarse shell-tempered ware. Both could be either late Saxon or early medieval. Animal bones and oyster shells were also present in the same deposit. The topsoil horizon through which the pits were dug yielded a late Saxon or early medieval sherd with sand and shell tempering (the latter having dissolved, leaving lacunae).

35. Two of the sherds, distinctively Middle Iron Age and in Little Waltham fabric H (Drury 1978), were found in the buried soil horizon sealing the primary silting. The exact locations of the other sherds in relation to the section is uncertain: two are Middle Iron Age, and the other is of Early Iron Age type.

36. *Trans. Essex Archaeol. Soc.* 1 (1858), 137.

37. Accn. No. 5044.25. *Colchester Mus. Rep.* 1926, 21.

38. Inf. from the late Major Brinson.

39. *ibid.* and other local informants.

40. A manuscript report by John H. Hope is lodged in the County Sites and Monuments Record, Chelmsford.

41. Marked on the archaeological record maps in Colchester Museum.

42. This could be misleading: it is possible that the geophysical survey merely located an old quarry.

43. The selectivity of finds' retention and reported evidence on older excavations in Essex is a recurrently biassing factor. Excavations on the Roman villa at Rivenhall and on the Roman towns at Chelmsford and Kelvedon in the 1940s, '50s and early '60s, all failed to take note of pre-Roman features and artifacts. More recent excavations on these sites have yielded ample prehistoric evidence.

44. In the 1960s Professor Hawkes had already recognised - although not published - the significance of the Witham pottery as an indicator of Middle Iron Age ceramic tradition in Essex, and had compared it to the assemblage recently discovered at Ardleigh (Erith and Holbert 1970).

45. This find recalls the equally fortuitous discovery in 1928 of a unique silver penny of Cnut in the churchyard at Ashingdon, Essex. The site is claimed, on the basis of highly equivocal evidence, to be that of Canute's minster church, built in 1020. The coin is in Southend Museum: Rodwell 1993 forthcoming.

46. Medieval pottery was certainly found in the rampart during the 1930s excavations, but it was not considered to be of interest and no attention was paid to it.

47. ERO T/B 71.

48. The road was called Maldon Lane in 1608: *ibid.*

49. See note 125.

50. ERO T/B 71.

51. Colchester Museum, CM 4.55.

52. If the river formed the east side of the enclosure, the area would have been increased to nearer 70 ha (180 acres); but topographically this arrangement is highly unlikely.

53. While it is just possible that the two main ditches represent successive phases of construction, rather than a bivallate earthwork, this interpretation seems improbable.

54. Western Estate Map, Rivenhall, 1716: ERO D/DFg 1/10. Rivenhall Tithe Award, 1839: ERO D/CT 290. Faulkbourne Tithe Award, 1839: ERO D/CT 136. In the Faulkbourne Tithe Award the naming of 'Bergey Field' and 'Brakey Field' have been erroneously transposed (land parcels 120 and 127).

55. A farm was established in the southern angle of the Rivenhall End crossroads, probably in the early sixteenth century; and another in the eastern angle in the seventeenth century. The northern angle remained undeveloped until the nineteenth century. For development plans of Rivenhall End, see Rodwell and Rodwell 1992, fig. 87; for Burgate Field see Rodwell and Rodwell 1985, fig. 127. Subsequent work has indicated the need for minor modifications to the latter, for which see here Fig. 31.

56. The hall and one cross-wing survive, albeit much altered. The pond has been infilled in the present century, and road levels were changed in the 1960s.

57. The original survey notes are held by the National Monuments Record, London.

58. A circular building shown here on the 1874 Ordnance Survey map (1:2,500) was presumably a dovecote. The field adjoining on the west was called Dovehouse Field in the eighteenth and nineteenth centuries.

59. Not noted by Trump (1961): ERO T/M35 and T/M34.

60. ERO T/B 71.

61. In a previous discussion of this estate the possibility was raised that the 2½ hide manor was located at Cressing (Rodwell and Rodwell 1985, 173). This is now seen to be erroneous.

62. Will of William Sone: ERO D/ACW 6/152. This property had formerly been owned by Robert Hutt(es), and may be traceable back to the sixteenth century, through family names. In 1593 John Hutt left an unspecified house to his son Robert, who was apparently a weaver: ERO D/ABW 19/231. I owe these references to Mrs Janet Gyford.

63. For discussion of 'Halton' names, see Ekwall 1936, 202–3. The Witham name is presumably descriptive of an Anglo-Saxon settlement with a notable pond, situated on a spur or promontory.

64. The south-east pond was almost certainly a quarry pit, and on the Tithe map a brick kiln was marked in the adjacent field. ERO D/CT 405, land parcels 804 and 805.

65. Essex County Council, Sites and Monuments Record.

66. ERO T/M 35.

67. ERO T/M 34.

68. For related field names, see Field 1972, 247.

69. The origin of the naming of Canewdon Dyke has not been traced. The feature is marked on the Tithe map as 'Hollow Ditch': ERO D/CT 344, land parcel 509. It is similarly named on early editions of the Ordnance Survey maps.

70. *ibid.*

71. There are cropmark enclosures, with Roman and

Anglo-Saxon finds, close to Little Braxted mill, hall and church (Fig. 2, no. 3). This is an archetypal Essex manorial complex. At Cressing, which was formerly the northern part of Witham parish, there are two complexes where features and artifacts from the Early Iron Age onward have been recorded in small-scale excavations (unpublished). One is the environs of Cressing churchyard; the other is the large moated manorial complex at Cressing Temple (currently under investigation; see also Hull 1963, 123).

72. Unfortunately, the finds are ill-recorded, and now lost: Hull 1963, 187.

73. Rivenhall End lies on the border between Kelvedon and Rivenhall, and its Roman site is distinct from the villa at Rivenhall and the small town at Kelvedon. The site at Rivenhall End has yielded a peacock-decorated bronze strap-end, for which see Hawkes 1972. The late Roman Christian find from Brentwood is a ring bearing a Chi-Rho monogram: see Hull 1963, 57. The ring is now in the British Museum.

74. The only notices of this site so far published have been in local literature, where the building is referred to as a 'villa'. A plan has appeared in the newspaper *Essex Archaeology*, issue 7, p. 1 (Essex County Council, 1990). An interim report is forthcoming: N. J. Lavender, 'A Late Iron Age and Roman Site at "The Grove", Boreham', *Essex J*. There, the excavator favours interpretation as a *principia*, although conceding the possibility of a religious use. Reinterpretation of the site as a late Roman church and baptistery is suggested by the present writer. Boreham is set in a villa-dominated landscape and it would be difficult to sustain a case for an imperial estate in this area of Essex, or for 'The Grove' as a likely administrative centre.

75. Noted by M. R. Hull in his Essex topographical file in Colchester Museum.

76. Thoroughly robbed Roman structures beneath heavily used churchyards are notorious for escaping detection by grave diggers (cf. Rivenhall: Rodwell and Rodwell 1985, 7–8). Witham churchyard has long been closed to burial, and thus opportunities for the discovery of archaeological material have not been lately forthcoming.

77. This is ill-recorded; for the only published reference see Morant 1768, 115, or Hull 1963, 129. Faulkbourne Hall still lies amidst a tract of undeveloped eighteenth-century parkland.

78. Casual finds, as well as structural remains, indicate a greater density of high-status settlements in central and northern Essex than might initially be expected (Rodwell 1978b). A considerable number of medieval parishes contain one Roman villa site within their bounds, while some have two. There is nothing improbable in the suggestion that there were villas in close proximity at both Witham and Faulkbourne (especially since they would have been on opposite sides of the Brain valley). Moreover, the adjacent parishes on the west have yielded further evidence of well-appointed villas: there was a large one at White Notley Hall (Hull 1963, 164), and the ill-recorded site of another in Terling Place Park. The latter site has

also yielded an exceedingly rich hoard of late Roman gold and silver coins and jewellery (Hull 1963, 186).

79. What might appear to be an exception - and it is far from typical of early Anglo-Saxon cemeteries - is the recently excavated site at Springfield, north-east of Chelmsford: Buckley and Hedges 1987. This is not purely a pagan-period cemetery: it appears to have served a small community over a very long period, during which time the Christian rite of burial was adopted; see also p. 75.

80. Unpublished excavations by Mr John Hope alongside the Cressing Brook, east of Cressing Church.

81. *Historia Ecclesiastica*, 1 ch. 26.

82. Mapped in 1752 and 1812: see notes 48 and 49. In 1450 part of this area was 'Moor called Aldehope' (Blunt's Hall court roll, 29 Hen. 6): ERO T/B 71.

83. In the 1803 sale particulars the property was described as 'Ivy Chimney House, lately put into complete repair'. One of the adjacent fields was 'Ivy House Field'. Unfortunately the map that accompanied the particulars is missing. ERO B780.

84. See notes 66 and 67.

85. Lower Moors was not in fact labelled on these estate maps, the parcel having been transferred to an adjacent holding.

86. The process of estate fragmentation at this period has been studied locally at Rivenhall: see Rodwell and Rodwell 1992, forthcoming.

87. Medieval farmhouses in central Essex were almost invariably substantial timber-framed structures; many are still standing after 600 years or more.

88. As late as the eighteenth century, it was recalled that the lands of Howbridge Hall once extended up to the Roman road, and to Witham Bridge (Morant 1768, 109).

89. The only other candidate for the lesser holding is perhaps Dengie Farm (Fig. 29).

90. RCHM 1921, 267, no. 13. Stenning 1989, 98.

91. I am grateful to Mrs Janet Gyford for discussions concerning the problem of Witham manor, and for confirming that neither the so-called Manor House in Newland Street nor the Old Manor House at Chipping Hill has a sustainable claim to being an early manorial seat.

92. There is no extant record of the parochial severing of Faulkbourne from Witham. By the time of the Domesday Survey there is no hint of manorial links; but the interlocking of the parish boundaries leaves little doubt that fragmentation took place at an early, if unspecifiable, date.

93. Survey of the Manor of Witham, 1608. ERO T/B 71.

94. Walthamstow, Stow Maries and Michaelstow (in Ramsey).

95. See Rodwell and Rodwell 1992, forthcoming, section 10.5, land parcel no. 326 (with refs.).

96. Part of the small holding of Hungry Hall, which spanned the boundary between Witham and Cressing. For the extent of the Church Fields, see Witham Tithe map, parcels 548–9, 552 and 556.

97. One was in Broad Mead (Tithe land parcel 359); the other was in Inham's Mead and has not been located.

98. Faulkbourne Tithe Award, 1839. ERO D/CT 136.

99. The grounds for exemption, and the precise extent of exempt lands, are not made explicit in the Tithe Awards. In Cressing, *c*. 850 acres of former Templars' land were listed, but only 764 acres were tithe exempt. That was 40% of the entire parish. In Rivenhall, there were 120 acres of exempt Templars' land, abutting Cressing. In Witham, however, only 39 acres out of the Templars' very considerable holding enjoyed exemption, and that land appears to have been contiguous with Cressing.

100. RCHM 1921, 68. On architectural grounds, the twelfth-century date assigned here to Faulkbourne Church is too late.

101. Anglo-Saxon churches were commonly laid out from the centre-lines of walls, and that this was the case at Witham is clear from the length-to-width ratio of the sides of the nave: the 3:1 proportion obtains precisely. Measurements based on the external or internal dimensions of the nave fail to exhibit meaningful ratios.

102. Again, it is only measurements based on wall centre-lines that yield 'round' numbers of feet. Other measurements conspicuously fail to relate to round numbers, whether considered in Northern feet or Imperial feet.

103. It is not uncommon for a church to lie just off-centre in its graveyard, either to north or south, and for components of the historic topography to point towards a lateral shift having taken place from the original central focus: examples include Hadstock, Essex (Rodwell 1976d), Wickham St Paul, Essex (Rodwell and Rodwell 1977, 123) and Tidenham, Glos. (Rodwell 1989, 144). For discussion of this phenomenon in relation to a large circular churchyard at St Brelade, Jersey, see Rodwell 1990, 130–4. It may also be noted that the highest part of Witham churchyard is immediately east of the chancel. The possibility that the church was sited with a pre-existing structure on this spot as its eastern focus is equally worth considering.

104. The site has been denuded by centuries of ploughing, but the distribution of Anglo-Saxon features (Buckley and Hedges 1989, fig. 11) argues for the presence of a ditchless mound that influenced patterns of activity on the site for one and a half millennia after the demise of the Bronze Age settlement. I am grateful for the benefit of discussion on Springfield with David Buckley.

105. *Bull. C.B.A. Churches Cttee.* 16 (1982), 7–8.

106. Discoveries at Little Braxted are sadly ill-documented. Roman and early Saxon finds were made in 1973, when gravel quarrying took place alongside the river immediately adjoining the enclosure discussed here. Some of the finds were seen by the writer: the pottery was third and fourth century. Inhumations accompanied by iron spears and shield bosses were described.

107. The same is generally indicated on the Little Braxted Tithe map of *c*. 1844; but this map is not trigonometrically accurate. ERO D/CT 49.

108. Little Braxted is another example of a proprietary chapel with no contiguous glebe: the 7 acre field which was presumably given to maintain the church after its independence from the hall is 1.1 km distant.

109. *op. cit.* note 105.

110. Kellington church was totally excavated in 1990–91, and the earliest feature recorded was a single north-south burial, apparently under a stone cist; this was followed by an Anglo-Saxon pre-church cemetery: C. Atkins, R. Morris and W. Rodwell, *The Archaeological Investigation of the Parish Church of St Edmund, Kellington: A Preliminary Note* (1991). University of York. It may be relevant to note that grave-diggers reported finding two or three north-south orientated skeletons outside the west end of Hadstock church. The association of occasional north-south burials with early Christian sites is becoming more widely recognised.

111. Letter from Reaney to Cottrill, 15 October 1933 (Colchester Museum). Reaney says, 'My enquiries have led me to ignore completely *Guithavon*. There is no evidence of its use for Witham, and I understand that the name of the street was due to an etymological conjecture of a former vicar'. Guithavon Street was created in 1841.

112. Whether there was a bridge here before the conquest is very doubtful. The parish on the north side of the river, immediately opposite Maldon is Heybridge, the 'high bridge', first mentioned *c*. 1200 (Reaney 1935, 304).

113. While Whitelock's translation of 'borough' for *burh* has the merit of being consistent, it is an evocative term. Not every Edwardian *burh* was a fully fledged borough, and a duality of use of the word seems certain.

114. There are a few other Essex place-names incorporating 'burgate' (Reaney 1935, 263).

115. In the language of Domesday *burgus* superseded *burh* as one of the terms used in connection with defensible enclosures: thus the *burgus* of Colchester referred to the walled town (Round 1903, 414).

116. Rodwell and Rodwell 1992, forthcoming. Land parcels 298–300.

117. *ibid.* Land parcels 301, 303–5 and 305a.

118. While most of this block was Faulkbourne land, it also enveloped a detached parcel of Witham land, and was pierced by a tiny, intrusive tongue from Rivenhall. For convenience in the present discussion, the block is regarded as a 'floating' unit of Faulkbourne land.

119. The parish of Little Braxted is clearly cut out of Great Braxted, and the Domesday Survey, unusually for Essex, records the presence of a priest as having arrived here between 1066 and 1086. Little Braxted also had its mill by the latter date, but the wording of the Survey is not explicit as to whether it existed at the time of the conquest (Round 1903, 441). The general impression gained is that Little Braxted progressively acquired status during the eleventh century.

120. Rodwell and Rodwell 1992, forthcoming. The first block comprises land parcels 354–62, 388–403 and 405–9, and the second block parcels 363–70, 384–6, 410–17 and 422–30. 'Hitchings' is parcel 411.

121. A suggestion made long ago by B.E. Hildebrand (*Anglosachsiska Mynt* (1881), 408, no. 213), that a coin of the reign of Harthacnut, from an unidentified mint, was struck at Witham (cf. Reaney 1935, 300n) has been discredited. The inscription was misread, and is now known to refer to the mint at Bath: the correction was made by R. H. M. Dolley in *SNC* 71 (3) (1963), 45. I am grateful to Miss Marion Archibald for discussion of this point.

122. The date is unspecified, but must have fallen between 1136 and 1146.

123. Essex County Council 1990. The Barley Barn is now dated *c*. 1200–20 and the Wheat Barn *c*. 1260. The construction of the moat lay between these dates; its course is not fully defined.

124. Record Commission 1837, *Rotuli Chartarum*, p. 188, cited in Beresford 1967, 436.

125. Colchester Borough Muniments: Register of St John's Abbey, Colchester, f. 150d; cited in Britnell 1968, 16, n.30.

126. P.R.O. DL43 14/1. Discussed in Britnell 1968, 15.

127. The division of basic units of measurement into thirds and sixths is well established as an Anglo-Saxon predeliction; the move towards subdivisions into halves and quarters may not have occurred until well after the conquest; see generally Huggins *et al.* 1982.

128. *Loc. cit.*, note 66.

129. *Loc. cit.*, note 125.

130. ERO T/B 71.

131. The main road at Witham would undoubtedly have been carried on a bridge in the Roman period, but a return to a ford during the Anglo-Saxon era is attested by 'Wulfhere's ford'. The bridge must surely have been reinstated by the middle of the eleventh century,

since the place-name *Hobruge* (Howbridge) in the Domesday Survey attests the presence of the less important Saul's Bridge further down-river; see p. 41.

132. Tithe Award, parcel no. 345. There was also a Hither Town Field at the south-west extremity of the town, parcel no. 471.

133. ERO T/B 71.

134. More than one hundred can be counted or implied from nineteenth-century maps.

135. ERO T/B 71.

136. There was another mill further upstream in Faulkbourne parish, towards White Notley. This was more likely the Domesday mill of Faulkbourne manor.

137. Omitted from the plan in Rodwell and Rodwell 1985, fig. 123; the same applies to the suggested lower mill site at Faulkbourne. An additonal mill site at Rivenhall End has now been suggested near the lower end of the Cressing Brook, south of Hoo Hall (Rodwell and Rodwell 1992, forthcoming).

138. '... Charter indented of demise of the manor of Blonteshale, the whole mill in Wytham called "Machonesmelle" ...' *Cal. Close Rolls 1422–9*, 206. I owe this reference to Mrs Janet Gyford.

139. The tithe maps of the Witham area are all generally similar in the volume of detail shown. Their surveyors were primarily interested in functioning boundaries and the calculation of acreages. They tended to plot large ponds and moats only when water-filled; they generally ignored earthworks, tree lines, footpaths, tracks and private drives to houses.

140. The development of this and adjacent properties can be deduced from various early nineteenth-century maps : notes 66 and 67.

141. ERO B780.

Bibliography

Aldsworth, F., and Freke, D., 1976. *Historic Towns in Sussex: An Archaeological Survey*. Institute of Archaeology, London.

Allcroft, A.H., 1908. *Earthwork of England*. (London).

Allen, D.F., 1971. 'British Potin Coins: A Review', in Jesson and Hill (eds.), 1971, 127–54.

Anon. [Cromwell, T.K.], 1818. *Excursions in the County of Essex*, 1. (London).

Anon. 1844. 'Proceedings of the Central Committee of the British Archaeological Association', *Archaeol. J.* 1, 379–404.

Anon. 1845. *The Parish of Witham*. Privately printed. (London).

Armitage, E.S., 1912. *The Early Norman Castles of the British Isles*. (London).

Arnold-Forster, F.E., 1899. *Studies in Church Dedications*. (London).

Aston, M., and Bond, J., 1976. *The Landscape of Towns*. (London).

Bailey, R.N., Cambridge, E., and Briggs, H.D., 1988. *Dowsing and Church Archaeology*. (Wimborne).

Baker, D.B., Baker, E., Hassall, J., and Simco, A., 1979. 'Excavations in Bedford, 1967–77', *Bedfordshire Archaeol. J.* 13, 1–309.

Barrett, J.C., 1980. 'The Pottery of the Later Bronze Age in Lowland England', *Proc. Prehist. Soc.* 46, 297–319.

Bedwin, O., 1991. 'Asheldham Camp — An Early Iron Age Hillfort: Excavations 1985', *Essex Archaeol. & Hist.* 22, 13–37.

Benson, D., and Miles, D., 1974. *The Upper Thames Valley: An Archaeological Survey of the River Gravels*. Oxon. Archaeol. Unit, Survey 2. (Oxford).

Beresford, M.W., 1967. *New Towns of the Middle Ages: Town Plantation in England, Wales and Gascony*. (London).

Biddle, M., and Hill, D., 1971. 'Late Saxon Planned Towns', *Antiq. J.* 51, 70–85.

Blair, J. (ed.), 1988a. *Minsters and Parish Churches: The Local Church in Transition, 950–1200*. Oxon. Univ. Cttee Archaeol. Mono. (Oxford).

Blair, J., 1988b. 'Introduction: from Minster to Parish Church', in Blair 1988a, 1–20.

Blair, J., 1992. 'Anglo-Saxon Minsters: A Topographical Review', in J. Blair & R. Sharpe (eds.), *Pastoral Care before the Parish*, 226–66. Leicester U.P., Studies in the Early History of Britain. (Leicester).

Blair, J. and McKay, B., 1985. 'Investigations at Tackley Church, Oxfordshire, 1981–4: the Anglo-Saxon and Romanesque Phases', *Oxoniensia* 50, 25–46.

Blunt, C.E., Stewart, B.I.H., and Lyon, C.S.S., 1989. *Coinage in Tenth-Century England from Edward the Elder to Edgar's Reform*. British Academy.

Bowen, H.C., and Fowler, P.J. (eds.), 1978. *Early Land Allotment in the British Isles*. Brit. Archaeol. Reps. 48.

Bridgland, D.R., 1988. 'The Pleistocene Fluvial Stratigraphy and Palaeogeography of Essex', *Proc. Geol. Assoc.* 99, 291–314.

Britnell, R.H., 1968. 'The Making of Witham', *Hist. Stud.* 1, 13–21.

Brooks, H., 1989. 'The Stansted Temple', *Curr. Archaeol.* 10 (no. 117), 322–5.

Brooks, R.T., and Stokes, A.H., 1976. 'Excavations at Witham Lodge, Essex, 1972', *Essex J.* 10, 107–28.

Brown, G.B., 1915. *The Arts in Early England, 4*. (London).

Brown, N., 1983. 'Southend-on-Sea, Prittlewell', in D. Priddy (ed.), 'Work of Essex County Council Archaeology Section, 1982', *Essex Archaeol. & Hist.* 15, 119–56.

Brown, N., 1988a. 'A Late Bronze Age Settlement on the Boulder Clay Plateau: Excavations at Broads Green, 1986', *Essex Archaeol. & Hist.* 19, 7–15.

Brown, N., 1988b. 'A Late Bronze Age Enclosure at Lofts Farm, Essex', *Proc. Prehist. Soc.* 54, 249–302.

Brown, N., 1991. 'Prehistoric Pottery', in Bedwin 1991, 27–8.

Brown, N., forthcoming. 'Prehistoric Pottery', in J. Wymer and N. Brown, *Excavations at North Shoebury: Settlement and Economy in South-East Essex*. East Anglian Archaeol.

Brown, P.N., 1986. *The Maldon Burh Jigsaw*. Maldon Archaeological Group.

Buckley, D.G. (ed.), 1980. *Archaeology in Essex to AD 1500*. CBA Res. Rep. 34.

Buckley, D.G., and Hedges, J.D., 1987a. *The Bronze Age and Saxon Settlements at Springfield Lyons, Essex: An Interim Report*. Essex County Council, Occ. Paper 5. (Chelmsford).

Buckley, D.G., and Hedges, J.D., 1987b. *Excavation of a Cropmark Enclosure Complex at Woodham Walter, Essex, 1976*. E. Anglian Archaeol. 33.

Buckley, D.G., Major, H., and Milton, B., 1988. 'Excavation of a possible Neolithic Long Barrow or Mortuary Enclosure at Rivenhall, Essex', *Proc. Prehist. Soc.* 54, 77–92.

Bullock, P., Murphy, C.P., and Waller, P.J., 1985a. *The Preparation of Thin Sections of Soils and Unconsolidated Sediments*. (Harpenden).

Bullock, P., Fedoroff, N., Jongerius, A., Stoops, G., and Tursina, T., 1985b. *Handbook for Soil Thin Section Description*. Waine Research. (Wolverhampton).

Casey, P.J., (ed.) 1979. *The End of Roman Britain*. Brit. Archaeol. Reps. 71.

Christy, M., 1928. 'The Essex Hundred-Moots: An attempt to identify their Meeting-Places', *Trans. Essex Archaeol. Soc.* new ser. 18, 172–97.

Coller, D.W., 1861. *The People's History of Essex*. (Chelmsford).

de Coninck, F., 1980. 'Major Mechanisms in the Formation of Spodic Horizons', *Geoderma* 24, 101–28.

Cornwall, I.W., 1953. 'Soil Science and Archaeology with Illustrations from some British Bronze Age Monuments', *Proc. Prehist. Soc.* 19, 129–47.

Cornwall, I.W., 1958. *Soils for the Archaeologist*. (London).

Cotton, M.A., [1960]. 'Observations on the Classification of Hill-Forts in Southern England', in Frere (ed.) [1960], 61–8.

Cottrill, F., 1934. 'A Trial Excavation at Witham, Essex', *Antiq. J.* 14, 190–1.

Courty, M.A., and Fedoroff, N., 1982. *Proceedings of the Second Nordic Conference of Scientific Methods in Archaeology, Denmark, 1981*.

Crummy, P., 1984. *In Search of Colchester's Past*. Second ed. Colchester Archaeol. Trust. (Colchester).

Crummy, P., 1990. 'A Roman Church in Colchester', *Curr. Archaeol.* 10 (no. 120), 406–8.

Cunliffe, B., 1976. *Iron Age Communities in Britain*. Second ed. (London).

Cunliffe, B., 1984. *Danebury: An Iron Age Hillfort in Hampshire 2*. CBA Res. Rep. 52.

*Cunliffe, B., and Rowley, T. (eds.), 1976. *The Beginnings of Urbanisation in Barbarian Europe*. Brit. Archaeol. Reps. S-11.

Curwen, E.C., 1929. *Prehistoric Sussex*. (London).

Dimbleby, G.W., 1962. *The Development of British Heathlands and their Soils*. (Oxford).

Drury, P.J., 1972. 'The Romano-British Settlement at Chelmsford, Essex: *Caesaromagos*. Preliminary Report', *Essex Archaeol. & Hist.* 4, 3–29.

Drury, P.J., 1976. 'Braintree: Excavations and Research, 1971–76', *Essex Archaeol. & Hist.* 8, 1–143.

Drury, P.J., 1978. *Excavations at Little Waltham, 1970–71*. CBA Res. Rep. 26.

Drury, P.J. (ed.), 1982. *Structural Reconstruction: Approaches to the Interpretation of the Excavated Remains of Buildings*. Brit. Archaeol. Reps. 110.

Drury, P.J., 1984. 'The Temple of Claudius at Colchester Reconsidered', *Britannia* 15, 7–50.

Drury, P.J., 1988. *The Mansio and other sites in the South-Eastern Sector of Caesaromagus*. CBA Res. Rep. 66.

Drury, P.J., and Rodwell, W.J., 1973. 'Excavations at Gun Hill, West Tilbury', *Essex Archaeol. & Hist.* 5, 48–112.

Drury, P.J., and Rodwell, W.J., 1978. 'Investigations at Asheldham, Essex: An Interim Report on the Church and the Historic Landscape', *Antiq. J.* 46, 133–51.

Drury, P.J., and Rodwell, W.J., 1980. 'Settlement in the Later Iron Age and Roman Periods', in Buckley (ed.) 1980, 59–75.

Drury, P.J., and Wickenden, N.P., 1982. 'An Early Saxon Settlement within the Romano-British Small Town at Heybridge, Essex', *Medieval Archaeol.* 26, 1–40.

Dugdale, J., 1819. *The New British Traveller, 2*. (London).

Dyer, J., 1972. 'Earthworks of the Danelaw Frontier', in Fowler (ed.), 1972, 222–36.

Eddy, M.R., and Petchey, M.R., 1983. *Historic Towns in Essex. An Archaeological Survey of Saxon and Medieval towns, with Guidance for their Future Planning*. Essex County Council. (Chelmsford).

Ekwall, E., 1936. *The Oxford Dictionary of English Place-Names*. (Oxford).

Elsdon, S.M., 1975. *Stamp and Roulette Decorated Pottery of the La Tène Period in Eastern England*. Brit. Archaeol. Reps. 10.

Erith, F.H., and Holbert, P.R., 1970. 'The Iron Age "A" Farmstead at Vinces Farm, Ardleigh', *Bull. Colchester Archaeol. Group* 13, 1–26.

Erith, F.H., and Longworth, I.H., 1960. 'A Bronze Age Urnfield on Vinces Farm, Ardleigh, Essex', *Proc. Prehist. Soc.* 26, 178–92.

Essex County Council, 1990. *Cressing Temple: A Brief Guide*. (Chelmsford).

Evans, J., 1864. *Coins of the Ancient Britons*. (London). Supplement, 1890.

Fedoroff, N., 1968. 'Genèse et Morphologie des Sols à Horizon B textural en France Atlantique', *Science du Sol* 1, 29–65.

Field, J., 1972. *English Field Names: A Dictionary*. (Newton Abbot).

Fowler, P.J. (ed.), 1972. *Archaeology and the Landscape*. (London).

Fowler, R.C., 1907. 'Religious Houses', *History of the County of Essex*, 2, 84–202. Victoria History of the Counties of England. (London).

Fowler, R.C., 1911. *The Church of St. Nicholas, Witham*. (Colchester).

French, C.A.I., 1988. 'The Southwest Fen Dyke Survey Project', *Antiquity* 62, 343–8.

French, C.A.I., forthcoming. 'Soil Analysis of the Ditch Deposits at Tattershall Thorpe, Lincolnshire'.

Frere, S.S. (ed.), [1960]. *Problems of the Iron Age in Southern Britain*. Univ. of London, Occ. Paper 11.

Frere, S.S., 1970. 'A Romano-British Votive Relief from Witham', *Britannia* 1, 267.

Gibson, E. (ed.), 1695. [W. Camden], *Britannia*. (London).

Gifford, P.R., 1984. *Witham in Old Picture Postcards*. European Library. (Zaltbommel, Netherlands).

Going, C.J., 1987. *The Mansio and Other Sites in the South-Eastern Sector of Caesaromagus: The Roman Pottery*. CBA Res. Rep. 62.

Gough, R. (ed.), 1789. [W. Camden], *Britannia 2*. (London).

Gould, I.C., 1903. 'Ancient Earthworks', *A History of Essex*, 1, 275–314. Victoria History of the Counties of England. (London).

Grant King, D., 1963. 'Bury Wood Camp. Report on Excavations, 1960', *Wilts. Archaeol. & Natur. Hist. Mag.* 210, 185–208.

Greenwood, P., 1989. 'Uphall Camp, Ilford, Essex: An Iron Age Fortification', *London Archaeol.* 6, 94–101.

Grimes, W.F., 1960. *Excavations on Defence Sites, 1939–45. I. Mainly Neolithic and Bronze Age*. HMSO. (London).

Gyford, J. (ed.), 1985. *Domesday Witham*. Privately printed. (Witham).

Haberey, W., 1942. 'Spätantike Gläser aus Grabern von Mayen', *Bonner Jahrbücher* 147, 249 ff.

Haslam, J., 1983a. 'The Origin and Plan of Bedford', *Beds. Archaeol.* 16, 29–36.

Haslam, J., 1983b. 'The Development and Topography of Saxon Cambridge', *Proc. Cambridge Antiq. Soc.* 72, 13–29.

Haslam, J., 1988. 'The Anglo-Saxon Burh at *Wigingamere*', *Landscape Hist.* 10, 25–36.

Hawkes, C.F.C., and Hull, M.R., 1947. *Camulodunum*. Soc. Antiq. Res. Rep. 14.

Hawkes, S.C., 1972. 'A Late Roman Buckle from Tripontium', *Trans. Birmingham & Warks. Archaeol. Soc.* 85, 145–59.

Henderson, T., 1986. *The Parish Church of St. Nicolas, Witham, Essex*. Privately printed. (Witham).

Henig, M., Loring, L.E., and Wadhams, M.C., 1972. 'Romano-British Finger Rings at Witham', *Essex J.* 7, 106–7.

Hewett, C.A., 1973. 'A Medieval Timber Kitchen at Little Braxted, Essex', *Medieval Archaeol.* 17, 132–4.

Hill, D., 1981. *An Atlas of Anglo-Saxon England*. (Oxford).

Holgate, R., 1988. *Neolithic Settlement of the Thames Basin*. Brit. Archaeol. Reps. 194.

Hope, J.H., 1984. 'Excavations at All Saints Church, Cressing, Essex, 1979', *Four Church Excavations in Essex*. Essex County Council, Occ. Paper 4. (Chelmsford).

Horsley, J., 1733. *Britannia Romana 3*. (London).

Huggins, P.J., 1978. 'Excavation of Belgic and Romano-British Farm with Middle Saxon Cemetery and Churches at Nazeingbury, Essex, 1975–6', *Essex Archaeol. & Hist.* 10, 29–117.

Huggins, P.J., Rodwell, K.A., and Rodwell, W.J., 1982. 'Anglo-Saxon and Scandinavian Building Measurements', in Drury (ed.) 1982, 21–65.

Hull, M.R., 1963. *A History of Essex, 3: Roman Essex*. Victoria History of the Counties of England. (London).

Hurst, J.G., 1955. 'Saxo-Norman Pottery in East Anglia', *Proc. Cambridge Antiq. Soc.* 49, 43–70.

Isings, C., 1957. *Roman Glass from Dated Finds*. (Groningen).

Jesson, M., and Hill, D. (eds.), 1971. *The Iron Age and its Hill-Forts*. (Southampton).

Jongerius, A., 1970. 'Some Morphological Aspects of Regrouping Phenomena in Dutch Soils', *Geoderma* 4, 311–31.

Jongerius, A., 1983. 'The role of Micromorphology in Agricultural Research', in P. Bullock and C.P. Murphy (eds.), *Soil Micromorphology*, 111–38. (Berkhamsted).

Leech, R.H., 1975. *Small Medieval Towns in Avon*. Cttee for Rescue Archaeol. in Avon, Glos. & Somerset. (Bristol).

Lees, B.A. (ed.), 1935. *Records of The Templars in England in the Twelfth Century*. British Academy: Records of the Social and Economic History of England and Wales, 9. (London).

Limbrey, S., 1975. *Soil Science and Archaeology*. (London).

Lobel, M.D., 1975. 'Cambridge', *The Atlas of Historic Towns*, 2. (London).

Lucas, W.J., 1884. 'Some Account of the Town and Church of Witham', *Trans. Essex Archaeol. Soc.*, new ser. 2, 207–10.

Macphail, R.I., 1986. 'Palaeosols in Archaeology: their role in the Understanding of Flandrian Pedogensis', in V.P. Wright (ed.), *Palaeosols: Their Recognition and Interpretation*, 263–90. (Oxford).

Major, H.J., 1982. 'Iron Age Triangular Clay Loomweights', in D. Priddy (ed.), 'Work of the County Council Archaeology Section, 1981', *Essex Archaeol. & Hist.* 14, 111–32.

Matthews, C.L., 1976. *Occupation Sites on the Chiltern Ridge*. Brit. Archaeol. Reps. 29.

Meaney, A.L., 1964. *Gazetteer of Early Anglo-Saxon Burial Sites*. (London).

Meates, G.W., 1979. *The Roman Villa at Lullingstone, Kent, 1*. Kent Archaeol. Soc. Mono. 1.

Morant, P., 1768. *The History and Antiquities of the County of Essex, 2*. (London).

Morris, R., 1989. *Churches in the Landscape*. (London).

Morris, S., and Buckley, D.G., 1978. 'Excavations at Danbury Camp, Essex, 1974 & 1977', *Essex Archaeol. & Hist.* 10, 1–28.

Murphy, P., 1988. 'Plant Macrofossils', in N. Brown 1988b, 281–93.

Murphy, P., 1990. 'Springfield Lyons, Chelmsford Essex: Carbonised Plant Remains from Neolithic, Late Bronze Age, Iron Age, Roman, Early and Late Saxon Contexts'. *Ancient Monuments Laboratory Reports Series* 11/90.

Ordnance Survey, 1962. *Map of Southern Britain in the Iron Age*. (Chessington).

Petchey, M.R., 1977. 'Excavations in Hertford, 1973–4', *Herts. Archaeol.* 5, 157–75.

Petchey, M.R., 1980. 'The Archaeology of Medieval Essex Towns', in Buckley (ed.) 1980, 113–17.

Pollitt, W., 1953. *Southend before the Norman Conquest*. Second edn. Southend Museum Handbook 7.

Priddy, D., and Buckley, D.G., 1987. 'An Assessment of Excavated Enclosures in Essex together with a Selection of Cropmark Sites', in Buckley and Hedges 1987b, 48–77.

Rahtz, P.A., Harden, D.B., Dunning, G.C., and Radford, C.A.R., 1958. 'Three Post-Roman Finds from the Temple Well at Pagans Hill, Somerset', *Medieval Archaeol.* 2, 104–11.

Rahtz, P.A., and Watts, L., 1979. 'The End of Roman Temples in the West of Britain', in Casey (ed.) 1979, 183–201.

Rahtz, P.A., and Watts, L., 1989. 'Pagans Hill Revisited', *Archaeol. J.* 146, 330–71.

Reaney, P.H., 1935. *The Place-Names of Essex*. Eng. Place-Name Soc. 12. (Cambridge).

[Repton, J.A.], 1848. 'Proceedings of the Association', *J. Brit. Archaeol. Assn.* 3, 317–23.

Repton, J.A., 1854. 'Remarks on British and Roman Urns', *Archaeol. J.* 9, 59–62.

RCHM, 1921. Royal Commission on Historical Monuments (England), *An Inventory of the Historical Monuments in Essex, 2*. HMSO. (London).

RCHM, 1922. Royal Commission on Historical Monuments (England), *An Inventory of the Historical Monuments in Essex, 3*. HMSO. (London).

RCHM, 1975. Royal Commission on Historical Monuments (England), *An Inventory of the Historical Monuments in the County of Dorset, 5*. East Dorset. HMSO. (London).

RCHM, 1977. Royal Commission on Historical Monuments (England), *An Inventory of Historical Monuments: The Town of Stamford*. HMSO. (London).

Rodwell, K.A., 1988. *The Prehistoric and Roman Settlement at Kelvedon, Essex*. CBA Res. Rep. 63.

Rodwell, W.J., 1975. 'Milestones, Civic Territories and the Antonine Itinerary', *Britannia* 6, 76–101.

Rodwell, W.J., 1976a. *Settlement and Economy in the Territory of the Trinovantes, c. 500 B.C. to A.D. 50.* Unpublished D.Phil. thesis, University of Oxford.

Rodwell, W.J., 1976b. 'Coinage, Oppida and the Rise of Belgic Power in South-East Britain', in Cunliffe and Rowley (eds.) 1976, 181–367.

Rodwell, W.J., 1976c. 'Iron Pokers of La Tène II-III', *Archaeol. J.* 133, 43–9.

Rodwell, W.J., 1976d. 'The Archaeological Investigation of Hadstock Church, Essex: An Interim Report', *Antiq. J.* 56, 55–71.

Rodwell, W.J., 1978a. 'Relict Landscapes in Essex', in Bowen and Fowler (eds.) 1978, 89–98.

Rodwell, W.J., 1978b. 'Rivenhall and the Emergence of First-Century Villas in Northern Essex', in Todd (ed.) 1978, 11–32.

Rodwell, W.J. (ed.), 1980. *Temples, Churches and Religion in Roman Britain.* Brit. Archaeol. Reps. 77.

Rodwell, W.J., 1989. *Church Archaeology.* English Heritage. (London).

Rodwell, W.J., 1990. *The Fishermen's Chapel, Saint Brelade, Jersey: Its Archaeology, Architecture, Wall Paintings and Conservation.* Société Jersiaise. (Gloucester).

Rodwell, W.J., 1993 forthcoming. 'The Battle of *Assandun* and its Memorial Church: A Reappraisal', in J. Cooper (ed.), *The Battle of Maldon.*

Rodwell, W.J., forthcoming. 'The Witham Lodge Earthwork: Observations and Trial Excavations, 1970–72', in Turner, forthcoming.

Rodwell, W.J., and Rodwell, K.A., 1977. *Historic Churches: A Wasting Asset.* CBA Res. Rep. 19.

Rodwell, W.J., and Rodwell, K.A., 1985. *Rivenhall: Investigations of a Villa, Church and Village, 1950–1977, 1.* CBA Res. Rep. 55.

Rodwell, W.J., and Rodwell, K.A., 1992. *Rivenhall: Investigations of a Villa, Church and Village, 1950–1977, 2.* CBA Res. Rep., forthcoming.

Rodwell, W.J., and Rouse, E.C., 1984. 'The Anglo-Saxon Rood and Other Features in the South Porch of St. Mary's Church, Breamore, Hampshire.', *Antiq. J.* 64, 298–325.

Rogerson, A., and Dallas, C., 1984. *Excavations in Thetford, 1948–59 and 1973–80.* E. Anglian Archaeol. 22.

Round, J.H., 1903. 'Text of the Essex Domesday', *History of the County of Essex, 1,* 427–578. Victoria History of the Counties of England. (London).

Rowles, H.J., 1934. 'Excavations at Witham in 1933', *Essex Rev.* 43, 27–30.

Saville, A., 1983. *Uley Bury and Norbury Hillforts.* Western Archaeol. Trust, Mono. 5. (Bristol).

Slager, S., and van de Wetering, H.T.J., 1977. 'Soil Formation in Archaeological Pits and Adjacent Soils in Southern Germany', *J. Archaeol. Science* 4, 259–67.

Smith, M.L., 1970. *Markets, Manors and Manorial Court Rolls of Witham.* Privately printed. (Witham).

Spurrell, F.C.J., 1887. 'Withambury', *Essex Naturalist* 1, 19–22.

Stead, I.M., 1976. *Excavations at Winterton Roman Villa.* HMSO. (London).

Stenning, D.F., 1989. 'Early Brick Chimney Stacks', *Essex Archaeol. & Hist.* 20, 92–102.

Stenton, F.M., 1947. *Anglo-Saxon England.* Second edn. (Oxford).

Strutt, J., 1774. *A Compleat View of the Manners, Customs, Arms, Habits, etc. of the Inhabitants of England, 1.* (London).

Stukeley, W., 1725. *Itinerarium Curiosum.* (London).

Taylor, H.M., and Taylor J., 1965. *Anglo-Saxon Architecture, 1, 2.* (Cambridge).

Thomas, C., 1981. *Christianity in Roman Britain to A.D. 500.* (London).

Todd, M. (ed.), 1978. *Studies in the Romano-British Villa.* (Leicester).

Trump, D., 1961. 'Blunt's Hall, Witham', *Trans. Essex Archaeol. Soc.* ser. 3, 1, 37–40.

Turner, R., 1982. *Ivy Chimneys, Witham: An Interim Report.* Essex County Council, Occ. Paper 2. (Chelmsford).

Turner, R., forthcoming. *Excavation of an Iron Age Settlement and Roman Religious Complex at Ivy Chimneys, Witham, Essex, 1978–83.* E. Ang. Archaeol.

Van Arsdell, R.D., 1989. *Celtic Coinage of Britain.* (London).

Wadhams, M.C., 1972. 'The Development of Buildings in Witham from 1500 to circa 1880', *Post-Medieval Archaeol.* 6, 1–41.

Welch, M.G., 1989. 'A Ring-Brooch and Penannular Brooch Pin from Kelvedon, Essex', *Medieval Archaeol.* 33, 151–2.

Wheeler, R.E.M., 1935. *London and the Saxons.* London Museum Cat. 6.

Wheeler, R.E.M., 1943. *Maiden Castle, Dorset.* Soc. Antiq. Res. Rep. 12.

Wheeler, R.E.M., 1954. *The Stanwick Fortifications.* Soc. Antiq. Res. Rep. 17.

Whimster, R., 1981. *Burial Practices in Iron Age Britain.* Brit. Archaeol. Reps. 90.

Whitelock, D. (ed.), 1961. *The Anglo-Saxon Chronicle: A Revised Translation.* (London).

Wickenden, N.P., 1986. 'Prehistoric Settlement and the Romano-British "Small Town" at Heybridge, Essex', *Essex Archaeol. & Hist.* 17, 7–68.

Wickenden, N.P., 1992. *The Temple and Other Sites in the North-Eastern Sector of Caesaromagus.* CBA Res. Rep. 75.

Williamson, T., 1986. 'Parish Boundaries and Early Fields: Continuity and Discontinuity', *J. Hist. Geog.* 12, 241–8.

Williamson, T., 1987. 'Early Co-axial Field Systems on the East Anglian Boulder Clays', *Proc. Prehist. Soc.* 53, 419–32.

Wilson, D.M., 1964. *Anglo-Saxon Ornamental Metalwork, 700–1100, in the British Museum.* (London).

Wright, T., 1836. *The History and Topography of the County of Essex, 1.* (London).